398568

KT-130-596

COLOR CORRECTION FOR VIDEO

Second Edition

777.55 HUL

COLOR CORRECTION FOR VIDEO

Using Desktop Tools to Perfect Your Image

Second Edition

STEVE HULLFISH

JAIME FOWLER

ELSEVIER

AMSTERDAM • BOSTON • HEIDELBERG • LONDON • NEW YORK • OXFORD
PARIS • SAN DIEGO • SAN FRANCISCO • SINGAPORE • SYDNEY • TOKYO

Focal Press is an imprint of Elsevier

Focal Press is an imprint of Elsevier
30 Corporate Drive, Suite 400, Burlington, MA 01803, USA
Linacre House, Jordan Hill, Oxford OX2 8DP, UK

Copyright © 2009 by Elsevier Inc. All rights reserved.

No part of this publication may be reproduced, stored in a retrieval system, or transmitted in any form
or by any means, electronic, mechanical, photocopying, recording, or otherwise, without the prior
written permission of the publisher.

Permissions may be sought directly from Elsevier's Science & Technology Rights
Department in Oxford, UK: phone: (+44) 1865 843830, fax: (+44) 1865 853333,
E-mail: permissions@elsevier.com. You may also complete your request on-line
via the Elsevier homepage (http://elsevier.com), by selecting "Support & Contact"
then "Copyright and Permission" and then "Obtaining Permissions."

 Recognizing the importance of preserving what has been written, Elsevier prints its books on acid-free
paper whenever possible.

Library of Congress Cataloging-in-Publication Data
Hullfish, Steve.
   Color correction for video : using desktop tools to perfect your
image / by Steve Hullfish and Jaime Fowler. — 2nd ed.
        p.   cm.
   Previous ed. published under title: Color correction for digital video.
   Includes index.
   ISBN 978-0-240-81078-2 (pbk. : alk. paper)   1. Digital video—
Editing—Data processing.   2. Video tapes—Editing—Data processing.
3. Color computer graphics.   I. Fowler, Jaime.   II. Hullfish, Steve. Color
correction for digital video.   III. Title.
   TR899.H85 2009
   778.59′3—dc22

2008030500
British Library Cataloguing-in-Publication Data
A catalogue record for this book is available from the British Library.

ISBN: 978-0-240-81078-2

For information on all Focal Press publications
visit our website at www.elsevierdirect.com

09 10 11 12 13   5 4 3 2 1

Printed in China

Working together to grow
libraries in developing countries

www.elsevier.com | www.bookaid.org | www.sabre.org

ELSEVIER   BOOK AID International   Sabre Foundation

778.
593
HUL

398568

CONTENTS

ACKNOWLEDGMENTS

Although writing is a fairly solitary task, the production of a book is not. We want to acknowledge the efforts of many people for their contributions to bringing this book to print.

Many experts from around the world generously offered their knowledge and wisdom, in particular Roy Wagner, Tal at Chainsaw, Thomas Madden at Kodak, Stephen Nakamura at Technique, Bob Sliga at Film and Tape, Randy Starnes, Mike Most, Peter Mavromates, Ed Colman of SuperDailies, Craig Leffel at Optimus, Alex Scudiero at I3, Robert Lovejoy at Shooters, Rob Currier of Synthetic Aperture, Andre Brunger of 3-Prong, and Karl Sims of GenArts. For great assistance with all things "wave and vectorscope," we send a special thanks to John Pierce of Tektronix and that company's brilliant engineers. My neighbor and friend, Greg "Tech Support" Gillis, provided invaluable support and guidance. I'd also like to thank Thomas Madden from Kodak for his careful review of the theoretical aspects of the book and for providing invaluable technical expertise and guidance.

For great contributions of video examples, I'm lucky to know Gary Adcock, an international expert on video and data cameras and workflow.

I'd like to thank my editor at *DV* magazine, Jim Feeley, for buying the original pitch that a series of articles on color correction would be something that would interest his readers. That original series was the impetus for CMP Publications to begin discussions for this book.

I would like to thank the book's original editor, Dorothy Cox, for providing a guiding hand through the creative process. Also for the revised edition, the folks at Focal Press, including Paul Temme, Dennis McGonagle, and their very capable team took on the task of turning lots of words and images into a final, marketable product.

I would like to thank my parents, William and Suzanne Hullfish, for instilling in me the importance of writing and creative thought. They also taught me that any journey begins with a single step and that the journey itself is often more wondrous and fulfilling than the destination. Those were important lessons to have tucked into my belt during the making of this book.

My coauthor, Jaime Fowler, was a constant source of support and a great sounding board and cheerleader. Jaime's experience as an author, editor, and teacher is evident throughout the book. In a field where being a storyteller is one of the biggest compliments someone can pay another person, Jaime is one of the best storytellers I know.

Finally, my wife, Jody, was the greatest force behind this book. She endured many months of being a *de facto* single parent to our two children, and she was more sympathetic to the strains and struggles that this book placed on our family than I had a right to expect. Without her patience, love, and understanding, I would not have been able to complete this book. Thank you, Jody.

Thanks also to many of the colorists and directors of photography that I interviewed for my second color correction book, *The Art and Technique of Color Correction,* for their knowledge that made its way into this new edition in one form or another and to the people who provided footage for the tutorials and examples, including Torey Loomis at Silverado, for acting as the conduit for the "Susannah" footage, and Julie Hill at Artbeats.

Steve Hullfish

My wife, Peggy, and children, Lauren, Brendan, and Joshua, all helped by leaving me be during the crunch stage of the book, feeding me leftovers, and basically letting me take over the dining room table *again* for a few crucial months.

My colleague and coauthor, Stephen Hullfish, managed to motivate and occasionally talked me down from writing "theory" into writing in the "real world." Steve was also great for our first-time collaboration. It was kind of fun—in an evil sort of way—to watch him go through the same pain as I did during the writing of my first book. More important, I hope his wife, Jody, and the kids will let me borrow him for a few other concepts that are in the hopper.

Dorothy Cox was amazingly patient. She knew we had the right stuff and just waited for it to come out. Also I must thank Trish Meyer for quietly championing this book. Trish was our behind-the-scenes promoter—I can't thank her enough for that.

The colorists in this book are amazing. My special thanks to Jim Barrett and Julius Friede for shining light on the black art and to my friend and fellow editor, Lisa Day, who has always been very kind and helpful to me. Also thanks to DK and the Buda Bunch for occasionally bringing some "colorful" memories to light. Special thanks to Steve Bayes, whose cat analogy was borrowed for this book.

Joel Fowler (no relation) has been a teacher and mentor who never gave up and was always inspiring to me. Dave and Bettie Fowler (yes, they're my parents) have always been my guiding light, telling me to do what I want and have fun—pretty much what I've always done since Day One.

Jaime Fowler

INTRODUCTION

Who Should Read This Book?

Any good communicator will tell you that knowing and understanding your audience are the most important things in communication. The original audience for this book, originally written in 2002, was very easy to define: *nearly everyone*. That's because very few people had been exposed to the small array of tools that allowed real color correction power at the desktop level. Avid and Final Cut Pro released their first versions of applications with color correction tools within months after Jaime Fowler and I first signed the deal to write this book. At the time, Avid Symphony was probably the only piece of gear under $250,000 with much color correction power.

Since then, numerous companies have started delivering color correction systems, hardware, software, plug-ins, and workflows. The list of players at this point is extensive. However, in the spirit of the original publication, this book is aimed at an audience who wants to understand how to do good color correction "on the desktop." With that said, if you are a beginning colorist or student who aspires to play with the "big iron" systems, this is also a good starting place for you because the basic concepts are identical. *Beginning colorist* is a term that can easily be applied to plenty of veteran editors and effects artists. Even if you know how to use the interface of your color application but you don't always get the results you want as quickly as you would like, this is the book for you.

The difficulty in understanding the audience for this revised edition is that the audience has matured a bit and has been exposed to more options in the last few years. However, it's difficult to assess every individual reader's body of knowledge. Even skilled and seasoned professionals probably have something to learn. After the first edition came out, I received plenty of emails from veteran colleagues who learned things about video levels, setting up monitors, and using waveform and vectorscopes that they were amazed that they didn't know. The book also found a wide following among After Effects users, which was a completely unintended audience.

So to answer the question of the book's intended audience, let me tell my personal story of learning color correction. I was one of the original beta testers for Avid's Symphony. In an early release, Symphony included a powerful color correction mode. When I first saw it, it looked intimidating. There were lots of controls that could deliver a huge amount of power, but I had no idea where to

Big Iron
This is industry jargon that indicates an expensive and very powerful system. In the color correction industry, the historical Big Iron system would be the da Vinci 2K.

start. The instruction manual covered all the basics of what the knobs and buttons did, but I didn't know what I was looking for in the image itself or how to use the power that had been delivered to me. If that describes you, you should read this book.

If you have ever wondered how you can make your productions look "network ready," this book is for you, too. As I learned color correction at the feet of some very talented senior colorists, notably Bob Sliga, the one big "take away" that I got from my training was that understanding what all the knobs and buttons do is not nearly as important as training your eye to see the deficiencies and strengths of each image and understanding where the image wants you to take it or how far you can push it from its intended direction. This is the origin of the impression that color correction is some "unlearnable" black art. The breakthrough that this book delivers is that there are several tricks to learning exactly what to look for.

This book is also designed to be "product and platform agnostic." In other words, we don't care what color correction application or NLE you use or on which computer operating system you are running it. The book is based on principles that should be applicable to any gear that can do color correction. Because of the general nature of the book, it is not a substitute for reading the color correction section of your user's manual for your application. However, one of the criticisms of the original edition that we seek to repair with this edition is the complaint that specific step-by-step instruction was lacking. Therefore, throughout the book we show step-by-step tutorials for a number of applications. I'll try to hit several of them, but we'll stick to the ones with the most widespread acceptance and distribution. That includes Final Cut Pro, Apple's Color, Avid, and Color Finesse (which often ships as an included plug-in with Adobe's After Effects and Premiere). If you are using an application other than one of those, you should see that the interface that your application uses is probably very similar to these.

How to Use This Book

The structure of this revised edition is quite changed from the original. In this edition, we want to quickly get you started making your first corrections, so we start the book with a couple of quick tutorials that will get you off to a good start with the basics. After that, the book follows in a specific order with more detailed explanations that should probably be read "linearly." The order of the book after the first chapter should help you build one skill on top of the other.

The first edition started out with a several chapters of theoretical knowledge. That information is still included in this book, but in this edition, some of that theory is introduced "as needed" throughout the book. The rest of the content of the first three chapters are left for Chapters 9 and 10.

Also, instead of delivering the glossary as a whole unit in the back of the book, we've included the glossary items in the margins, usually on the same page where the words are encountered in the body text. Each glossary item is also referenced in the book's index, so the index can be used almost as a standard glossary.

Throughout the book you will see three icons. The icon

indicates a running glossary throughout the book, the

icon indicates video tutorials available on this book's DVD, and

the icon indicates a tip or important advice.

The Icons Used in This Book

 Glossary Item—Provides definitions of industry jargon and technical terms.

 Video Tutorials—Check out the DVD included with this book to watch more than two hours of video tutorials. Plus, there are additional tutorials on the DVD that are not referenced in the book. All tutorials are iPod ready.

 Technical Tips—How-to's or important advice on how to get the job done.

A Note about The Color Images in This Book

Color video is additive. As a result, some of the images in this book—which is printed subtractively with color inks—might not reproduce accurately on the printed page. For a more complete explanation of this issue, please refer to the "Additive and Subtractive Color" section in Chapter 10 of this book.

GETTING STARTED WITH COLOR CORRECTION

Quick Start

Nobody wants to wade through the entire text of a book before they feel they've learned anything, so this first chapter of the book is designed to get you started color correcting quickly. We'll gloss over a few important details in this chapter, but we'll cover those things in more depth in the remaining chapters. This chapter is an overview of the chapters to follow. The goal of this chapter is for you to make as much progress as quickly as possible.

> *The goal of this chapter is for you to make as much progress as quickly as possible.*

The Goals of Color Correction

> *There are two primary objectives in basic color correction: spread your tonal range and balance the colors.*

There are two primary objectives in basic color correction: spread your tonal range and balance the colors. There are a lot of other important goals, including matching shots from one to another, helping to tell the story, and making the images "pop" or "read." But we'll focus on spreading the tonal range and balancing colors in this initial chapter.

Spreading the tonal range means that you take full advantage of the tonal range of your display medium. In most cases this means maximizing the number of levels of gray between the deepest black and the brightest white that your display or broadcast specifications can reproduce. For most people reading this book, that means a TV screen or maybe a computer display. It can also mean prepping the image for a digital intermediate transfer to film. Tonal range corrections do not always have to spread completely from 0% black to 100% white, but oftentimes they do. The other goal of tonal range corrections is determining if certain parts of the tonal range should be compressed while other parts

Tonal Range

Tonal range is sometimes also called the dynamic range, luminance range, or contrast range, though these terms can have slightly different technical definitions. The tonal range is the difference between the brightest and darkest areas of the image. The tonal range of the image—and how those tones are spread throughout the tonal range—defines its contrast. For some applications of this phrase, tonal range indicates the actual number of *levels* of tones that a recording medium can record (256 per channel in the case of RGB 8 bit, or 1025 per channel in the case of RGB 10 bit). For our purposes, we will refer to tonal range (singular) as the range of tones between brightest and darkest. Ansel Adams and other proponents of the Zone System break the tonal range of an image into 11 distinct tonal ranges.

should be expanded. We'll do a quick tutorial on this in a moment.

Balancing the colors means that any unwanted color casts are eliminated. The reason for the term "balancing" will become more obvious as we start to examine and analyze our images with a number of different tools. Color casts in images are sometimes desired, for example, the warm, red tones of a sunset or the sad, blue, coolness of a rainy day. These are color casts that often serve the story, so we need to be careful not to eliminate them. Examples of color casts that are undesirable are usually caused by video cameras that haven't been white balanced properly or film footage shot with the wrong filter for the combination of film stock and light temperature.

Spreading the Tonal Range

Much of the information that viewers use to understand and interpret the image is based on the tonal range or contrast between brights and darks. In most cases we want to give viewers as much information as possible, but sometimes you don't, like the case of a thriller or horror movie where you may be trying to hide things in the shadows.

The first step in determining the proper tonal range where your image should "live" is setting the proper level for blacks or shadows.

The first step in determining the proper tonal range where your image should "live" is setting the proper level for blacks or shadows. Setting the black level is almost always the place where any experienced colorist starts a correction. So the question for a beginner is, "Where do I set the proper black level, and how do I know what I should set it to?"

This book is product and platform agnostic. In other words, this book is less about what buttons to push on specific pieces of hardware or software and more about understanding the process so that you can feel comfortable color correcting on almost any application that exists now or in the future. Because of that, I'll show you the right buttons in a few applications. Hopefully you're using one of the apps that I used as an example. Otherwise, look for similar parameters in the software or hardware that you use.

Blacks are also known as shadows, pedestal, set-up, or lift, depending on the application.

Blacks are also known as shadows, pedestal, set-up, or lift, depending on the application. Setting the black level usually involves adjusting a slider called either "blacks," "shadows," "set-up," "lift," or "pedestal," such as the controls in the screen shots that are shown here from several of the most widely distributed applications with color correction capabilities.

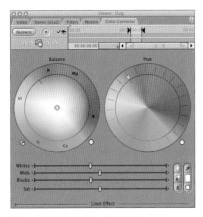

Figure 1-1 FCP Color Corrector.

Figure 1-2 Color Primary room Basic Tab.

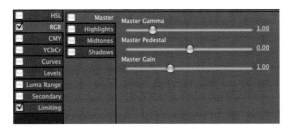

Figure 1-3 Color Finesse HSL Controls Master Tab.

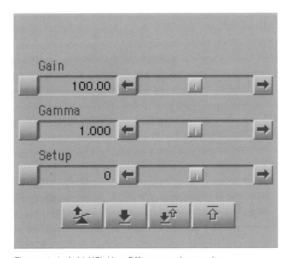

Figure 1-4 Avid HSL Hue Offsets tonal controls.

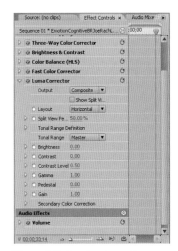

Figure 1-5 Premiere Luma Corrector.

Waveform Monitor

A waveform monitor displays the amplitude level—brightness and darkness—along the vertical axis with the dark parts of the image near the bottom and the brighter parts of the signal near the top. Technically, the horizontal axis of the waveform displays time, but practically speaking, the horizontal axis of the waveform corresponds to the horizontal placement of picture elements across the image with no regard to the vertical placement of elements in the image. The waveform monitor also displays chroma levels, but these are easier judged on a vectorscope.

How to Determine the Proper Black Level

When I started to learn color correction, the biggest mystery to me was simply "How do you know what's right?" To set black levels you need some tools for proper analysis of the black level. Basically that means a waveform monitor, though there are other tools that would work. We'll get into the full range of analytical tools later in the book. For now, a simple waveform monitor will do. Don't panic. You don't need to be an A/V geek or slide rule engineer to understand this display. We just need to know how low we can go legally, and that's pretty simple.

Firstly, you need to know what "legal black" is on your system or waveform monitor. For most waveform monitors, black is at 0 IRE or 0% or 0 millivolts. In the United States, which defines black as 7.5 IRE for composite analog NTSC signals, black can mean 7.5 IRE or 0 IRE depending on the type of video signal. The easiest way to tell which is right for your system is to feed "filler" (the black signal your system generates whenever it doesn't have real video to send) to the waveform monitor.

The easiest way to tell which is right for your system is to feed "filler" (the black signal your system generates whenever it doesn't have real video to send) to the waveform monitor.

If "filler" is 0 IRE, then your goal in most color correction shots is to get at least some portion of the picture down to 0 IRE. If you get black *lower* than 0 IRE, your program may not pass quality control (QC) if you are sending it for broadcast or mass duplication.

Some waveform monitors have configuration settings that allow you to choose whether black displays as 0 IRE or 7.5 IRE (some-

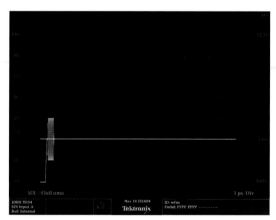

Figure 1-6 This figure shows a waveform monitor displaying blacks at 0 IRE. All waveform and vectorscope images are captured courtesy of a Tektronix WFM7120, which can be viewed as a traditional external scope or can be monitored remotely via a web browser.

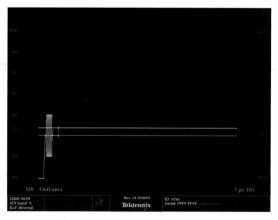

Figure 1-7 This figure shows a waveform monitor displaying blacks at 7.5 IRE.

More on Waveform Monitors

External Scopes versus Internal Scopes

Figure 1-8 Tektronix WFM7120 external video scope.

I always suggest that color correction be done with external scopes, such as those by Tektronix, Leader, VideoTek, OmniTek, and others.

I always suggest that color correction be done with external scopes, such as those by Tektronix, Leader, VideoTek, OmniTek, and others. These scopes generally have more power and information than internal scopes and give you a true sense of the levels coming out of your system because they are downstream from the video card. All internal monitoring, such as the scopes in Color or Final Cut or Avid, do not represent the actual video signal as it has left your system, and software scopes usually do not represent the entire signal. Due to limitations in the amount of computational power required for these displays, software companies often only display every other line or only every fourth line of video. Sometimes, having real time scopes enabled on your chosen NLE (non linear editing system) can actually impede the performance of the NLE itself as it tries to do the important tasks that it is actually designed for. So you can make your editor or compositing software run better by turning off the internal scopes and running with a good external scope.

Flat Pass versus Low Pass (Luma)

External waveform monitors have a button that allows you to "filter" the incoming signal so that the display shows either luma only (Low Pass), or whether the signal includes chroma information (Flat Pass). In Flat Pass, the chroma information can make the trace (the squiggly lines representing the signal) appear to go beyond legal. When you are trying to determine the luminance of your signal on a waveform monitor, you should be in Low Pass, not Flat Pass. Look at the two images of a waveform display fed by color bars in Low Pass and Flat Pass to understand the difference.

Vectorscope

A vectorscope displays chrominance and hue. The saturation (or gain) of the chroma (or color) is measured by how far it extends from the center of the scope. Neutral images (black, white, and all levels of gray) register as a dot in the middle of the vectorscope. Hue is indicated by the position of the trace around the perimeter of the circle. Vectorscopes have graticules that show each of six different colors (red, green, blue, magenta, cyan, and yellow) in a different, fixed vector (position) around the vectorscope. Color includes a cool 3D vectorscope that allows you to rotate the vectorscope in 3D space to see luminance displayed as well. 2D vectorscopes cannot display luminance information.

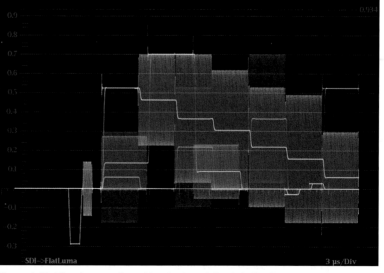

Watch the video tutorial "Spreading the tonal range" on the DVD.

times called "with NTSC setup"). The Tektronix WFM7120 that I use is configurable, and I have it set to display blacks at 0 IRE. This is how I will display black throughout the book unless otherwise noted.

If your black levels are generally higher than 0 IRE, then your picture may look washed out and flat. We'll get more into the complexities of the waveform monitor later in the book.

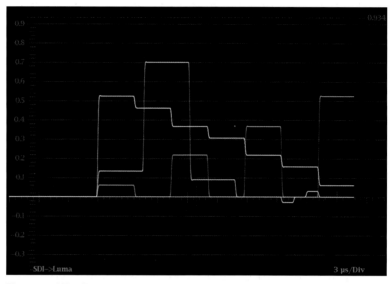

Figure 1-9 Waveform monitor with color bars fed to it in Low Pass.

Figure 1-10 Waveform monitor with color bars fed to it in Flat Pass.

Setting the Black Level

Using your waveform monitor in luma only mode, and knowing where your black level should be by looking at filler, you can use one of the tools in Figures 1-1 to 1-5 to set your black level to the proper position on some real video.

You can use your own video footage for this exercise, or load one of the video examples from the DVD. For the purpose of this tutorial, we'll use the FCP Color Corrector filter and the file from the DVD called "ChromaDuMonde_overbal.mov."

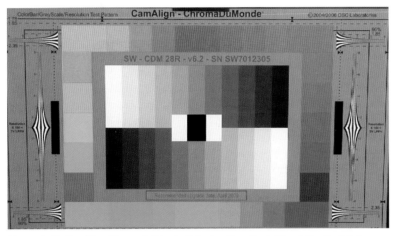

Figure 1-11 CamAlign ChromaDuMonde Color bar/Gray Scale/Resolution Test Pattern chart. Copyright 2004/06 by DSC Laboratories. Used with permission. Shot with a Panasonic HVX200. This is commonly called a "chip chart" because of the "chips" of various colors and shades.

I suggest you drag all of the tutorial video files to your internal hard drive or a media drive from the DVD now.

1. Launch Final Cut Pro (or whatever application you want to use to follow along with the tutorial)
2. Import the "ChromaDuMonde_overbal.mov" file, dropping it into a sequence.
3. Then go to Effects>Video Filters>Color Correction>Color Corrector.
4. Go to Tools>VideoScopes to call up your internal scopes if you do not have external scopes.
5. In the Viewer, switch to the Filters tab to see the controls for the effect. You can view this filter in either Numeric mode or Visual mode.

Legal Levels

Legal levels apply to video images that will be broadcast or duplicated. There are "legal" limits for black levels, white levels, and the strength of colors (saturation). These limits are determined by international committees and national governing bodies, such as the FCC. They can be further stipulated by specific broadcasters, such as PBS or the Discovery Channel. If you are creating a program for broadcast, check with your outlet for specifics. Some replicators or duplicators also have legal levels that videotape masters must adhere to.

IRE

This is a unit of measure for waveform monitors. It is named for the Institute of Radio Engineers, which defined the unit. The scale starts in negative numbers and goes beyond 100 IRE.

Millivolts

This is another unit of measure for waveform monitors. It is not as easy to use as the simple IRE scale or a simple percentage scale, so we will not use this scale to describe video levels.

Trace

The trace is the portion of the waveform or vectorscope that indicates the levels of the video signal. It is the portion that responds to level adjustments. On most scopes, the trace tends to be green or sometimes white. Sometimes the trace is actually referred to as the "waveform," while the actual device that displays it is referred to as the "waveform monitor." The traditional color for the trace is green. More colorists don't like the green trace, so on many monitors the color of the trace is user selectable. Many colorists choose a neutral gray or white color for the trace.

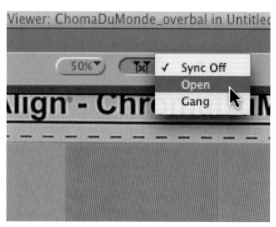

Figure 1-12 Open button in Canvas.

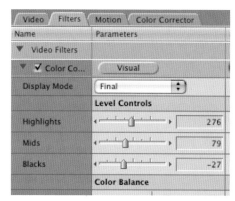

Figure 1-13 Color Correction Filter in Numeric Mode.

Graticule

The graticule is the fixed lines on the waveform and vectorscope that provide scale and positioning information, for example, the IRE lines on the waveform monitor or the color targets on the vectorscope. The graticule is often orange as a contrast to the green of the trace. This word is not limited to video. Graticule also defines the network of longitude and latitude lines on a map.

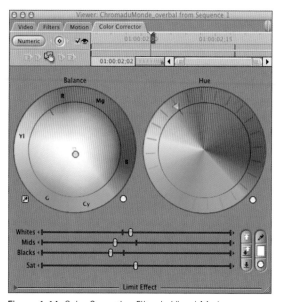

Figure 1-14 Color Correction Filter in Visual Mode.

6. Adjust the "Blacks" slider down until the shape at the bottom of the center of the waveform monitor reaches the bottom orange line labeled "Black" or 0%.

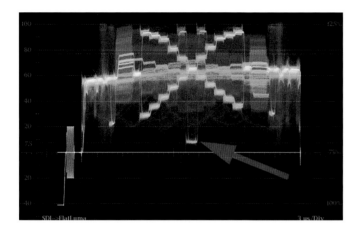

Figure 1-15 This shape at the arrow represents the starting point for the pure black "chip" in the middle of the ChromaDuMonde camera chart. It should be on the "black" line (0 IRE) of the waveform monitor, not above or below it.

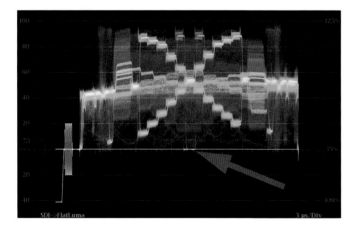

Figure 1-16 This figure represents the image when the black level has been brought down too low. The flattening of the shape at the arrow indicates clipping or crushing of the signal, which results in a lack of detail in the shadows.

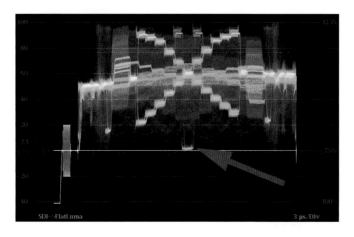

Figure 1-17 This figure represents the proper black level. The signal is neither too high above the black (0 IRE) line nor is it crushed.

Chip Chart

A camera test chart with small "chips" of different colors and shades. Each small block of color is called a chip. The charts used throughout this book are high quality camera charts from DSC Laboratories.

TIP

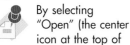

By selecting "Open" (the center icon at the top of your Canvas is a pulldown menu) on your Canvas, your Viewer will stay linked to your Canvas, updating effects status as you move in your timeline, making it easier to color correct multiple shots.

TIP

Adjusting levels when color correcting is like focusing a camera. You can never really be sure you're "in focus" unless you pass the proper point, so pull down your black level until the shape starts to flatten out at the bottom or goes past the line that indicates 0 IRE or 0% black. Then bring it back up to the proper level.

The ChromaDuMonde chart is really a test pattern. Bring in a real world image from your own footage or from the DVD that accompanies this book and try to set the black level. Remember to watch the bottom of the waveform monitor as you slowly lower the black level, making sure that you don't "flatten out" the trace of the waveform monitor along the bottom. Try to keep the basic shape of the trace from distorting too much.

In future lessons, we will break this rule about not flattening out the waveform shapes as we attempt to create certain looks, such as blown out highlights and crushed blacks, but for now, the goal is to maintain as much detail as we can in our video images, and that means that the shape of the trace on the waveform monitor should not flatten out.

Determining the Proper White Level

Determining the proper white level is a little easier because there aren't any strange choices about black levels being at different legal levels depending on your country or type of video signal. With white level it's always 100 IRE or 100%.

There are certainly times when you may not want to bring your level up as high as 100%. You need to look at the image itself and determine if there's anything that actually deserves to be completely bright white. Sometimes, with a simple head shot interview, for example, the brightest part of the image should be a highlight on someone's skin, which may not belong past 80% or 90%.

With your black level set, you can bring your white level up to the maximum legal level and see if the image appears too contrasty or harsh. If it does, then back it down to a comfortable level. On the other side of that, if your image appears to be underexposed or flat, then the white level should be brought up to its highest legal level. Also, remember that the white level—or highlight level—is not the final adjustment that we'll make to determine the overall brightness of the image, so if you're not happy with the brightness of your image at this point, or if it seems like your white levels are correct but your skin tones are now too bright, we will fix that in another step.

Another special circumstance to consider when determining white level is if your footage was shot overexposed, the whites and other bright highlights will be clipped. This can be seen as a thin, bright line along the top of the waveform monitor. In this case, you can attempt to bring your video levels down somewhat to cut the glare, but you shouldn't bring your levels much below 100% because having a clipped signal that is much lower than 100% will look very strange.

Figure 1-18 This sky on the left side is overexposed to the point of being clipped.

Crush

When the black level is lowered so that the shadows lose detail, this is known as crushing the signal or creating a crushed look. It is a form of clipping or taking a signal beyond its correct range.

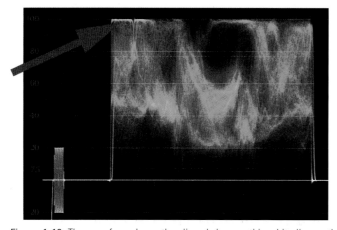

Figure 1-19 The waveform shows the clipped sky as a thin white line on the left side of the trace as indicated by the arrow. The sky on the right side is also bright, but it is not heavily clipped because the waveform doesn't form a thin, compressed line.

Setting the Proper White Level

Setting the white level is very similar to setting the black level. Let's go back to our "ChromaDuMonde overbal" clip in Final Cut Pro using our same Color Corrector filter that is already applied.

1. Using either the Numeric view or the Visual view, adjust the Highlights slider (as it is called in Numeric view) or the Whites slider (as it is called in Visual view) until the brightest portion of the signal sits no higher than the 100% line in the waveform monitor.

2. Drag an RGB Limit effect or Broadcast Safe effect on to the clip. Now, instead of having the white levels go beyond 100% you'll see the upper portions of the trace begin to distort or flatten out as you move them up near the 100% line. As with "crushing" the black levels, you want to avoid

Clip (clip, clipping, clipped)

A clipped signal means that the image was exposed too bright for the imaging technology or recording technology. The result is a loss of detail that can be identified on a waveform monitor by a thin, sharp line at the top of the trace.

this distortion because it indicates that the signal is clipping and losing highlight detail. With this specific ChromaDuMonde file, you want to make sure that the ratio or steps between the lines of the trace that represent the brightest chips doesn't change. If you go too high, the lines representing the chips will actually flatten out to be on the same level.

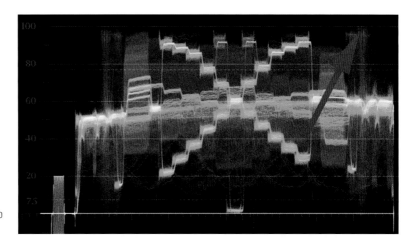

Figure 1-20 These whites are set correctly. Though they don't quite go all the way to 100%, any higher setting caused the highlights to begin to compress, especially on the right side, which was lit slightly brighter than the left. I stopped raising the whites when the area near the arrow began to compress into a thin line.

3. You may have noticed that your black levels have come up a bit. Use your blacks slider to put them back where they were before you raised your white levels. This is a little dance that you will always have to do if you are color correcting with a mouse or single trackball. Professional colorists usually use a color correction interface similar to the JLCooper Eclipse or Tangent Devices CP-200-BK that allows them to simultaneously adjust black and white levels, so as they bring white levels up, they are holding down the black levels with another control.

Figure 1-21 This is JLCooper's Eclipse CX panel. The rings indicated by the arrows allow simultaneous adjustment of the whites, mids, and blacks.

Determining the Proper Gamma or Mids Level

With your white and black levels set (sometimes referred to as your highlight and shadow levels) the next step is to determine your "mid" or "gamma" levels. With the brightest and darkest portions of the picture often determined by legal levels, the gamma or midrange is the portion of the tonal range that can be set to give the shot its true overall tone.

With the brightest and darkest portions of the picture often determined by legal levels, the gamma or midrange is the portion of the tonal range that can be set to give the shot its true overall tone.

There are several reasons for changing the gamma or mids. One is that raising the mids can make a shot that already has the whites set as high as they can go seem brighter. Another is that lowering gamma can help provide additional richness to an image that already has blacks set as low as they can go. Additionally, it is possible to "play" the gammas against either the highlights or the shadows so that a specific portion of the tonal range exhibits greater contrast. This can be accomplished in the shadows, for example, by crushing the blacks down and stretching the mids up—to accomplish greater contrast in the lower mids—or by clipping the highlights up and stretching the mids down—to accomplish greater contrast in the upper mids.

Think of your tonal range as a rubber band.

Think of your tonal range as a rubber band. First you want to stretch the top and bottom out to their safe or legal limits. Then you can grab the middle of the rubber band and stretch and compress the top or bottom within those limits. We'll deal with this concept in greater depth in later chapters.

Setting the Proper Gamma or Mids Level

Returning to Final Cut Pro and the same Color Correction filter that we started working with to set the blacks and whites, we'll finish the tonal correction on the file by adjusting the gamma, or mid, slider.

For now, let's just set the gamma or midrange of the image so that it looks pleasing. For our ChromaDuMonde file, we want the middle gray tones (the thick band of the trace that extends all the way across the middle of the waveform monitor) to average out to 50%. With our blacks set to 0% and our whites set to 100%, the middle grays are between 55% and 65% (similar to Figure 1-20).

Drag the Mids slider (which may be called the gamma slider in some other software) so that the waveform monitor looks more like Figure 1-22, with the average closer to 50%.

When you are done adjusting the mids down, you may find that it's necessary to adjust the blacks and whites up a little bit.

Gamma

This term has two meanings that are somewhat tied to each other. One meaning for gamma is the curve or transition between white and black. The other meaning describes the middle of the tonal range between shadows and highlights. The reason that these meanings are tied is that by altering the position of the midtones, the curve between white and black is also altered.

Figure 1-22 Note that the midtone grays are now between 40% and 60% with the center gray chip, indicated at the arrow, around 55%. Note that the tonal range is spread out between 0% and 100% and that the steps between the lines representing the chips on the chart are much more evenly distributed than in the original waveform image (Figure 1-15). Also note that no portions of the image are clipped or crushed.

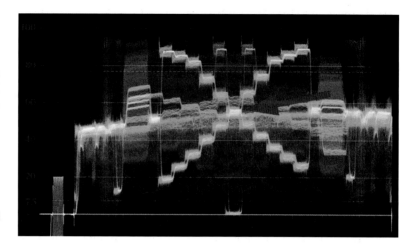

Now look at the waveform monitor and the image itself as you check and uncheck the Color Correction check mark at the top left of the filter in the viewer. When it is unchecked, you are seeing the original camera image. When it is checked, you are looking at your correction. Your correction should be much more pleasing.

My final settings for the numeric view of the filter were:

Highlights: 276
Mids: 80
Blacks: −27

Try setting the tonality of a different video clip. With the camera chart, the instructions that came with the chart indicated where the gray should be positioned on a waveform monitor. With a real world image, the choice is not quite so cut and dried. The positioning of the gamma or mids is set completely by eye with most images because there is no legal level for the middle of the image. Setting the gamma is done "to taste" or can be done to help better match the current shot to the surrounding shots in the sequence.

TIP

When you are adjusting any specific tonal range (shadows, mids, highlights) you need to focus more of your attention on the portion of the picture that has those kinds of tones. Look at what happens to the shadows as you adjust the blacks. Look at the midtones (skin tones, for example) as you adjust your mids. And look at the brightest portions of the picture as you adjust the highlights.

Balancing the Colors

With the tonal range set nicely, the next step in most color correction is to balance the colors.

With the tonal range set nicely, the next step in most color correction is to balance the colors. This means that any unwanted color casts are removed. When I started doing color correction, I didn't understand how to *see* unwanted color casts unless they were pretty obvious. Some people are very good at doing this without any training. Some people need some practice. The good thing is that the tools to analyze color casts are always right at the colorist's fingertips, so if someone says, "The blacks look a little green," and you don't really see what they're talking about, don't worry. I'll show you several ways to check out these color casts.

Analyzing Color with the Vectorscope

Please do not get freaked out by scopes. Think of the waveform and vectorscope as creative tools. They are there to help you.

A vectorscope is a simple analytical tool with the sole purpose of analyzing the strength and hue of colors in the video signal. It's easiest to understand by superimposing a color wheel on top of the vectorscope.

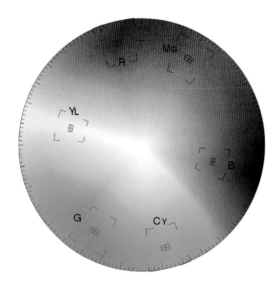

Figure 1-23 A vectorscope with a color wheel superimposed on top. Note that the unsaturated colors are in the center of the scope.

The strength or saturation of the color is relative to the distance of the trace from the center of the vectorscope. The direction of the trace around the perimeter of the circle tells what hue it is. Think of the vectorscope in terms of a clock face. If part of the trace extends toward 11:00, that means it's red. Toward 1:30 is magenta, 3:00 is blue, 5:30 is cyan, 7:30 is green, and 9:00 is yellow.

So with that knowledge in hand, you might ask, Where is white? Where is gray? And where is black? The seemingly bizarre answer is that black, white, and gray are all exactly in the middle because they are completely neutral. Remember: Saturation is indicated by the distance from the middle. Because black, white, and gray have no saturation at all, that means they are all in the exact middle of the vectorscope.

> ***Because black, white, and gray have no saturation at all, that means they are all in the exact middle of the vectorscope.***
> ***Balancing colors in color correction means that colors that are supposed to be neutral are neutral.***

Balancing colors in color correction means that colors that are supposed to be neutral are neutral. And because neutral colors are so easy to define on a vectorscope—they're in the middle—balancing them should be easy to do. You just center neutral colors

TIP

Centering the trace on the vectorscope is usually easiest to do when the gain or zoom on the vectorscope is increased so that it's easier to see the center. All good external scopes have a way to increase the gain or the zoom on the vectorscope, but not all software scopes can do this.

on the vectorscope. This does not mean that a perfectly balanced image doesn't have portions of the trace that extend out toward red or blue or green. You want those colors if there are skin tones or grass or sky in your picture. It just means that most images have neutral tones in them, and those tones should be centered on the vectorscope.

Analyzing Color with the RGB Parade Waveform

When I wrote *The Art and Technique of Digital Color Correction*, I interviewed dozens of great colorists. One of the questions I asked them was: "If you were stranded on a desert island with only one scope, which would it be?" Most of them said they'd want an RGB Parade waveform.

What is the advantage of the RGB Parade waveform monitor? It gives you information on brightness (tone) as well as important information on color balance, so it's the one scope that can really do it all.

The RGB Parade works very similarly to the waveform monitor that we used earlier in this chapter already, except that it displays each of the channels of color information—red, green, and blue—individually in a "parade" across the display. The first image or "cell" shows the red channel, the second shows the green channel, and the third shows the blue channel.

Figure 1-24 This is a graphic I created in Photoshop and imported into Final Cut Pro.

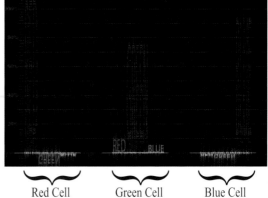

Red Cell   Green Cell   Blue Cell

Figure 1-25 This is the RGB waveform display of Figure 1-24. Note that in the first red cell, only the RED word is displayed, in the green cell, the GREEN word is predominant, and in the blue cell the BLUE word is predominant. Because each word was created only from a pure color, the smaller, or inversed, words are probably only showing up due to an error in the way the color spaces were translated when the file was imported.

We're still talking about needing to balance the colors, and the RGB Parade gives some great information when it comes to balancing colors. As I mentioned, each of the cells is similar to the regular waveform monitor that you already used, except that each cell only gives a level for one color.

The thing to realize with video is that when the three color channels (red, green, and blue) are equal, there is *no* "color." Equal levels of red, green, and blue means there is no saturation.

Equal levels of red, green, and blue means there is no saturation.

So when you are looking at an RGB Parade waveform display, you usually want the top and bottom of all three cells to line up. That indicates balanced colors.

Cell

The display of the individual color channels of the RGB Parade waveform monitor are referred to as cells. There are three cells: red, green, and blue. Sometimes there is a fourth cell for Y or luma. That cell is usually displayed first in left to right order, followed by red, green, and blue.

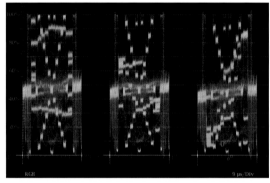

Figure 1-26 This is a properly white balanced ChromaDuMonde chart displayed on an RGB Parade waveform. The image is balanced and neutral. Note that all three cells are essentially the same levels. Remember: From left to right, the three waveforms are red, green, and blue.

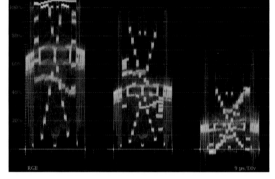

Figure 1-27 This is an improperly white balanced ChromaDuMonde chart displayed on an RGB Parade waveform. The image is warm. Note that the red cell is higher than the green and blue cells.

Analyzing Color with the Eyedropper

It is also possible to analyze colors with an eyedropper in many applications. This is a popular method amongst Photoshop retouchers. Analyzing color with an eyedropper is similar to using the RGB Parade waveform. You sample a color that should be neutral (a black, white, or neutral gray) with the eyedropper and then take note of any color channel that is higher or lower than the others.

There are some tricks to this technique because the RGB values that you will get from an eyedropper can vary quite a bit from one pixel to the next, so you have to kind of average them out in your head as you drag around an area that you feel should be neutral.

Retouchers

A retoucher is the print equivalent to a colorist in the film and TV world. The tools of the retoucher are often analogous to the colorist's tools, but sometimes the retoucher can do things that colorists cannot do because of the static nature of print.

Let's analyze three images with an eyedropper. You can do this in Apple's Color, Color Finesse, or in almost any Adobe application. I will do this in Avid's color correction mode.

On the DVD are three files of a DSC Labs Grayscale Test Pattern chart shot with a Panasonic HVX200. The files are called "grayscale_neutral.mov," "grayscale_warm.mov," and "grayscale_cool.mov." They are all HD files. Import them into your color correction application of choice and look for a way to sample colors with your eyedropper. I will walk you through this with specific instructions if you're on an Avid, but you should be able to follow along with other applications.

After importing the three shots into the Avid, cut them into a sequence and go into color correction mode or choose Toolsets > Color Correction.

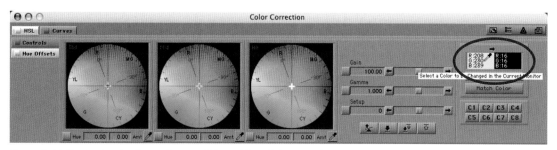

Figure 1-28 To sample with the eyedropper, click on either of the two color patches indicated by the red circle. Your cursor will change to an eyedropper, and you can click and drag to a color in one of the monitors in the Composer window.

TIP

You can opt-drag (Mac) or alt-drag (PC) the color swatch you just saved into a bin for later matching or reference.

Click and drag from one of the color patches in the upper right corner of the Color Correction window to a neutral color in the Current window and release. This will save the RGB values of that color temporarily.

For the purposes of this tutorial, let's sample a black, gray, and white "chip" from the grayscale_neutral chart. I'll sample the middle gray chips and the black and white chips that are right in the center of the chart. These are 8-bit RGB values.

My RGB values for the grayscale_neutral.mov are:

White: 205, 226, 237

Gray: 140, 136, 140

Black: 27, 33, 37

(Your values may be slightly different. Mine varied between 3 and 7 values inside of each of the three chips as I dragged around.)

Watch the video tutorial "Analyzing with the Avid eyedropper" on the DVD.

The preceding numbers tell us that the white balance on our "neutral" image is not really quite neutral. In the whites and blacks, the blue is slightly elevated (237 for whites and 37 for blacks), and red is a little deficient (205 for whites and 27 for blacks). If you really wanted to get this image looking absolutely neutral, you'd need to add some red in the whites and the blacks and maybe pull back on the blues in the whites and the blacks as well. In the grays, as I dragged around, the blues and greens were pretty similar most of the time, with red a little lower, so maybe you could add just a touch of red in the midtones as well, though the preceding sample would indicate that adding a little green is the right thing to do. Remember that you're never going to get all of these numbers to match, so we're just looking to get a general idea of which colors are slightly stronger or weaker.

Let's also sample the warm and cool chip charts. Here are the numbers I came up with:

Grayscale_cool
    White: 146, 226, 253
    Gray: 81, 133, 192
    Black: 23, 33, 51
Grayscale_warm
    White: 254, 204, 127
    Gray: 162, 120, 72
    Black: 32, 28, 25

These values give you a real clue about what's wrong with these images. In the cool file, blue is elevated across all three tonal ranges. Red is also more deficient than green, and green is also lower than blue. In the warm file, the red channel is elevated in the whites and grays, though the blacks are actually pretty close between the lowest and highest channel.

So what about yellow casts, cyan casts, and magenta casts? How do you know if you have one of those? Take a look at a vectorscope (Figure 1-29). The primary colors of red, green, and blue form a triangle on the vectorscope. The secondary colors—cyan, magenta,

TIP

 Color casts are rarely the same strength across all three tonal ranges. This means that each tonal range should be balanced separately.

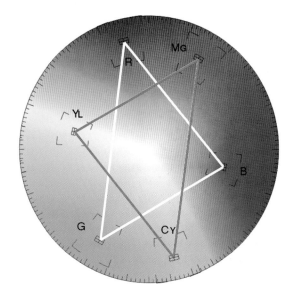

Figure 1-29 Note the position of the primary colors of red, green, and blue on the vectorscope. Note the position of the secondary colors of magenta, cyan, and yellow between the primary colors. And note the secondary colors that are opposite the primary colors. Memorize these relationships. If memorizing these are difficult, remember that you can always see these relationships on a vectorscope.

TIP

If you find a bright or dark patch in some video that you're sampling, and the numbers don't move much as you scrub around in the area, that is an indicator that that area is clipped. If all of the whites are pegged at 235 or 255 or the blacks bottom out at 0 or 16, then that area has no detail because it is clipped.

and yellow—are positioned between each of the primary colors. The secondary colors are made up of equal amounts of each of the primary colors that they're between. Yellow is equal parts red and green, cyan is equal parts green and blue, and magenta is equal parts red and blue. If you look at the gray values of the preceding grayscale_neutral clip, you will see that the red and blue values are equal to each other and higher than green. That means that there could be a slight magenta cast (red + blue = magenta) to the midtones. Another way to check on secondary colors is to look at the color directly opposite the primary color on the vectorscope. In the case of the gray values in our neutral image, if you look opposite of green, which is slightly low, you see magenta, so once again you know that there could be a slight magenta cast to the midtones of that image.

Balancing with the Color Wheels (Color Balance Controls, Hue Offset Wheels)

The tools that colorists are being exposed to in the last several years have changed fairly dramatically. For most experienced colorists, the "real" tool for fixing color casts are the color wheels.

For most experienced colorists, the "real" tool for fixing color casts are the color wheels.

Most of these experienced colorists practiced their craft on the gold standard da Vinci telecine/color systems. The three trackballs in the various da Vinci models basically did the same thing that the color wheels do in so many software color correctors now. As a matter of fact, several manufacturers, such as Tangent Devices and JLCooper, make manual user interfaces that allow the manipulation of the color wheels in many applications with triple trackballs (see Figure 1-21).

Using the color wheels to balance colors is very easy if you are looking at a vectorscope or eyeballing your corrections just looking at your monitor. Using the color wheels while monitoring an RGB Parade waveform monitor or while sampling with an eyedropper is a bit more challenging, but it is worth the effort and practice.

Using the color wheels while monitoring a vectorscope is simply a matter of grabbing the cursor in the middle of the color wheel. In Avid and Color Finesse, these are called the Hue Offset wheels, in Final Cut Pro's Color Corrector 3 Way effect they're called Color Balance controls. Apple's Color also calls them Color Balance controls. Adobe products refer to them as Color wheels.

Let's balance the cool gray chip chart using the Color Balance controls in Apple's Color. Once again, you can follow along in any application that has similar wheels.

In Color, import the "grayscale_neutral.mov," "grayscale_warm.mov," and "grayscale_cool.mov" that we just used in the eyedropper exercise.

Select the Grayscale_neutral clip in the time line and go in to the Primary In room (tab) of Color (Figure 1-30). Take a look at the RGB Parade waveform monitor and the vectorscope. We're going to try to match the warm and cool grayscale images to this one.

Watch the video tutorial "Balance Grayscale with Color Wheels" on the DVD.

Select the Grayscale_cool clip in the time line. Notice that the vectorscope on the neutral image creates a nice dot in the center of the scope, while vectorscope of the cool image is more of a streak that extends out between the blue and cyan "targets" (Figure 1-31). Also on the red cell of the RGB Parade, the level is low, while in the blue cell, the levels are so high that they are clipped along the top. If you are doing this exercise in Color, you can see in the cool 3D vectorscope that the neutral image stays very close to the center line between white and black, while the cool image swoops away.

To balance the cool image, we'll use the Color Balance wheels in Color's Primary In room (tab). Start with the Shadow wheel (to the left) and drag the center crosshairs away from blue while watching the vectorscope image. You will see that the part of the trace that is closest to the center of the vectorscope will get even closer. Notice the effect you have on the center portion of the trace as you drag around in that Shadow wheel. The goal is to get it into the center.

Now we'll balance the highlights with the Highlight wheel (to the right). This time we're trying to drag the far end of the trace back to the middle. This will take a much more extreme move because the highlights are farther away from "normal" than the shadows were. Keep your eyes on the white chips on the chart to make sure they don't become too red or yellow.

Finally, we'll balance the midtones (the center wheel). Try to create the same nice tight point in the vectorscope that you saw when you were looking at the neutral clip. You won't be able to match them perfectly because the blue highlights clipped and some color data was permanently lost when that happened.

It will take a little bit of work going back and forth between the shadow, midtone, and highlight wheels to get this file looking good. You'll notice on the RGB Parade that the blown out highlights in the blue cell can't really be recovered, but the levels for the gammas all match across all cells, and the levels of the shadows also match across all three cells (Figure 1-32). A screen grab of the trackballs from my final correction are also included (Figure 1-33). Note that I also moved the Master Lift down a bit and the Master Gain up a bit to stretch the contrast a little.

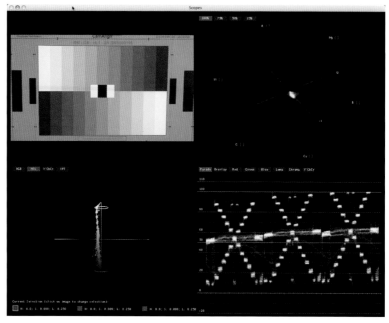

Figure 1-30 Apple Color's displays for the neutral grayscale image.

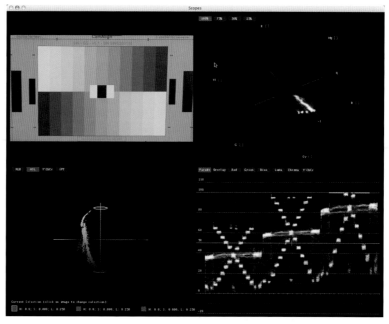

Figure 1-31 Apple Color's displays for the cool grayscale image.

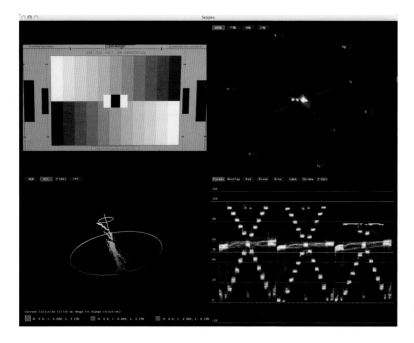

Figure 1-32 Apple Color UI with RGB Parade indicating clipped highlights in the blue cell (farthest to the right in bottom corner).

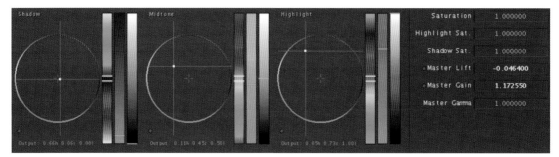

Figure 1-33 Apple Color UI of the Primary In room showing positions of the Color Wheel corrections and Master Lift and Master Gain corrections.

Try this same exercise with the warm chart and with any of your own footage that has a color cast in it.

> ***Balancing with the Color Balance controls is much easier to do while watching the vectorscope.***

Balancing with the Color Balance controls is much easier to do while watching the vectorscope. With experience and practice, you'll be able to balance using the wheels while watching the RGB Parade waveform, but until then it'll be a little like trying to draw a circle on an Etch A Sketch®.

Balancing with RGB Levels

Another way to correct color balance is to use red, green, and blue levels controls. Basically these are controls—usually sliders—

that allow you to adjust the highlight, midtone, and shadow amounts of each of the color channels individually. In Color, this is done in the Primary In room by clicking on the Advanced Tab along the right side. In Final Cut Pro, you would use the Video Filters>Color Correction>RGB Balance effect. In Color Finesse, you would use the RGB Master tab. In Avid (other than Symphony and DS) there are no controls to do this, though using Curves is similar, as you will see in the next section of the book. In Adobe Premiere and After Effects, these controls are in Effects>Levels (Individual Controls). Then inside the effect, spin down the "twirlies" for red, green, and blue to reveal the individual sliders for black, white, and gamma for each color channel.

Using these sliders seems very intimidating and way too technical, but if you watch the RGB Parade waveform monitor while adjusting these controls, you'll see how very easy this is to do.

If you didn't read the earlier part of this chapter recently, you may want to go back and check out the section on Analyzing Color with the RGB Parade Waveform.

 Watch the video tutorial "Balance grayscale with RGB sliders" on the DVD.

Let's use the same files we just used in the Balancing with the Color Wheels section. You can continue to work in Color, if you have access to it, by using the Advanced Tab in the Primary In room, but I will do the rest of this tutorial in Color Finesse (plugged in to Final Cut Pro).

1. Import the "grayscale_neutral.mov," "grayscale_warm. mov," and "grayscale_cool.mov" into Final Cut Pro—or any NLE that has Color Finesse as a plug-in, like Adobe Premiere or After Effects—and cut the files into a sequence. Select the "grayscale_warm.mov" clip in the time line and select it. Add an Effects>Video Filters>Synthetic Aperture>SA Color Finesse 2 effect to the clip. In the Filters tab, choose the Full Interface for the Color Finesse effect (or you can drag way down on the list of controls to RGB Master where you will see gamma, pedestal, and gain controls for each color channel.

2. When balancing a chip chart that is essentially all neutral tones, the goal is to make each of the three color channels, or cells, on the RGB Parade waveform match one another. You can also use these sliders while analyzing your image with the eyedropper. While most real world images have colors that are of different levels of red, green, and blue, you can still balance colors using the same technique. You just need to be cognizant of the differences that *should* be kept between the color channels, for example, a blue sky will make the blue channel higher than red or green and it *should* be that way. A predominant skin tone (for example in a close up) will have higher red and yellow channels. But if there is something black and something white in the frame, you can balance the three color channels to those

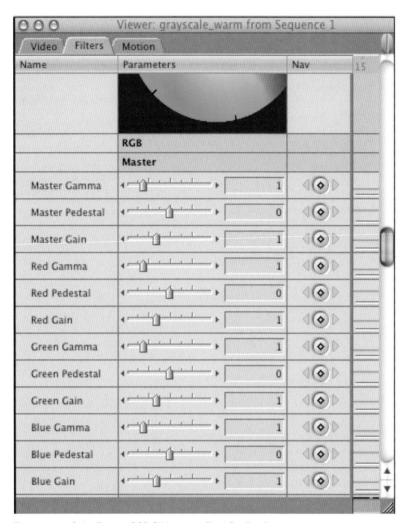

Figure 1-34 Color Finesse RGB Sliders as a Final Cut Pro filter.

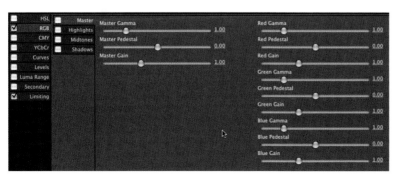

Figure 1-35 Color Finesse's full user interface. The RGB sliders are in the RGB tab.

black and white references. Legendary colorist Bob Festa calls these references his "visual signposts." They tell him where to go.

> ***Legendary colorist Bob Festa calls these references his "visual signposts."***

3. Start by adjusting the black levels of all three color channels so that you have a nice black on all three channels. If you're working in Color Finesse with an external scope, you can't use the full interface because the changes aren't updated to the output video card until you complete the correction, but if you use the Filters controls in Final Cut, they update in real time. I brought the overall pedestal down to –0.05, the red pedestal down to –0.03, and the green pedestal down to –0.03.

4. Now let's adjust the highlights or "gain" controls for each channel while we watch the top of the RGB Parade. The red channel is clipped at the top, so you shouldn't place the red channel all the way up. It's already too high because the image is so warm.

5. Finally, adjust the gamma controls for each color channel, trying to get the bar that runs through the middle of the trace to average out at about 50 IRE. When you do this, it will radically affect some of the other levels that you've already set. Go back and tweak them back into position. If you don't have a panel, like the Tangent Devices CP-200 or JLCooper Eclipse, this could take some time. The final figures I ended up with are as follows:

Master pedestal: –0.05
Red pedestal: 0
Green pedestal: –0.05
Blue pedestal: –0.13
Red gain: 0.9
Green gain: 1.32
Blue gain: 2.22
Red gamma: 0.93
Green gamma: 0.93
Blue gamma: 1.25

With the "chip chart" under your belt, try this same exercise with some of your own footage, or footage from the DVD, that has color casts in it. Remember, the order that you adjust levels should normally be blacks first, then whites, then midtones.

Balancing with Curves

Finally, you can balance with Curves. This is very similar to balancing with RGB levels. The easiest way to balance using Curves is to keep an eye on your RGB Parade waveform level. Pairing Curves and the RGB Parade will make your correction very intuitive. Many applications have Curves controls now. Avid was the first to popularize this method for video corrections (though they've been in Adobe apps forever), and Avid still has the "sexiest" of the Curves UIs with a nice color coding that lets you know that pulling down the blue curve will make your correction more yellow.

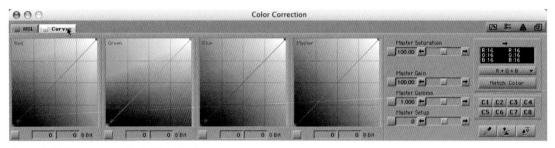

Figure 1-36 Curves control in Avid Media Composer.

We'll use the Avid to balance color using Curves, but you can also use Color's curves in the Primary room, or Color Finesse's Curves control. In After Effects and Premiere use Video Effects>Color Correction>RGB Curves. Final Cut doesn't have Curves controls except by using Color or the Color Finesse plug-in.

The theory behind using Curves is identical to using RGB levels. With Curves, the thing to understand is the relationships of the graphs to the video image and which axis controls what. Looking at Figure 1-36, the colors of the graphs help you to understand the relationships a little better. Let's consider the Master graph first. That's the one on the far right. It controls the levels of all three color channels, so it essentially does the same thing as a Master Gain, Master Set-Up, and Master Gamma control all rolled into one. To adjust set-up (blacks), drag the small purple dot at the lower left corner of the graph. To bring blacks up, drag straight up. To bring blacks down, drag to the right. To bring whites down, grab the small purple dot at the upper right corner of the graph and drag it down. To bring whites up, drag to the left. If you want to alter the gamma or midtones, you can click on a point along the line to add a point and then drag that point in any direction. Dragging it up or to the left will brighten the gammas. Dragging it down or to the right will darken the gammas.

Most software that uses Curves also has numerical readouts of the direction that the points on the graph are being moved.

Let's use the same files we just used in the Balancing with RGB Levels section. You can continue to work in Color, if you have access to it, by using the Advanced Tab in the Primary In room, but I will do the rest of this tutorial in Avid.

Watch the video tutorial "Balance color with Curves" on the DVD. Some video tutorials are done in a different application than the text tutorials, but the principles are the same.

8-bit Color

8-bit color is one of the two primary color depths of video. 8-bit color refers to the number of bits that define a single color channel of video. 8 bit is sometimes mistakenly referred to as 24 bit (8 bits times three channels of color). 8-bit color has 256 levels of gray in each color channel. The number of colors that 8-bit color depth can reproduce (mathematically) is $256 \times 256 \times 256 = 16.8$ million colors.

10-bit Color

While it may sound only slightly better than 8 bit, 10-bit color has 1024 levels of gray per color channel, or $1024 \times 1024 \times 1024 = 1$ billion+ colors!

1. Import the "grayscale_neutral.mov," "grayscale_warm. mov," and "grayscale_cool.mov" into Avid and cut the files into a sequence. Go into color correction mode, or choose Toolset>Color Correction to enable the color correction workspace. Park the time line indicator on the "warm" clip.

2. At the top of the Composer window, click on the word "Previous" or "Next" at the top of the screen and choose "RGB Parade" from the resulting pulldown window. If you have an Avid that has real video output (Mojo DX or Nitris DX, for example) and external scopes, then use the external scopes instead.

3. The RGB Parade should look similar to the screen grab in Figure 1-39. Note that the red channel is very hot. The top of the red cell is clipped, the shadows are lifted, and the gamma is at almost 75% instead of 50%. Green is fairly close to where it should be. The midtones are just a touch low, the blacks are elevated similar to the reds, and the highlights are just a little low. The blue channel has the blacks at about the right level, and the midtones and highlights are only about halfway to where they should be.

4. As with all other corrections, the black levels are the first thing to worry about, then highlights, and then midtones. Which color channel to start with doesn't really matter, but I like starting with green or whichever channel is closest to being correct. Then I can use that as a guide for the other two channels. We want to drag the bottom corner of the green Curve to the right just a bit to lower the black level of that channel. We want to get it down to the 0% mark, *not* the bottom orange line. If you can't get fine enough control, you can type in the numbers in the boxes just below the Curve. My final number in the first box was 8. This essentially lowered the black level of the green channel by 8 levels on a scale of 256 (8-bit color).

5. Now raise the top right corner point on the green Curve to the left. This will raise the level of the highlights. We want to get them to about 100% without "flattening" any of the trace, which would indicate clipping. Do not take it all the way to the top orange line. My final number in the first box was 235. With those two levels correct, the gamma is absolutely perfect, averaging outright at 50%.

6. Now do the same for the blue channel. The blacks in the blue channel look good. The highlights have to come way up. I took the top right part of the blue curve and pulled it back to 145. That brought my blacks up a bit, so I moved my black point down to 10. Then I placed a point in the middle of the blue Curve and brought it up. I brought a

point at about 77 up to 135 to get the blue and green channels to match.

7. Finally, work on the red channel. Blacks first. I moved the Curve to the right by 10 "bits," matching the green and blue channels. I am going to skip jumping straight to the highlights of the red channel because it is so clipped, so I will set my midtones next by clicking on a spot in the middle of the blue Curve and pulling it down to match the other two curves. This pulled the blacks down too much, crushing them, so I'm going to move the black point back a little from where I had it. Bringing it all the way back to 0 matches the other two channels and unclips (or "uncrushes") the red channel's black level. The highlights are still too high, so click on the top of the Curve and pull it down. I brought my level down to 191. That meant I had to raise the midpoint back up a little to get it to match the other two channels again. I set the white point of the red channel by seeing that only three of the chips above the midtone were unclipped, so I matched the top of the third chip of the red channel to the same level as the third chips of the blue and green channels. That makes the "steps" of chips in the RGB Parade look evenly matched except for the two clipped chips in the red channel.

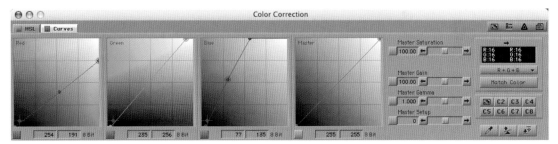

Figure 1-37 Here is what my Curves look like for the final correction. The numbers under the Curves indicate the level changes for the selected point on the Curve. The selected point is indicated by a small circle around the point. For the red, green, and master Curves it is the top point in my example. For the blue Curve, it indicates the middle point.

Take some time to try to use the Curves in your favorite app to adjust some of your own footage. The RGB Parade waveform is probably the easiest tool to analyze your results, but you could also use the eyedropper. In Color, you can select three simultaneous points on the image to monitor, and they update in real time as you either make adjustments or play through a scene. You can also try your hand at doing this correction using a vectorscope if you want a little more of a challenge.

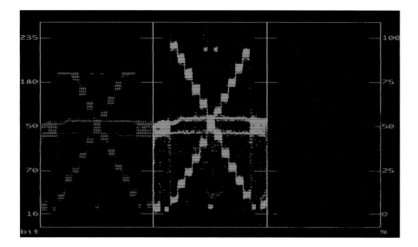

Figure 1-38 Here is the Avid internal RGB Parade waveform with the final correction.

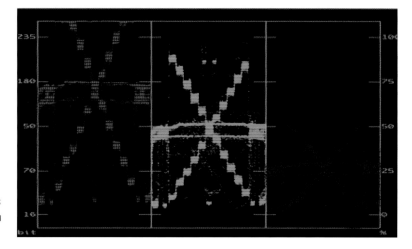

Figure 1-39 For comparison, this is the Avid RGB Parade waveform of the original image.

Conclusion

You've learned that analyzing your footage with several tools is the key to doing good color correction.

You've learned that analyzing your footage with several tools is the key to doing good color correction. With lots of experience and a very long-term relationship to a great high-end monitor, you can use your eye more to guide these corrections, but even experienced pros rely on the waveform monitor and vectorscope because your eyes can fatigue and lose reference. The scopes and other tools provide hard, unyielding reference points that will guide you even after a long grading session.

The scopes and other tools provide hard, unyielding reference points that will guide you even after a long grading session.

Using these references, there are many different tools to affect your grades. Which ones you use will depend somewhat on personal preference and somewhat on the situation or image at hand.

With this basic understanding of what we're trying to accomplish and how it is generally done, let's delve deeper into the world of color correction in the following chapters. We still have a lot to learn, including becoming more adept at the tools already mentioned and discovering how much can be accomplished with great color correction, including enhancing storytelling and creating images that stop viewers in their tracks.

Grade (used as both a verb and a noun)

To grade is the act of doing color correction. This is the widely accepted worldwide term, though it has enjoyed more popular support in the European postproduction community. As a noun, it indicates the color correction applied to a single shot. "On this grade, I went after more of a sunset feel." Or, "How do you want me to grade this shot?"

2

ANALYZE THIS—
YOUR MONITOR

In the Getting Started chapter, I explained that analyzing your image is an important first step toward good color correction. The next three chapters will be a more in-depth discussion of the analytical tools. We'll start with the most obvious choice for analyzing your image: using your eyes and your monitor.

The first way that the desktop editor usually analyzes the video image is to simply view the image on the computer screen. This is not recommended, though, because the gamma response of a computer display is different from a TV set or video monitor. Also, this image has not yet passed through the video card as it will when it goes to tape. A properly adjusted video monitor is definitely the preferred way to look at your image unless your project is going to be delivered solely via the web or to computer monitors. There is also a section later in this chapter on properly calibrating your video monitors.

The gamma response of a computer display is different from a TV set or video monitor.

Since this book was originally written, the industry has stopped manufacturing cathode ray tube (CRT) monitors. These monitors were the industry standard for color correction for their entire history until about 2008. Now, liquid crystal displays (LCDs)—and to a smaller extent, plasmas, DLP (digital light processing), and projection—are the only alternative, though numerous new technologies are about to hit the shelves, including OLED (organic light-emitting diode), SED (surface conduction electron-emitter), and LCDs with full RGB light emitting diode (LED) backlights. Choosing an LCD monitor for critical viewing is difficult with the current state of technology. Some manufacturers are employing extraordinary technical methods to get enough performance from LCD technology, and other LCDs have very poor performance despite claims from the manufacturers.

Liquid Crystal Displays

Why do LCD displays have a bad rap with image professionals? The main concerns are twofold: (1) blacks are not usually as rich on LCD displays as were traditionally delivered with CRT displays, and (2) the colors and contrast of most LCD displays change—sometimes drastically—with slight viewing angle changes.

To understand both of these problems, you need to understand how LCD technology works. Generally, the LCD displays that you would use as a video monitor work by placing a small light, like a fluorescent tube, at the bottom of the display and shines it up against a reflective, angled screen to "backlight" the monitor. All of the light that comes out of your screen, of any color, originates from this backlight. When the backlight bounces light out toward you, it is diffused by a screen to even out the light output across the screen. From there, a polarizing filter orients the light so that the waves are only going in one direction, let's say vertically. Then the light passes through the actual liquid crystal panel. If there is no electrical current applied to a specific pixel on the panel, then the light stays in this vertical orientation. On the other side of the LCD panel is another polarizing filter that is oriented 90 degrees from the first so that any light that passes through it must be horizontal. The LCD panel, when voltage is applied to it, is capable of "twisting" the light from one orientation to the other in degrees (this kind of LCD is known as a "twisted nematic" LCD). With no change in voltage, the light is completely blocked by the second polarizer. With the full voltage applied, it is twisted completely so that all of the light energy passes through the second polarizer. Between the "full off" and "full on" positions, varying amounts of "twist" to the light result in varying brightnesses. You can see that the light that is reaching your eye is going through several filtering layers. Because the angle with which the light comes through those filters is critical, the angle with which you view these kinds of monitors is also usually critical.

Some manufacturers have created several solutions to the viewing angle problem with varying degrees of success. With some displays, instead of orienting the polarizers at 0 degrees and 90 degrees, the polarizers are oriented at 45 and 135 degrees to give a greater side-to-side viewing angle. Other manufacturers employ special films that compensate for the direction of light, but these films can have a tendency to make off-axis viewing look yellow.

Be aware of the limitations of the technology and carefully select monitors. One of the most important tests you can do—and most manufacturers do *not* want you to see their monitors in this way—is to feed the monitor a nice, pure, even gray image to the entire monitor and look for unevenness and changes in color and brightness as you move your head up and down and from side to side. Sometimes even slight adjustments in the viewing angle can yield noticeable differences when looking at a pure gray image. Also, check to see how deep the blacks on the monitor are by looking at a pure black image. Oftentimes monitors appear to have very nice, rich blacks, but it is only because the people who are demonstrating the monitor have fed an image that also includes very bright whites, which—next to even a dull black—will appear rich.

Monitor Environment

Before we get into too much of a discussion about the monitors themselves, there is an important concept of color theory that affects the image as we perceive it on the monitor. The concept— which will be addressed further in the final chapters on color theory and video—is that the colors and contrast of the surrounding environment of the monitor can make a drastic difference in the way the image on the screen is perceived. Most color correction suites are designed so that the colors and lighting that surround the monitors do not influence the way the colors on the monitor are perceived.

Colors and contrast of the surrounding environment of the monitor can make a drastic difference in the way the image on the screen is perceived.

The color temperature of the lighting near the monitor and the paint colors near the monitor can affect the way the colorist perceives the colors that are on the screen. The color temperature and amount of light reflected onto the face of the monitor from elsewhere in the room should be controlled as much as possible. This affects LCD displays even more than CRT displays.

The color correction suite shown in Figure 2-1 was fairly brightly lit when this photograph was taken, but during a session the lights would be dimmed to reduce flare light. Although the walls appear slightly bluish in this publicity photograph, the monitor actually sits in front of a neutral gray field. The light that can be seen shining from behind the central monitor is daylight balanced.

Color Temperature
Measured in degrees kelvin (K), color temperature is based on an object called a black body radiator, which emits light when heated. The color of the light depends on the temperature to which the black body is heated. Black bodies heated to about 3500 K appear reddish, whereas those above about 7000 K appear bluish.

Figure 2-1 Color correction suite, not photographed under working conditions. Image courtesy of The Film & Tape Works.

Viewing conditions have evolved over the years. Randy Starnes, a veteran colorist who worked on projects like *NYPD Blue*, remembers the comfortable surroundings of his first color correction suite:

> *To relate how important the surround is, when I first started, we worked in a room that was designed to resemble the living room. The thought was: you're going to watch television in an environment similar to this, so let's color grade in this environment.*
>
> *The monitor was set in a bookcase. It was a warmly lit room with a desk lamp and overhead tungsten lights. It was a beautiful room. It was very comfortable, like a den or a gentlemen's smoking room.*

Daylight Balanced
This generally indicates that the light has a white point of 6500 K, which is generally the color of daylight, though the color of daylight actually varies enormously depending on time and location and other local conditions. "Daylight balanced" is sometimes used to describe light that is lower than 6500 K. Oftentimes 6000 K is used as a daylight reference. Sometimes light as "warm" as 5500 K or even 5000 K is described as being "daylight."

The longer you would color correct something in that room, the more red you would put into the pictures because your eyes became desensitized. The color receptors became desensitized to the warm environment. At the start of the day, skin tones would look normal, but after 6 or 8 hours, you were correcting skin tones oversaturated, like basketballs, because your perception had changed.

It is real-life experiences like Starnes's that create a strong case for understanding the principles of color theory when designing an ideal color correction suite or simply adapting a basic edit suite to be suitable to the task of color correction.

According to Thomas Madden, an imaging scientist with Eastman Kodak Company, Starnes's anecdotal example of color surrounds has a strong foundation in scientific principle. The viewing environment alters the adaptive state of the observers' visual system—the way they perceive color. This subject is addressed thoroughly in a book written by Madden and his colleague Edward Giorgianni called *Digital Color Management.*

Figure 2-2 This is a modern color correction suite that is attuned to the need for a neutrally color balanced viewing environment. Note the neutral gray wall behind the main monitor and the daylight balanced light that backlights the monitor. This is the da Vinci color correction suite at CBS News NY. Neal Kassner, who is featured in *The Art and Technique of Digital Color Correction* grades *48 Hours* in this suite. During a session the warmish overheads are turned off, and the overall lighting is dimmed. Image courtesy Neal Kassner.

The Eyes Have It

Madden says:

A given color stimulus, the light that reaches your eyes, presented to an observer under different viewing conditions may very well have different color appearances in each condition. So in the example where the same color stimulus is presented in two different viewing environments, an instrument would sense each stimulus and say, "These are the same," and a viewer may well look at each and say, "Well, no, they're not. They look entirely different to me." That result has to do with image luminance levels and surrounds as well as other factors. So, the viewing conditions have a big influence on color management.

If you start with a live scene that was captured by a digital camera and the digital image was brought to a monitor on a workstation, and then the image was going out to film, and then to be projected in a dark theater, you've got three very different viewing conditions for the same image: the original scene, the monitor, and the theater conditions. An observer in each of those viewing conditions is going to be under different adaptive states. If I reproduce the same colorimetry in those three environments, the viewer will have a different impression of each presentation. So, the question I've got to ask is, "What colors do I need to produce in each viewing condition that will evoke in the observer the same visual impression of the original colors?"

For the colorist, this task is ultimately complicated further by the fact that we rarely have control over the final viewing environment. This would not seem to be very significant, but consider the fact that some video monitors have been tested to have contrast ratios as high as 1000:1 when tested with contact instruments, unaffected by the viewing environment. Yet that same monitor would be perceived to have only a 100:1 contrast ratio under poor viewing conditions. According to Madden, even flare light as low as 0.5% of a white image displayed on the screen can have a significant impact on the quality of the image.

In the previous example, *flare light,* or the light that falls on the face of the screen from various lights and sources in the room, effectively lowers the contrast ratio of the image. But that's not the only effect. In addition, the colors on the monitor appear to be desaturated because of the addition of white light to the colors being transmitted from the monitor itself. The problem of flare light polluting the saturation and contrast of an image is especially evident and damaging in the darker portions of the picture.

For many color critical applications, people work in near total darkness. This is not always practical for those working with clients, but many video professionals, when they do not worry about entertaining clients during the creative process, work completely in the dark. This even extends to the 3D lighters on animated films. After the modeling and animation are completed, the lighting specialists step in to really determine the final look of the images by determining how much light bounces off the characters and sets from various directions. This lighting process is carried out almost entirely in the dark, similar to the environment where the footage will eventually be shown: a darkened movie theater.

Another interesting phenomenon that applies to the perception of video images is that softness in image detail is also perceived by the viewer as lowered contrast and even decreased saturation. This phenomenon is exploited by numerous graphics programs that offer the ability to sharpen a fuzzy image. Many of these programs rely on algorithms that increase contrast to create part of the perception that the picture is sharper.

Further complicating the reproduction of "correct" colors is that, in reality, nobody wants the true color of the scene most of the time! Madden explains:

In reality, nobody wants the true color of the scene most of the time!

There are other factors that affect color reproduction. There's color memory and color preference. With regard to color memory, studies have shown that we don't remember colors exactly as they were if we're removed from the original scene. We tend to remember colors as being somewhat more saturated than they originally were. So when we design a system that reproduces original scene colors, they tend to be reproduced at a higher saturation level because that's what people remember. We also have preferences for the reproduction of certain colors, particularly skies and grass. Grass and foliage we tend to prefer being reproduced a little cooler—more cyan than they really are. If we reproduced grass accurately, people would tend to think it was yellow and pale looking.

Colorists often exploit this human preference; the colors we *want* to see may not be the colors that are actually there. Therefore, the job of finding the right color is not a completely technical exercise.

Let's take a look at some real-world visual examples and how they can affect our perception of color. The phenomenon of surrounding color can be demonstrated with simple blocks of color.

In Figure 2-3 notice that the gray square in the black border seems brighter than the exact same shade of gray with the light gray border. The black surround in Figure 2-4 increases the perceived luminance of both reddish blocks compared to the lighter surround. Notice in Figure 2-5 the shift in hue of the two identical blocks of green when surrounded by blue and yellow. Surrounded

TIP

For an example of how this preference can be exploited, check out Randy Starnes's use of secondary color correction on page 153.

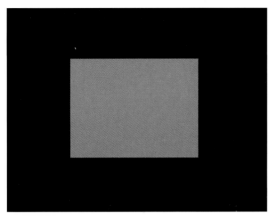

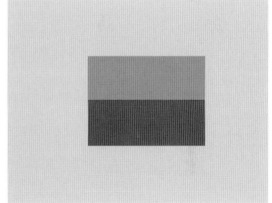

Figure 2-3 Grays surrounded by black and light gray.

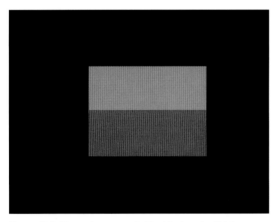

Figure 2-4 Two reds surrounded by black and a lighter gray.

Figure 2-5 Greens surrounded by blue and yellow.

by blue, the green seems more yellow, and surrounded by yellow, it appears more blue.

Understanding what these surround colors can do to your perception of the color within them explains the care that most colorists—or at least the care of the people who designed their rooms—take in eliminating any false perception of color. Lighting in a colorist's suite is carefully chosen and monitored. Specialized lamps are ordered to emit a smooth, consistent light in the 6000 K range, which is considered to be daylight—or even a little beyond daylight. Most colorists agree on a temperature of 6500 K. But some color professionals use white references as low as 5000 K. Walls surrounding the main monitor that the colorist uses are painted a specific neutral gray. The care taken in eliminating surrounding colors even extends in many cases to using waveform and vectorscopes that do not have the traditional green trace color but a white or neutral color instead. Some colorists even put tape over bright red or green power buttons or indicators.

These surrounds affect the colorist day in and day out. Randy Starnes explains:

> *The reason you have the neutral background is that you keep the same perception all along. You refer to something that is neutral. Otherwise, if you bathe the area in blue, you're going to compensate for that. You're going to lose your sensitivity to blue, and then you become desensitized to that. If you sit in a yellow room, your pictures are going to end up yellow. Or you're going to be constantly fighting what you perceive. So the easiest way to compensate for that is to surround the monitor with something that is neutral and daylight.*
>
> *You can also take your monitor to black and white to refresh your perspective. or Sometimes I'll use the switcher to put a gray border or a white border around my image to judge what pure white should look like or pure gray. Sometimes that helps the colorist, and sometimes that helps clients, whose perception is just as important to the process because they might feel like a white shirt needs to be whiter, looks dingy. Doing commercial work, selling laundry soap, sometimes you might add a little blue to the whites to make them whiter than white, depending on how the set is designed. If you have an environment that is not neutral, the hardest thing to get right is going to be the white scenes.*

You can also take your monitor to black and white to refresh your perspective.

Colorists who work on green screen or blue screen color corrections that are destined to be keyed over another background are well aware of how the large amount of background color floods their eyes and can affect the way they correct the foreground images. That is why many colorists will key out the backing color to black or a neutral gray before attempting their correction.

When I wrote my second color correction book, *The Art and Technique of Digital Color Correction*, I used high-quality reference monitors from eCinema. The monitors actually came with backlights that were calibrated to the exact color temperature of the backlights inside the monitors themselves.

The Real and the Ideal

For many people working in established rooms or even improvised spaces, these surround issues will not be easy to resolve. But at least you should understand the consequences of color correcting next to a warm table lamp, under fluorescents, or adjacent to a huge red movie poster. Try to limit flares, lights, and distracting surrounding colors to assist your eyes in presenting your brain with the most accurate colors.

Setting Up Your Computer Monitors

Before viewing any images on a computer monitor, you'll need to set it up. Usually your monitor will come with some sort of setup procedure from the manufacturer. Also, most computers have settings that adjust the graphics card that feeds your monitor. This setting is usually referred to as a *profile*. These profiles attempt to ensure that the colors on the image in your monitor match the colors of the image that is sent from your computer. Even if you are monitoring your main output color on a video monitor, the computer monitor should be set up as accurately as possible.

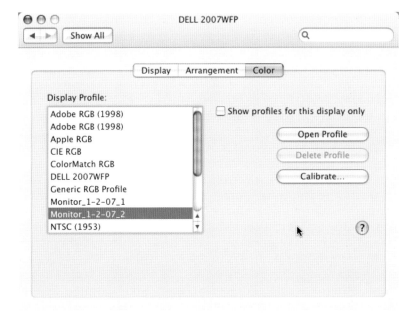

Figure 2-6 Monitor profiles in System Preferences>Displays on a Mac. There are many factory preset profiles to choose from. The ones labeled "monitor_1-2-07_1" and "monitor_1-2-07_2" were created by calibrating my monitor using the GretagMacbeth Eye-One Display 2 calibrator and software.

ICC Profiles

ICC stands for International Color Consortium. Their goal, as stated on their web site, is "making color seamless between devices and documents." To do this they promote a cross-platform, cross-product standard for creating and using profiles to match color reproduction at all stages of production: acquisition, display, and output. Their web site (www.color.org) is very informative on issues of color management.

LUT

Look-up tables. These are numerical arrays that allow for the translation of colors so that inputs, monitors, and outputs all look the same. The complexity of look-up tables can vary and include 3D look-up tables, which are the standard in matching displays and film ingest and output for feature films. LUTs compensate for the latent strengths, weaknesses, and display limitations of a given medium or device. For example, if your flatbed scanner tends to create yellowish highlights, a LUT could be created to automatically eliminate those yellowish highlights.

Print retouchers and graphic artists who must deal with computer images matching print images on a daily basis have very carefully created ICC profiles of their scanners, monitors, and printers so that they have a consistent reference throughout the process. These profiles are essentially LUTS, or look-up tables. To create your own profile for your monitor, it is good to invest in—or borrow—a calibration device, like X-Rite's GretagMacbeth Eye-One Display. It's a little device that looks kind of like a computer mouse, and it can be placed on your monitor to sense the color coming from the monitor. This, along with the accompanying software and calibration images that come with the device, allow you to quickly and easily set up a monitor profile that is fairly close to your video monitor. Matt Allard of X-Rite explains, "For editors viewing video on computer LCD displays, the monitor should be set to a 2.2 gamma setting and should use the D65 standard for white. D65 means that white is at 6500 K color temperature."

"For editors viewing video on computer LCD displays, the monitor should be set to a 2.2 gamma setting and should use the D65 standard for white."

Calibrating Your Video Monitors

Making sure that your viewing monitor properly represents the image you're correcting is critical. Because this book is aimed at a wide range of editors, we should point out that using a consumer-grade TV set as a monitoring device is far from optimal. One reason is that broadcast video monitors have a far better picture than most consumer TV sets, and the color of consumer sets is often skewed—most often going bluish. These consumer sets are also set up very specifically to hide certain errors in the picture that you need to see. They are also generally tweaked to provide a much more colorful picture than the signal fed to them is actually delivering. Studies show that this is how people remember color and prefer color to be portrayed, whether it's accurate or not. Consumer TVs also rarely allow for as much "tweaking" as professional video monitors.

Broadcast or professional monitors more accurately represent the image the camera sees. They have tighter tolerances than a regular TV set. Monitors usually have less overscan (usually 2%–5%), allowing you to see more of the picture. In addition, most monitors have underscan functions to allow you to see all of the picture area for critical analysis of the entire frame.

Professional monitors also conform to color standards. Color temperature is preset to 6500 K, which is the broadcast standard.

In addition to color and tonal accuracy and sharpness, one of the advantages of a professional quality video monitor is the presence of the Blue Only button. The purpose of Blue Only is to allow

Figure 2-7 Simulated image of SMPTE bars viewed as Blue Only.

the correct adjustment of the color, hue, and brightness controls on the monitor using a SMPTE color bar signal (see Figure 2-7). On some monitors Blue Only is also called Blue Check. With still other monitors, you achieve this by pressing buttons that disable the red and green guns. Viewing an image as Blue Only allows you to easily see phase errors or video signal level errors. Blue Only mode turns off the red and green signals and feeds the display only the blue signal.

If you don't have a monitor that allows you to select only the blue channel in some manner, you can also view the monitor through a dark blue filter, like those used by veteran lighting directors to check for contrast differences. A Tiffen or Wratten 47B dark blue photographic filter would work as well.

The blue photographic filter or blue filter button on the monitor have the same effect, which is that a SMPTE color bar pattern viewed as Blue Only shows a series of bars that alternate in brightness. Attempting to adjust chroma and hue with the full spectrum of colors is a very subjective judgment, but adjusting chroma and hue while monitoring only the blue channel becomes "black and white."

But adjusting chroma and hue while monitoring only the blue channel becomes "black and white."

How does this work? The order of the colors in the color bars signal is not random. These color bars (SMPTE color bars) have certain features that some other color bar signals do not (see Figure 2-8). The order of the colors is always the same, though some other color bar signals include a black bar to the right of the blue bar. They are arranged by brightness, with the brightest to the left and the darkest to the right (white, yellow, cyan, green, magenta, red, and blue).

There are also some other interesting arrangements of the bars that are evident only when viewing specific color channels. If you have a monitor that can turn off individual channels, check it out on your monitor. Otherwise, refer to Figure 2-9. Look at the pat-

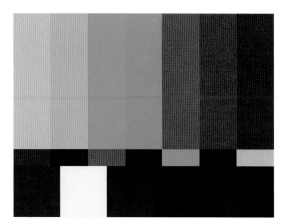

Figure 2-8 SMPTE color bars.

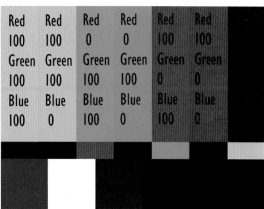

Figure 2-9 SMPTE color bars. Each bar indicates the percentage of red, green, and blue in it. Note the patterns of red, green, and blue as you read the numbers from left to right.

terns in the percentages of red, green, and blue in each colored bar. Notice that all of the colored bars are made up only of combinations of either 0% of a color or 100% of a color. Also, notice that the bars alternate from having 100% blue to having 0% blue with every bar. The red and green values show similar patterns. The red values alternate in pairs, and the green values are all grouped together.

If you look at the blue channel only, SMPTE color bars are essentially black and white bars (actually, black and bright blue) that appear as white, black, white, black, white, black, and white. Why? Because the first bar in color bars is white. Pure white in video is made by having all three channels—red, green, and blue—at full level. For the sake of simplicity, let's use a scale from 0 to 100 for this discussion, so white has 100 Red, 100 Blue, and 100 Green. (For most computers and color levels, this is usually described with a scale from 0 to 255, but a scale based on 100 makes it easier to understand the math.) If you are only looking at the blue channel, that means you are looking at 100 brightness. The next bar in color bars is yellow. Yellow is made up of 100 Red, 0 Blue, and 100 Green. Monitoring Blue Only means that you are looking at a bar with 0 brightness. Cyan is a combination of 0 Red, 100 Blue, and 100 Green. This means the bar should have 100 brightness. The green bar is 0 Red, 0 Blue, and 100 Green. This gives this bar a 0 brightness if set up properly. Magenta is 100 Red, 100 Blue, and 0 Green, giving the green bar a 100 brightness when viewed as blue only. The red bar is comprised of 100 Red, 0 Blue, and 0 Green. That makes this bar appear as 0 brightness. Finally, the blue bar is made from 0 Red, 100 Blue, and 0 Green. That means that, when viewed as Blue Only, this bar appears at 100 brightness. EBU bars and some other color bars have a final bar of black to the right of the blue bar. That bar has no amount of

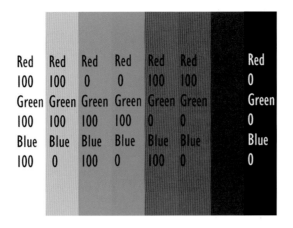

Figure 2-10 EBU color bars. Each bar indicates the percentage of red, green, and blue in it. Note the patterns of red, green, and blue as you read the numbers from left to right.

red, green, or blue, so it would also appear as black, or 0 brightness, as shown in Figure 2-10.

If you only look at the numbers in the blue row across the bottom of the color bars, you can see that whether the blue channel is on or not alternates from one color bar to the next. There are also patterns in the red and green channels. With red, the first two color bars have 100 Red, and the second pair of bars have 0 Red. The third pair of bars have 100 Red, and the final bar has 0 Red. With the green channel, the first four bars have 100 Green, and the last three have 0 Green.

So what do these patterns in the bars have to do with properly calibrating your monitor? A lot. To explain it, let's look at the RGB readings as we move along a color wheel. The color wheel in Corel Painter makes it easy to visualize (see Figure 2-11). As we rotate along the color wheel while monitoring the RGB levels of the colors on the wheel, the amount of blue increases or decreases. Similarly, as we rotate the hue of the video monitor, the amount of blue in each bar increases or decreases. The object is to match the brightness of each bar that should have 100 Blue (white, cyan, magenta, and blue) and to match the darkness of the bars that should have 0 Blue (yellow, green, and red). This is much less subjective than trying to determine if the yellow bar is a little too green or a little too red. In addition to being less subjective, the biology and anatomy of our eyes are much better tuned to perceive variations in brightness than they are in hue.

One trick to the Blue Only system is that Chroma controls also adjust how much blue is in each bar. To see this, let's go back to Corel Painter in Figure 2-12 and watch the blue level as we slide the amount of chroma down. Even though the color wheel indicates a pure blue hue, adjusting the intensity of the saturation changes the amount of blue in the pure blue hue. (Try saying that three times fast!)

So chroma and hue interact with each other in determining the brightness of each bar. The key to figuring out which control is

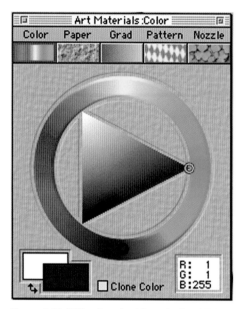

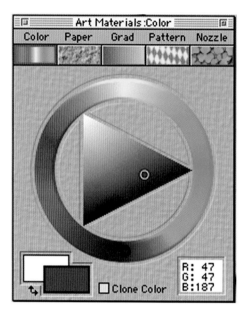

Figure 2-11 RGB color wheel from the Corel Painter user interface (UI). Note the RGB numbers in the bottom right corner that describe the dark blue color that's been selected.

Figure 2-12 RGB color wheel from the Corel Painter UI. Note the RGB numbers in the bottom right corner that describe the less saturated blue color that's been selected. While the hue has stayed the same as in Figure 2-11, the amount of red and green have both increased.

Figure 2-13 Properly set up full spectrum SMPTE color bars.

Figure 2-14 Properly set up SMPTE color bars viewed with the Blue Only function.

affecting the blue hue and which is affecting the blue saturation is to match the brightness of the smaller rectangles in SMPTE color bars with the longer bright bars above them, as shown in Figure 2-13. Notice that these smaller rectangles are the same colors that contained 100% blue in the longer bars. They are just in the reverse order from the regular full-length bars.

The Hue controls on the monitor will mostly affect the middle, short, bright bars, and the Chroma will mostly affect the longer

Figure 2-15 Full spectrum SMPTE color bars with the hue rotated by 10 degrees.

Figure 2-16 SMPTE color bars with the hue rotated by 10 degrees viewed with the Blue Only function. Note the subtle level change in the right-most dark blue bar.

Figure 2-17 Full spectrum SMPTE color bars with the chroma lowered by 10%.

Figure 2-18 SMPTE color bars with the chroma lowered by 10% viewed with the Blue Only function. Detecting a difference in this print image in the book may not be possible.

bright bars. Look at the following figures to see how bars look when correctly set up (see Figure 2-13 and 2-14) and then on an improperly set up monitor (see Figures 2-15 through 2-18).

Figures 2-15 and 2-16 have the hue rotated 10° off. To the untrained eye, 10° does not change the hue of the full spectrum bars that much, but it is quite noticeable when viewed as Blue Only. Notice that the third dark bar from the left is brighter than the others. Also, the tall, top bars vary in brightness from the shorter bars below them.

Figures 2-17 and 2-18 show chroma lowered by 10%. Once again, to the untrained eye, they look pretty good, but viewed as Blue Only, you can see the difference in the luminance levels between the top set of long bars and the shorter bars below them. Compare this to Figure 2-7 where you cannot see where the long bars end and the short bars begin.

With the Hue and Saturation controls set properly, we can now adjust the Brightness and Contrast controls. Brightness should be adjusted first. To do this, watch the three small black bars under the red color bar. This is called the *pluge* (rhymes with "huge" or "luge," depending on whom you ask). The goal is to adjust the contrast so that the middle bar is just barely distinguishable from the bar to the right, and then tweak it a bit more so that the two bars to the right just merge, while the third bar to the left is just a bit brighter than the two to the right. When tweaking Contrast, the key is to look at the only rectangle that is truly 100% white. That rectangle is at the bottom under the yellow and cyan bars. Set the contrast so that this bar appears very white but not annoyingly bright or glowing. Also, there should be a difference in brightness between the small bottom square, which is 100% white, and the other white rectangles, which are only 75% white.

Alternative Methods for Video Monitor Calibration

With the increased prevalence of LCD monitors, calibration of video monitors has actually gotten a lot harder and more complicated.

With the increased prevalence of LCD monitors, calibration of video monitors has actually gotten a lot harder and more complicated. The primary reason for this is the difference in backlight technology and the resulting color differences in the video image.

If you feel that setting up to color bars is not working for you, you could try one of several solutions being marketed to home theater enthusiasts. I was skeptical of this route myself, but I have been assured by several color scientists that the general principles of using these home theater setup solutions are completely viable.

The trick for using these setup programs is that home TV sets, and indeed most professional video monitors, don't allow software to automatically set the levels on the monitor itself, so the software can only guide a human being in changing the levels by hand (usually with the monitor or TV remote) to set the specific levels. This is best done with some kind of hardware calibration method. Some of them use the same sensor that I suggested in the section on calibrating your computer display along with special test patterns from a DVD. One source for doing this yourself is from a company called SpectraCal and their calibration software, CalMAN.

Another alternative to setting up your own monitor is to have it calibrated and set up by a professional who uses Imaging Science

Foundation (ISF) calibration and who is ISF certified. If you decide to go this route, make sure the technicians are certified and using test generators and color sensors like those by Sencore. This is not a job for the teenagers at the local big box electronics store. Many of these technicians can properly calibrate your computer monitors as well as your video monitors. Fees for this service are typically several hundred dollars—more for projectors.

3

USING SCOPES AS CREATIVE TOOLS

The next two important tools—after the video monitor itself—in analyzing a video image are a waveform monitor and vectorscope. There are three general categories of scopes available. The first type is completely hardware based, with the waveform and vectorscope trace and graticule presented on a screen built into the scope (see Figure 3-2). The second type uses dedicated hardware to display the scopes on a separate computer display or as an overlay on your video monitor (see Figure 3-1). This is often referred to as a rasterizer or hybrid. The third type is software based using a video card, with the resulting image of the scope displayed in the software UI on your computer monitor (see Figure 3-3).

Choosing Your Scope

One of the main aspects that distinguish good scopes from bad is the resolution of the trace.

One of the main aspects that distinguish good scopes from bad is the resolution of the trace. The trace, which is the scope's visual representation of the video signal on the monitor, has a much higher resolution in hardware-based scopes and rasterizers. The resolution of the trace is particularly important when analyzing the video signal to be color corrected. This is where almost all software scopes—and even some hybrid scopes that are displayed on the video monitor—suffer. Hybrid scopes presented on a computer monitor are preferable to those presented on a video monitor because of the increased resolution possible with computer CRTs or LCDs. Many CRTs and LCDs are switchable between two inputs so that an extra monitor is not needed. You can have your editing computer UI displayed on the A side and the scopes on the B side. This saves lots of monitor real estate.

Figure 3-1 Rackmountable
rasterizer with separate LCD
display. Courtesy Tektronix, Inc.

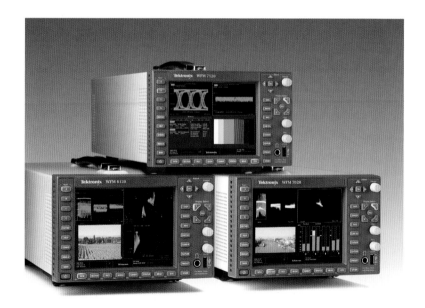

Figure 3-2 Rackmountable
integrated display scopes.
Courtesy Tektronix, Inc.

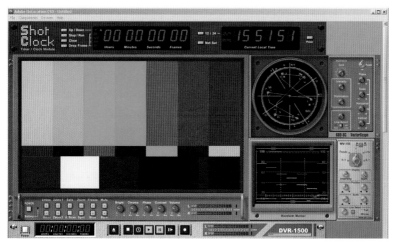

Figure 3-3 Adobe's OnLocation software-based scope user interface.

Another factor to consider is that most external scopes and hybrids offer a broader range of variables or settings that can be controlled or monitored, while many software scopes are set to a default configuration that cannot be changed. Often these software scopes are not designed to measure all of the elements of the video signal, such as blanking. Some of the analyses in this book are best performed on scopes that can be deliberately set out of calibration or that require specific settings, so users of software scopes will be somewhat limited in these examples.

Another common method for getting waveform and vectorscope information is to rely on the built-in scopes of the software itself. Apple's Color, Final Cut Pro, Adobe, Avid, and others all provide built-in scopes. There are several problems with these scopes. The main issue is that no matter how fast the computers get, the software designers want most of the "cycles" (computer power) to be assigned to the actual editing application, not to the scopes, so they do not usually monitor every single line of video. They are also limited in their ability to show customized views and settings. Although these scopes often very accurately portray the video information inside the application, they are not downstream of your video card, so they can't really give you a true indication of the signal that's going on to tape. Finally, by turning off the built-in scopes and using "real" scopes, you are freeing up computer power to be used for the real purpose of your application.

Many people cannot afford the cost of these hardware-based scopes or the rasterizer scopes. Fortunately for them, there are several software scopes—like ScopeBox's software scopes (Figure 3-4) or Hamlet's VidScope (Figure 3-5)—that allow you to see a waveform and vectorscope on your computer monitor. With a spare, low end computer and monitor, a video card, and this type of software, you can have a set of scopes that are "external" to your editing or color correction application. It has the benefit of not relying on your main editing computer for computational power, and it has the benefit of monitoring the signal downstream of the

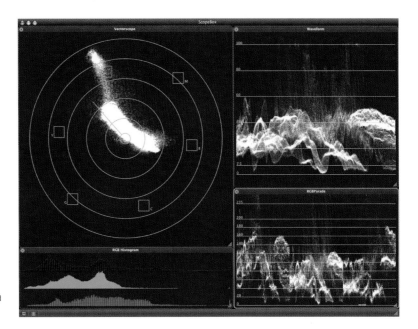

Figure 3-4 Screen shot of ScopeBox's software scopes on a Mac.

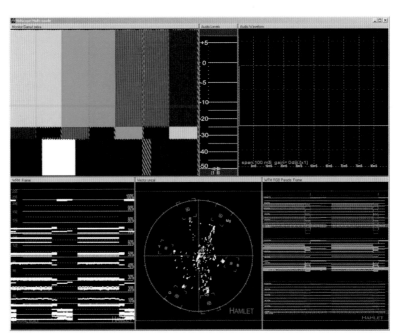

Figure 3-5 Screen shot of Hamlet VidScope software scopes on a PC.

video card on your editing computer. The drawback is that the resolution of these software solutions is still not as high as a standard scope from one of the main scope manufacturers. That may change over the coming years.

However, an important and often hidden problem with many software scopes built in to editing and color correction applications is that they may not present information on all of the lines of the video raster. Some scopes present just a single line, which is virtually useless. This is like trying to determine what a scene looks like through a paper-thin slit in a wall. Other scopes may *appear* to give you all of the lines but are in fact only presenting a quarter or a 16th of the number of possible lines, similar to viewing a scene through a set of half-closed venetian blinds. This is very dangerous for trying to establish broadcast limits because you could have illegal areas—like a bright specular point—that sneak in between the lines that are being analyzed by the scope. Software scopes are constantly evolving and being updated with greater capabilities, so we won't point out specific deficient scopes here because as computers increase in speed, they may increase their number of scanned lines. Be sure to read your user's manuals carefully for this information. Some manufacturers won't divulge this information at all.

> *Having access to the information that the waveform monitor and vectorscope provide is essential for proper color correction.*

Whatever style of scopes you choose, having access to the information that the waveform monitor and vectorscope provide is essential for proper color correction. The main reason is that, as an analytical tool, the scopes provide critical information that can guide you in fixing color correction problems. Scopes also provide a fixed, objective reference as you work and compare shots. Each audio edit may sound okay next to the one beside it, but over the course of a program, the levels could easily slip a substantial amount as you progress farther and farther from your initial point of reference. Or imagine completing a mix without audio meters, only to discover that the monitors were turned up very loud, making your mix much too low.

> *Imagine trying to maintain a consistent audio level throughout a program if you didn't have audio meters.*

Scopes also help you provide a legal output of your creative product. Part of the responsibility of the colorist is to ensure that the luma and chroma signals are within certain technical limits. Being a brilliant editor and colorist doesn't mean much if no one will air your product or if the dubs are not viewable. *Legal limits* are set by broadcasters and cablecasters and vary from one to the next. But even if your product isn't being broadcast, legal levels affect the proper duplication of your project and the way it will look on a regular TV monitor.

Legal

Legal means that the brightness and color saturation of an image does not exceed minimum or maximum levels. In general these levels adhere to national and international standards. Also, as our delivery systems become more and more digitally based, "gamut" is also included in "legal" levels. In addition to "legal" levels, there is a second, similar term called "valid" levels.

Valid Levels

Levels that remain legal when transferred, translated, or transcoded between formats.

Let's take a look at how the waveform and vectorscopes can help us as we analyze the images we are attempting to correct. There are probably two groups who are about to roll their eyes and flip ahead a few pages. The first group is experienced online videotape editors: crusty veterans who've been using scopes forever. They know all about sync pulse, blanking, back porches, and breezeways, and they aren't interested in sitting through the basics. The second group is the new wave of digital whiz kids who have no interest in all the hard-core video engineering stuff that is largely obsolete since the death of the quad machine. Well, we're not going to be discussing all that video engineering stuff, with the exception of a brief discussion on keeping levels legal. We want to show how these two pieces of engineering equipment can be put to good use as *creative tools*.

Waveform Monitor

First, let's explore the waveform monitor. To many, the waveform is simply a way to look at the luminance or brightness of the video signal, but it can also display the chrominance levels of the signal as well. This chrominance information can be used to minimize color casts in your images.

One of the most basic uses of the waveform monitor is to allow you to see that your luminance and setup levels are legal. This means that the brightest part of the luminance signal does not extend beyond the 100IRE mark—with occasional specular highlights allowed to reach 108IRE, more or less, depending on the individual broadcaster's specs—and that the darkest part of the picture does not drop below either the 7.5IRE mark for NTSC video with setup or below 0IRE for NTSC video without setup and for all digital video signals and signals in countries beyond the United States.

So how do you know if your video should be with or without setup? Well, with virtually all *analog* NTSC video, you need to have setup with blacks at 7.5IRE. However, no digital format has setup. From DV to HDCAM, setup is not used anywhere in the world.

In analog formats, only the United States still uses setup (broadcast specification RS170A). NTSC in other parts of the world may or may not have setup. PAL and SECAM do not use setup. Component analog video has different standards also. The SMPTE/EBU (N10) standard does not have setup. So what do you do if you have a digital VTR and are using the analog in/out connectors? You need to know what standards are being used by the other analog machines. Then match the In/Out settings for Add/Remove Setup to match the rest of the system.

Allowing your video to extend outside of the range defined by whatever form of video you are using can cause broadcasters to refuse to air your finished tape until corrections are made or for

Sync Pulse, Blanking, Back Porch and Breezeway

Luckily for you, gentle reader, I will not bother with the in-depth technical details of the signal that is displayed on the waveform monitor, but if you want to talk the lingo and impress the resident geek at your local SMPTE meeting, this diagram provides a look at everything you never wanted to know about your video signal and had no intention of asking.

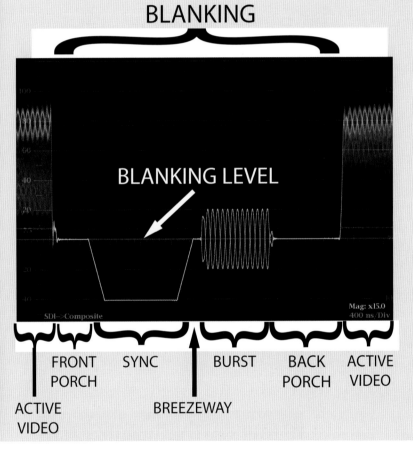

BLANKING

BLANKING LEVEL

SDI->Composite

Mag: x15.0
400 ns/Div

FRONT PORCH SYNC BURST BACK PORCH ACTIVE VIDEO

ACTIVE VIDEO BREEZEWAY

Figure 3-6 The technical anatomy of the waveform signal. Highly magnified, this is the portion of the waveform that is in the middle, between the two fields of video. None of these elements are critical to the "creative" use of the waveform monitor.

dubs to have quality issues, like sparkling, bleeding, bearding, and buzzing. Sometimes, if video levels are far enough astray, they can even cause buzzing in the audio channels.

There are also legal chrominance levels and other technical specifications regarding timing of the signals and other signal amplitudes and relationships. These all vary slightly from broadcaster to broadcaster. But let's leave this technical stuff aside and concentrate on how to use the waveform monitor for the fun stuff.

Chip Chart and Waveform Monitor

One of the important skills that is necessary to acquire is an understanding of what part of an image corresponds to a particular part of the trace on the waveform monitor. Because the waveform primarily is used to display luminance information, we will use an image that provides a full range of luma values, but little chroma information, to limit the confusion. The source image we will use is commonly referred to as a *chip chart*, in particular, the CamAlign GrayScale Test Pattern from DSC Laboratories.

On multicamera programs—like sports, soaps, talk shows, specials, concerts, and news—the cameras must be *matched* so that the colors from each camera angle match all of the other angles. To do this, usually all cameras are pointed at a chip chart comprised entirely of black, gray, and white chips. The process of setting up a camera to properly reproduce the chip chart is an excellent introduction to many principles of both color correction and the use of a waveform monitor.

Look at Figures 3-7 and 3-8: a chip chart and a waveform monitor of the same chart. Notice the unique pattern that the chip chart forms on the waveform monitor. When properly lit and set up—or *shaded*—the pattern is clean and uniform in shape. The

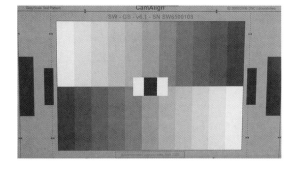

Figure 3-7 An image of the CamAlign GrayScale Test Pattern from DSC Laboratories, sometimes known generically as a "chip chart."

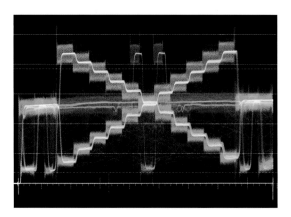

Figure 3-8 A waveform image of the chip chart captured from a Tektronix WFM7120 waveform monitor.

ultimate goal is that each gray square—or *chip*—is the same level on each camera.

Before we try to correct or color balance this image, let's examine it and figure out which parts of the image are represented by specific portions of the trace on the waveform. The trace shows an X shape with a thick band running horizontally through the center and a small straight line on the bottom of the waveform monitor, centered horizontally. The X is created by the two strips of chips. The top set of chips, which starts with bright chips to the left, creates the diagonal steps of the X that start in the upper left corner and ends in the lower right. The bottom set of chips is shown on the waveform as the diagonal series of steps that starts in the bottom left and ascends to the upper right.

The background gray color that makes up most of the chart surface is represented on the waveform by the thick horizontal line that runs around the 50IRE level. And the small black patch in the middle of the chip chart is represented on the waveform by the small horizontal line in the center.

When trying to analyze an image on the waveform monitor, it is important to remember that the horizontal positions of items in the image will correspond to the horizontal position on the trace but that vertical positioning in the image is inconsequential to the waveform display. The vertical positioning on the waveform monitor is completely determined by the brightness of the object—though sometimes also determined by chroma levels depending on the waveform settings. So an image with a gradation from black at the bottom and white at the top (or vice versa) will create a waveform with an even spread of the trace across its entire raster. A gradation from black on one side to white on the other side will create a diagonal line across the waveform monitor.

Figure 3-10 shows what a side-to-side gradation looks like on a waveform monitor. The gradation goes from black on the left to white on the right. Figure 3-12 shows how a gradation from top to bottom is represented on a waveform monitor. Whether the image was gradated from black to white or white to black in this case would not matter because vertical positions of images are not represented on a waveform.

For fun, let's look at an image of a simple title page with gradated text. This causes a distinct pattern on the waveform monitor (see Figure 3-14). This waveform was generated by typing the word "Wave" in Photoshop and gradating the image with white at the top of the word and black at the bottom. Switching the gradation with white on the bottom would have caused the word to appear upside down in the waveform monitor.

Although the primary point in monitoring the waveform is to match the gain and setup (brightness and blackness) of the signal, we can also use it to get important information on the chrominance of the signal, which would allow for the proper white balance and black balance of a live camera or a videotaped image. Most people do white balancing on their cameras using the automatic White Balance button while pointing the camera at a white target. Then they do a black balance by capping their camera and using the auto Black Balance button. It is also possible to manually do these corrections with the proper camera controls and the proper monitoring tools. Knowing how to accomplish this can help you understand a lot about color correction.

In a studio or in a remote truck, each camera control unit allows for individual control of each of the red, green, and blue channels of the camera for gain, gamma, and setup. Because you are reading this book for the purpose of color correction in the postproduction process, you can try these same experiments with color correction software and some footage of a chip chart or even a white sheet of paper that has bad white balance. The DVD included with this book has several files that can be imported and manipulated.

The important thing to remember when attempting to manually white balance or black balance a camera (or preexisting footage) is that black and white should be as achromatic as

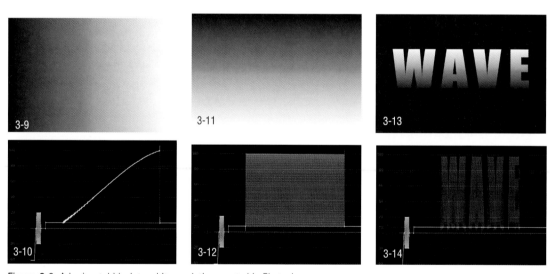

Figure 3-9 A horizontal black to white gradation created in Photoshop.
Figure 3-10 Waveform of the horizontal gradation shown in Figure 3-9 (captured using a Tektronix WFM7120).
Figure 3-11 A vertical black to white gradation created in Photoshop.
Figure 3-12 Waveform of the vertical black to white gradation shown in Figure 3-11.
Figure 3-13 Photoshop image of the word "WAVE" with a vertical gradation. Because we want the top of the word "WAVE" to be at the top of the waveform monitor, the white part of the gradation has to be at the top of the word. Otherwise the word would show up upside down on the waveform monitor.
Figure 3-14 Waveform of the word "WAVE" from Figure 3-13.

possible. That means "without color." Figures 3-15 and 3-16 show what a white piece of paper at 90IRE should look like on a waveform—with a Flat filter setting—and a vectorscope, respectively.

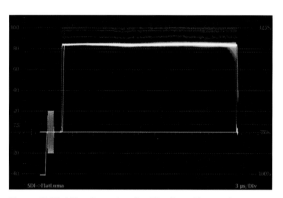

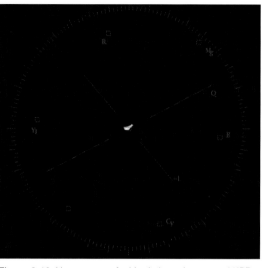

Figure 3-15 Waveform showing Flat Pass filter and luminance of white balanced paper at 90IRE.

Figure 3-16 Vectorscope of white balanced paper at 90IRE.

The image was shot with the luminance set at 90IRE instead of 100IRE because it's possible to destroy chrominance information by clipping the video levels. Even a poorly white balanced piece of white paper could look white if the luminance levels are cranked up high enough so that the chroma information is clipped completely. At 90IRE, there are obviously no clipped signals. Notice that the vectorscope in Figure 3-16 shows a single, fuzzy dot in its center, while the waveform monitor (Figure 3-15)—set to Flat—shows a clean, thin white line. Both of these are indications that the balance is good. We're primarily focusing on waveform monitors in this chapter, but comparing indications on both a waveform monitor and vectorscope is an important skill. Vectorscopes will be discussed in further detail starting on page 83.

The waveform monitor is capable of many different displays that are used for different purposes. To see the chrominance information on the waveform monitor, there are several different displays that can be used, including several parade modes. On an older model waveform monitor with limited display options, the key to seeing chroma information is to set the waveform's filter.

Figure 3-17 shows SMPTE color bars in Low Pass filter mode. This only displays luminance information. With SMPTE bars, each

Excursion is used to define the fact that something is causing the trace on the waveform monitor to deviate from a thin, straight line.—Rick Hollowbush, Vice President, Technical Services, VideoTek

bar is displayed in order of luminance, so you see an even stair stepping of levels from white on the left down to blue on the right. Figure 3-18 is generated from the same SMPTE bar signal, but the waveform is in Flat filter mode. This combines luminance with chrominance information. The thick vertical bars represent the chrominance or strong color signal of the color bars.

With the filter on the waveform monitor set to Low Pass, only luminance information is displayed. If it's set to High Pass, you don't see any luminance information, only chroma. If it's set to Flat, the filter passes both luma and chroma information. On some built-in waveform monitors, "Flat" mode is called Y/C mode, which stands for luminance and chroma combined. Many people set their waveform monitor so that it displays both types of information. However, if you are trying to look for legal luminance values, it is difficult to read the display in this mode because the chroma information will make the levels seem higher than they should be.

On some built-in waveform monitors, "Flat" mode is called Y/C mode, which stands for luminance and chroma combined.

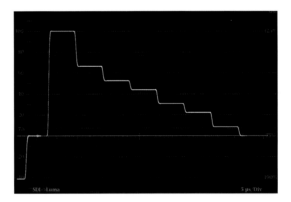

Figure 3-17 SMPTE color bars in Low Pass mode displaying only luminance information.

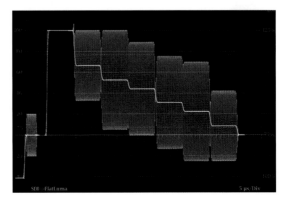

Figure 3-18 The same SMPTE bar signal but with the waveform in Flat filter mode, combining luminance with chrominance.

Tutorial—Balancing a Blue Cast on a White Piece of Paper

For the following tutorial, set the waveform monitor filter to Flat. Import the bluewhitebalancepaper.tiff file from the DVD into Color Finesse or your favorite color correction application that accepts still images. Or convert the tiff into a QT or other video file first. If the camera was not properly white balanced, the displays would look like they do in Figures 3-20 and 3-21. Figure 3-20 shows the waveform of a white piece of paper with a strong blue color cast. Notice the thickness of the excursion of the trace. This indicates the presence of chroma, though it doesn't indicate the specific hue. Compare this image with Figure 3-15. Figure 3-21 shows this same blue cast on a vectorscope. Notice the trace extending away from the center of the vectorscope toward the blue target of the graticule. Compare this with the properly balanced white displayed on the vectorscope in Figure 3-16.

Figure 3-19 A video capture of a piece of white paper that was improperly white balanced.

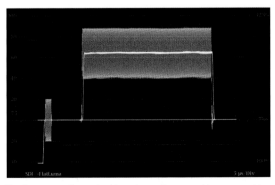

Figure 3-20 Flat Pass waveform of white piece of paper with a strong blue color cast and thick excursion.

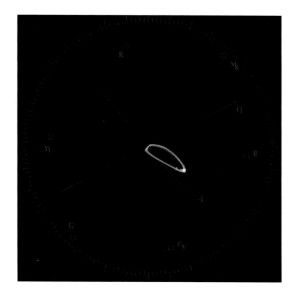

Figure 3-21 The same blue cast on a vectorscope.

Figure 3-22 An eyedropper sample of the 8-bit color RGB.

The vectorscope now shows that the trace is no longer in the center as it should be for a white piece of paper, but it extends out toward the color box that matches the color cast of the camera. (In this case, the white paper is fairly blue, and the vectorscope shows the dot approaching the blue target box on the vectorscope display.) The waveform also gives us clues that the paper is not white. Notice the difference in the thickness of the line between Figure 3-15 and Figure 3-20. (Your waveform needs to be set to the Flat filter to see the excursion of the chroma values.) The line has become fuzzy as the excursion is greater, showing greater amplitude. This is the indication on a waveform that there is chroma information in the signal. Eliminating the chroma information can be accomplished by trying to focus the fuzzy line into a sharp line. The technical term for this is *minimizing the excursion*. It is possible to do this using just the RGB gain controls.

Adjusting the green gain also moves the overall luminance of the signal.

One of the tricks to understand is that adjusting the green gain also moves the overall luminance of the signal. Because we were setting only the white balance, which is exclusively a *high* luminance signal, we did not adjust the gamma or setup controls. Adjusting gamma and setup are used to adjust midtones and dark shadows, so they shouldn't be used to adjust something that is supposed to be white. Attempting to adjust the gamma and setup levels when looking only at what should be a white piece of paper is a recipe for disaster because you will be making adjustments that you will only be able to see when you finally have an image that has some darker levels in it.

Two other waveform displays to look at are both defined as "parade" displays because it shows you different channels of information in a "parade" one after the next from left to right. The most common method, as we saw in the first chapter of the book, is the RGB Parade, which shows the red, green, and blue channels of color information horizontally across the display (Figure 3-23). You can also look at a YCbCr parade waveform, which shows the luma information in the first "cell," followed by the blue difference channel and the red difference channel (Figure 3-24). This is the way component video is often encoded for video: The luminance is sampled, then the color information is created by sampling the difference between the blue signal and the luminance and the red signal and luminance. It is fairly difficult to ascertain what is wrong with the picture from this type of parade. This display is also sometimes called a YPbPr display. The first cell shows the luma, the second shows that the blue channel is higher than the center line, which indicates the difference in strength from the luma channel. The third cell shows that the red difference channel is lower than the center line, indicating that red is lower than luma. If you want to use this display to balance the blue cast, the goal would be to bring the Cb channel down to the center line and the Cr channel up to the center line.

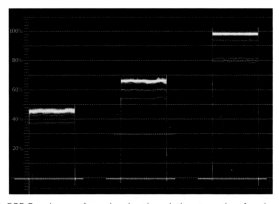

Figure 3-23 RGB Parade waveform showing the relative strengths of each color channel. From left to right: red, green, and blue. Because the white paper has such a blue cast, the RGB Parade shows it with much higher levels in the blue "cell" to the right.

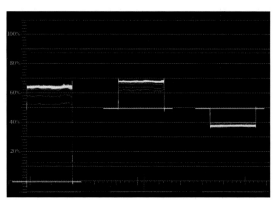

Figure 3-24 YCbCr (YPbPr) parade waveform. From left to right the cells indicate: luminance, the difference between luminance and blue, and the difference between luminance and red. In the second and third cells, the luminance difference is indicated by the distance from the center line (at 50%).

In attempting to white balance this image, try not to even look at the color of the image itself on the video monitor—because we are just working on a purely technical level—and rely completely on the scopes. You wouldn't want to do that in a real-life situation, but this exercise is to build confidence in using the tools correctly.

You can use some of the methods from the first chapter to attempt this correction. The easiest way to do this task manually is to use the red, blue, and green Gain controls while viewing the RGB Parade waveform display.

I will use the RGB master controls in Color Finesse as a plug-in to Final Cut Pro to walk you through this correction. In RGB Master controls it's a very straightforward correction when watching the RGB waveform. The only controls you need to use are the red, green, and blue gain controls. You can do this from the Color Finesse "simplified" controls in the Viewer's Filter tab, or you can call up the full interface and select the RGB tab.

I brought the green gain up until the green trace on the RGB waveform was at almost 100% without clipping. Then I brought down the blue gain control until the blue trace was even with the green. Then I brought the red gain control up so that the trace in the red cell (the first one) matched the trace of the other two cells. Figure 3-25 shows the levels I ended up with in Color Finesse.

Figures 3-26 through 3-29 show some other ways the scopes can be configured and other ways to view your correction. Figure 3-26 shows a Flat Pass waveform (which shows chroma information) with very little excursion around the luma informa-

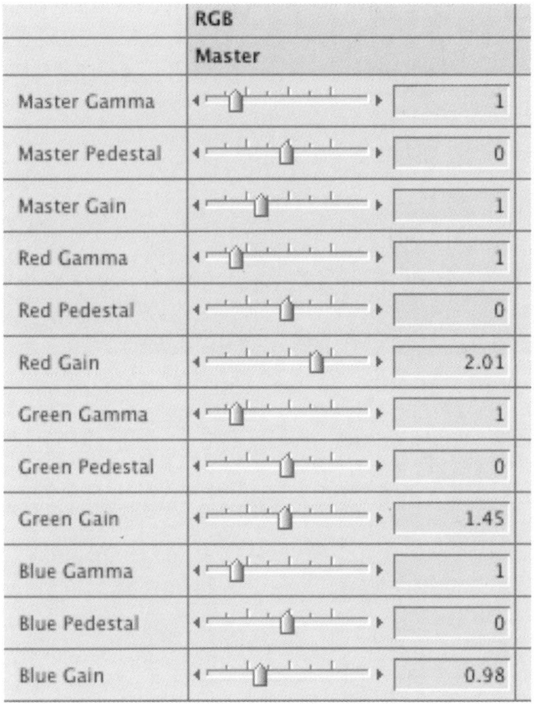

	RGB	
	Master	
Master Gamma	◄ ⟦slider⟧ ►	1
Master Pedestal	◄ ⟦slider⟧ ►	0
Master Gain	◄ ⟦slider⟧ ►	1
Red Gamma	◄ ⟦slider⟧ ►	1
Red Pedestal	◄ ⟦slider⟧ ►	0
Red Gain	◄ ⟦slider⟧ ►	2.01
Green Gamma	◄ ⟦slider⟧ ►	1
Green Pedestal	◄ ⟦slider⟧ ►	0
Green Gain	◄ ⟦slider⟧ ►	1.45
Blue Gamma	◄ ⟦slider⟧ ►	1
Blue Pedestal	◄ ⟦slider⟧ ►	0
Blue Gain	◄ ⟦slider⟧ ►	0.98

Figure 3-25 Color Finesse settings that fixed the white balance on the blue image.

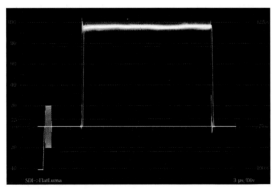

Figure 3-26 Flat Pass waveform display with very little excursion, showing that there is very little chroma, which means the whites are balanced. Compare this to Figure 3-20 from before the correction.

tion (the brighter line). Figure 3-27 shows an RGB Parade of the corrected image, with all three of the cells equal in height. This shows that the image is white balanced. Figure 3-28 shows a YCbCr waveform display. While this is a little hard to understand, the parade displays the luma information first. The Cb and Cr por-

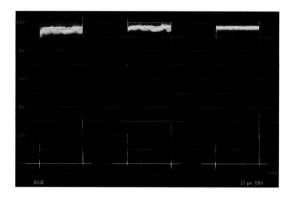

Figure 3-27 RGB Parade waveform display with all three cells even at the top, showing that they are balanced. Compare this to Figure 3-23 from before the correction.

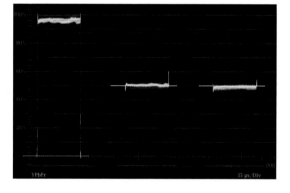

Figure 3-28 YCbCr Parade waveform (or YPbPr) with the Pb and Pr levels centered equally, showing that they are in balance. Compare this to Figure 3-24 from before the correction.

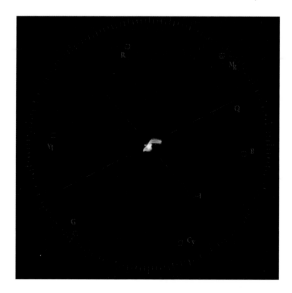

Figure 3-29 Vectorscope showing proper white balance. Compare this to Figure 3-21 from before the correction.

tions of the image show that the two color difference signals are of equal strength, centered in each cell.

Figure 3-29 shows a vectorscope display with the trace indicating chroma information centered tighter on the graticule as it should be, indicating proper balance.

The same process that we just went through for white balance is applicable to black balance. The vectorscope should show a slightly fuzzy black dot directly in the center, and the waveform monitor should show a clean, fine line at either 7.5IRE or 0IRE (see the "Waveform Monitor" section on page 58 for a refresher on the correct position for setup or black level for various video systems). For our discussion, let's assume that you want the blacks to be at 0IRE.

Proper Levels for Each Tonal Range

In addition to color balancing the cameras, the other important step in setting up a camera to a chip chart is in making sure that all of the whites are the same brightness from camera to camera and the blacks are the same blackness. Normally, in a remote truck this is checked by putting a vertical wipe between the signals of two cameras or by punching very rapidly between cameras. The same trick can be applied in post, though it is rare that you'll have these chip charts shot on tape. You can use wipes and punching back and forth between shots to check and compare other images side by side or in succession.

Figure 3-34 shows a waveform of two chip charts with a split wipe between them. Figure 3-33 shows the image of the chip chart split. The charts are identically balanced with identical levels, with the exception of gamma level, which is lower on the right side of the image. You can see that lowering the gamma has also pulled the level of the blacks and whites down noticeably.

Gamma controls must be set so that the middle grays from one camera are the same as all other cameras. Merely ensuring that the top and bottom levels are set is not enough to have the cameras match. Let's take a look at how some postproduction color correction controls can affect how the image looks—both on the waveform monitor and on the video monitor. Watching how the waveform monitor behaves and comparing it to the image on the video monitor while doing these adjustments will provide an excellent primer in how the various controls work as well as giving you experience in using the waveform monitor as a creative tool that will help guide your color corrections.

Experimentation

Try several different controls and several different analytical tools. Find what you are most comfortable with in certain situations. Until you gain experience, try several different approaches

TIP

When doing corrections to balance colors on a vectorscope, it is often helpful to zoom in or magnify the vectorscope so that you are only looking at the very center of the scope. Some scopes refer to this zooming or magnifying as "gain." The Tektronix WFR7100 shown in Figure 3-29 has a gain button for looking at the center (or other areas) of the vectorscope. You can program the gain button to jump to certain preset levels, like 2x gain or 5x gain.

Splits and Wipes for Matching

Doing a wipe between two images to match them is very easy in many applications. Apple's Color allows this in the Still Store room. The wipe can be angled and positioned.

Look for "Match color of chip charts" or "Match lions including secondary" on the DVD included with this book for a video tutorial on using split screens for matching.

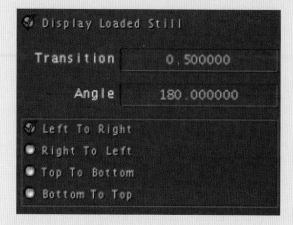

Figure 3-30 Interface for split screens in Apple Color's Still Store room.

In Color Finesse's full interface, you can split between a current correction and either the uncorrected source or a reference still. The screen shot (Figure 3-31) is from the top half of the Color Finesse UI.

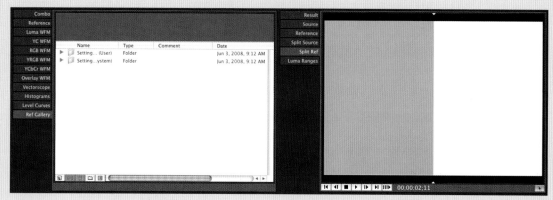

Figure 3-31 Interface for split screens in Color Finesse.

In Avid, you can also do a split between a current correction and the uncorrected source reference. Figure 3-32 shows the "Dual Split" button highlighted in purple under the cursor.

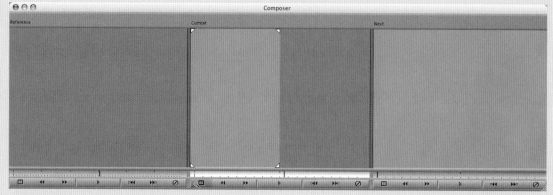

Figure 3-32 Interface for split screens in Avid Media Composer. The center portion of the figure shows a split between the "reference" frame to the left and the "next" frame to the right.

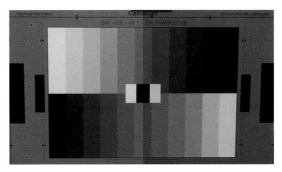

Figure 3-33 DSC Labs' grayscale chip chart with a split wipe between a neutrally balanced chart and a "correction" with the mids pulled way down.

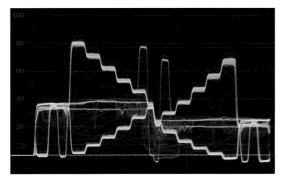

Figure 3-34 A luminance-only waveform showing the results of Figure 3-33.

while watching several different displays. Not every person likes to use the same tools for the same job, but it is dangerous to settle on a "favorite" tool for correction or a way to analyze the picture without experimenting with all of the options thoroughly. You'll need experience with many different color issues to discover which tools and which methods of analysis best suit the task and your way of thinking. Some things will be harder to learn at first, but in the long run they will provide faster corrections and better results. You may finally determine your favorite toolset, but be open to the idea that for some solutions, you're better off using a tool that is not in that toolset. Different problems are solved by different tools, and attempting to make one tool your all-purpose solution will limit your ability to solve all of the problems presented to you in the quickest or best way.

Until you gain experience, try several different approaches while watching several different displays.

When I wrote *The Art and Technique of Digital Color Correction*, many of the colorists that I interviewed worked quite differently from one another. Each had a unique way that they set up their scopes and chose specific tools with which they felt most comfortable, yet all of them left their comfort zone when certain problems called for tools that they didn't normally utilize for most of their work.

Viewing the Waveform While Setting Tonal Range Levels

We have already discussed how to watch for color casts in the waveform monitor. This will also be discussed in more detail when we get to the vectorscope. Now let's take color out of the discussion for a while and concentrate on an image that is supposed to be pure black and white. We'll use the waveform monitor and the chip chart to understand how the various controls affect the image and how some controls interact with others quite intimately, while other controls are designed to be more isolated in their affect on the image. While viewing the image of the chip chart on a waveform, let's try a few adjustments that are common to most color correction graphical user interfaces. The thing to remember here is that the sliders that give you the most *specific* control over *each* portion of the tonal range are the most desirable. Load file grayscale_neutral into your preferred color correction application.

We'll stick with the Master HSL controls in Color Finesse, Avid, Adobe, or FCP. These controls are essentially the same as a traditional time base corrector TBC. When you are controlling the Master levels, you will affect all of the image, but some controls will isolate level changes a little more effectively to certain luminance ranges. Apple Color doesn't have some of these controls for reasons that will become clear as you read about their failings. Understanding how to isolate the specific portion of the picture you want to affect is very important. Figure 3-35 is the proper exposure and balance for the chip chart. Notice the black—in the center—is set at 0. Midtones are around 50IRE, and whites are around 100IRE. Excursion is fairly minimal in Y/C mode on the left side of the image.

Understanding how to isolate the specific portion of the picture you want to affect is very important.

On the right side of Figure 3-35 is the waveform in Low Pass, Y or Luminance only. This eliminates the chrominance information, letting you concentrate on luminance levels. Notice that the excursion of each line—how blurry or fat it is—is almost nothing.

Figure 3-36 contains the identical viewing modes and chip chart *after* increasing the *brightness* control. Brightness is not the same as gain. Brightness is an additive function. If you have

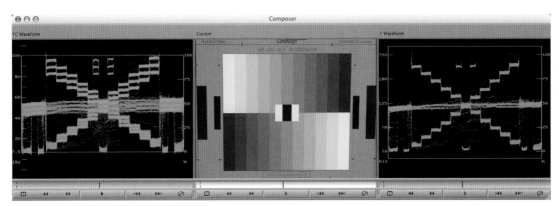

Figure 3-35 Chip chart with displays of a Y/C waveform monitor and a straight Luma or Y waveform, properly exposed and balanced. The chip chart that generated the image is in the middle.

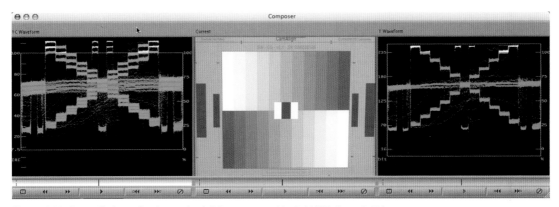

Figure 3-36 Same displays after increasing brightness control in Avid HSL Controls Tab.

a 0IRE black and a 100IRE white and you increase brightness by 10, you now have a 10IRE black and a 110IRE white. The entire signal is brought up. You may want to do this sometimes, but usually you want more control than to affect the image so globally. Using the gain controls in most applications is very different because it attempts to only affect the brightest parts of the picture. If raised or lowered enough, it will definitely affect the gamma or midtones of an image and can even alter the black level or shadows.

Figure 3-37 contains the identical viewing modes and chip chart after decreasing *contrast*. Contrast adjustments control two parameters at the same time. When contrast is decreased, shadow levels are raised and highlights are lowered, and when contrast is increased, shadow levels are lowered and highlights are raised. So decreasing contrast by 10 would make an adjustment of raising

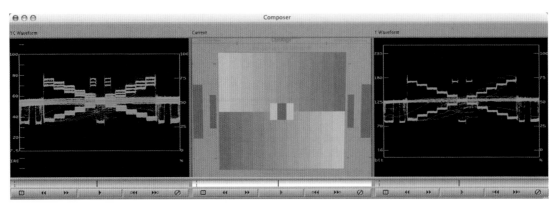

Figure 3-37 Same displays after lowering contrast control in Avid HSL Controls Tab.

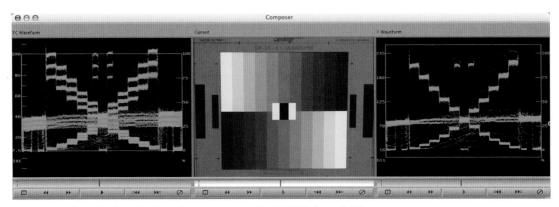

Figure 3-38 Same displays after lowering gamma control in Avid HSL Controls Tab.

blacks by 10 and lowering whites by 10. (This will depend on the algorithm used by the color correction engine to calculate the moves. Some engines use linear equations, and some are graded on a curve or allow you to set a center for contrast so that the contrast move could affect brightness and darkness differently.) Like brightness, you might want to use this occasionally, but usually it is better to control these functions separately by using the gain and setup controls (which may also be called something like highlights and shadows or gain and lift).

Figure 3-38 contains the identical viewing modes and chip chart *after* lowering midtones or gamma. Black levels and whites changed slightly. Pulling down the midtones has two effects on the picture. It compresses the range between black and the input midtone level, and it expands the level between the midtone level and the whites.

The Flat Pass waveforms in Figures 3-39 and 3-40 show a black level adjustment. The first image, Figure 3-39, shows blacks that have been lowered to the right level, but they have not yet started to be crushed. In Figure 3-40 the blacks are not only just *lower*, but the excursion in the black chips has been crushed to a tight, bright line. Look at the difference in the shape of the trace around the 0IRE line. This compression of the trace indicates a loss of detail.Looking at the specific shape of the trace as it starts to compress into a thin line is a good indication that you are compressing or clipping your image. This may be an effect that you are trying for, or it may be an indication that you have taken your correction too far.

This compression of the trace indicates a loss of detail.

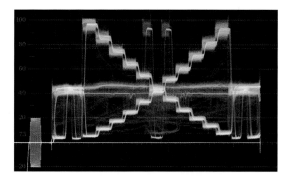

Figure 3-39 Black level adjustment. Note the thickness of the excursion in the center black chip.

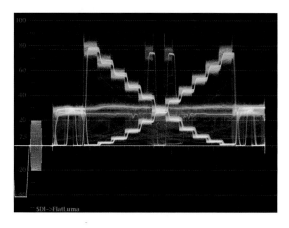

Figure 3-40 Black level adjustment with crushing. The excursion in the center black chip has been crushed to a thin line.

Just as the previous example shows how the waveform can see loss of detail as blacks are crushed, it can also show the fine line between crisp, bright highlights and blown-out whites. Sometimes these blown-out whites are desirable as a look, but usually they just mean lost detail.

Figures 3-41 and 3-42 are very, very similar. They are meant to show one small thing that acted as a signal as the gain was being raised. Note the shape of the top left and right chips in Figure 3-37, then compare them to the same chips in Figure 3-38. In Figure

3-38, the shape of that portion of the trace has changed slightly—flattening out somewhat—and the excursion has been minimized. That shows that the detail in those brightest chips is starting to get lost. You can use this compression of the trace as a sign that your highlights are probably high enough.

Now that we have shown how some basic adjustments appear on a waveform monitor, let's examine some real images and analyze them with the waveform monitor.

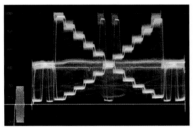 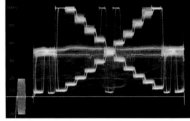

Figure 3-41 Note the shape of the top chips.

Figure 3-42 Now that gain has been raised, note the flattened trace for the top chips.

Figure 3-43 From Artbeats' Kids of Summer Collection, shot KS109. This file is available on the DVD in the Artbeats folder.

Figure 3-44 Waveform of Figure 3-43 with Flat filter (chroma and luma).

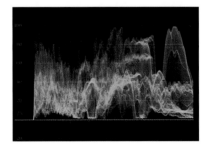

Figure 3-45 Waveform with luma only (Low Pass).

Figure 3-43 has nice, strong chroma values and a full range of luminance. Figure 3-45 is the Low Pass waveform view, showing only luma values. Figure 3-44 shows the Flat filter image, displaying chroma and luma information. The Flat Pass image is much harder to evaluate because of the large amount of chroma information. Because the horizontal orientation between the full raster image and the waveform always lines up, what I want you to try to do is judge which parts of the image (Figure 3-43) relate to each part of the trace in Figures 3-44 and 3-45.

Figure 3-46 is another image from Artbeats' Kids of Summer Collection. Figure 3-48 is a Low Pass waveform showing that the image sits primarily in shadows with some midrange values. To analyze various portions of the image, black wipes or garbage mattes were used to mask portions of the picture to more definitively conclude what portions of the image were being represented by which portions of the waveform trace. Compare the original image and its waveform with the masked images and their waveforms.

Figure 3-47 masks out the boy to let you compare the waveforms of Figure 3-48 and Figure 3-49. With the boy masked out, you can see the sweep of the sky that continues and the darker shadows that compromise the rest of the image in that same horizontal space where the boy was.

Figure 3-50 crudely masks the sky so that you can compare the waveforms in Figures 3-48 and 3-51. With the sky masked out, it becomes quite clear what part of the waveform in Figure 3-48 is sky.

Figure 3-46 From Artbeats' Kids of Summer Collection, shot 121.

As already discussed in this book, in addition to the traditional waveform displays, other displays, such as parade displays of RGB or YCbCr, provide substantial data on chroma values in a very usable form. The RGB parade scopes are useful and widely used by professional colorists. They show you the same waveform information that usually presents luminance information, but

Figure 3-47 From Artbeats' Kids of Summer Collection, shot 121, with boy masked out.

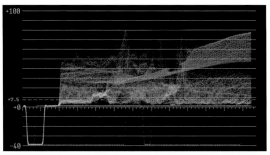

Figure 3-48 Low Pass waveform showing image from Figure 3-46 in shadows with some midrange values.

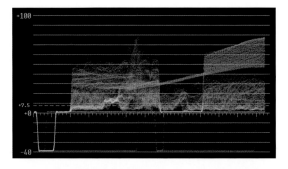

Figure 3-49 Waveform of Figure 3-47 revealing more sky and shadows.

Figure 3-50 From Artbeats' Kids of Summer Collection, shot 121, with sky masked out.

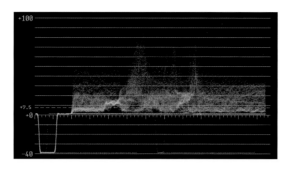

Figure 3-51 Resulting waveform monitor image of Figure 3-50.

they break it into three sequential images that show specific waveforms for each of the RGB channels. Because many of your corrections will be made using RGB controls, these scopes provide a very direct form of feedback.

The RGB parade scopes are useful and widely used by professional colorists.

Stephen Nakamura is a well-known colorist in Los Angeles. His feature film projects include *Leatherheads, Michael Clayton, The Bourne Ultimatum, Spiderman 3, Dreamgirls, Pirates of the Caribbean*, and David Fincher's *Panic Room. Panic Room* was one of the first features to be color corrected electronically using digital intermediate (DI). Nakamura swears by his RGB scope:

> *I just look at the waveform, vectorscope, and RGB Parade. The RGB Parade shows you where your cells are. It lets you see what you're driving up too high or too low or balancing your RGB channels. That's how you correct, by controlling the RGBs, so you need to be able to see those and what level they are and see if that coincides with the picture you're looking at.*

Digital Intermediate
A digital intermediate, or DI, has become an increasingly popular method of postproduction for feature films. Instead of the traditional method of cutting the camera negative and creating a timed interpositive and then release prints, the original film (OCN or original camera negative) is scanned at 2K, 4K, or higher, color corrected digitally, and printed back to film.

A Wave of Waveforms

The image of the boy swinging, from Artbeats' Kids of Summer Collection (Figure 3-52), is comprised of three distinct levels of red, green, and blue tones. There is the reddish color of the earth and some skin tones. There is the green of the trees and the swing supports. And there is the blue of the sky and the boy's shirt.

As you would guess from looking at the image, the red tones of the earth and the skin tones are fairly dark, as seen in the red channel, indicated in the left portion of Figure 3-53. The center "cell" in Figure 3-53 is the green channel with its strong green midtones and a darker level of green for the shadowed portions of the leaves. The black, vertical lines running through the green channel represent one of the swing chains blocking the tree and the swing supports blocking the trees. The blue channel (the "cell" on the right in Figure 3-53) displays the obvious bright blue luminance of the sky. The brightest part of the trace in the blue channel is broken up by the dark, vertical slices representing the chains of the swings and the swing supports.

Figure 3-52 Image with strong red, green, and blue tones. Courtesy of Artbeats' Kids of Summer Collection, KS133.

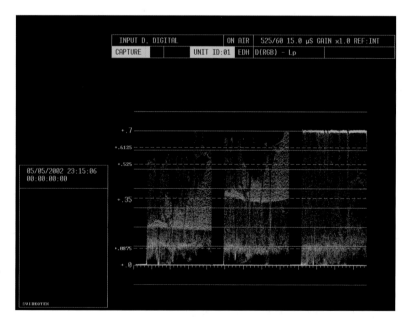

Figure 3-53 An RGB Parade waveform showing all three color channels of the image in Figure 3-52.

Isolating luminance information is a little easier to do on moving images. See Figures 3-54 through 3-57 for examples. It is quite apparent where the image of the boy is registering on the waveform when you see sequential images. Compare the waveforms in Figures 3-55 and 3-57 as the boy passes from one spot to another in horizontal space.

Another parade scope display is the YCbCr Parade, which we briefly discussed earlier in the chapter. To explain this display,

Figure 3-54 Swing shot in motion.

Figure 3-56 Subsequent swing shot.

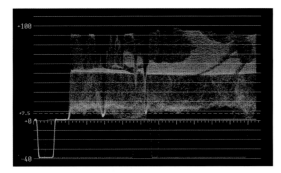

Figure 3-55 Waveform of Figure 3-54.

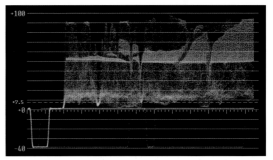

Figure 3-57 Waveform of Figure 3-56.

we'll go back to DSC Labs GrayScale Test Pattern. The image we'll use is one that was captured after taking the straight chip chart image. We'll turn just the highlights blue, leaving the rest of the image untouched (see Figure 3-58).

In Figure 3-58, there is little or no chroma information in the midtones and blacks. Only the highlights have been adjusted to show blue. This is seen on the YCbCr Parade in Figure 3-60. On the left is the luminance or Y value.

The next two parts of the parade image are harder to understand (Figure 3-60). The first cell indicates the luminance (Y) of the image. The middle cell in the waveform is displaying Cb, which is the difference between the luminance and the blue channel. The trace shows that there are elevated blue levels. The right image on the waveform is showing Cr, which is the difference between the luminance and the red channel. This display is showing that the red is deficient in portions of the image. If the image had no chroma values, the Cb and Cr traces would be centered on the line, showing no excursion as in Figure 3-61.

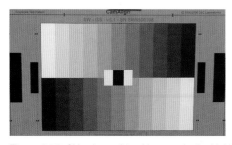

Figure 3-58 Chip chart with a blue cast in the highlights only.

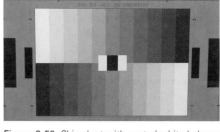

Figure 3-59 Chip chart with neutral white balance in all tonal ranges.

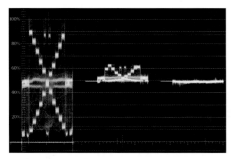

Figure 3-60 YCbCr Parade display of the chip chart in Figure 3-58.

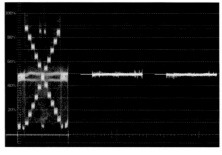

Figure 3-61 YCbCr Parade display of the chip chart in Figure 3-59.

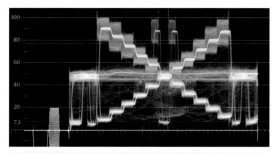

Figure 3-62 Flat Pass waveform display of the chip chart in Figure 3-58.

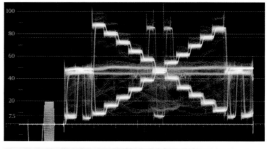

Figure 3-63 Flat Pass waveform display of the chip chart in Figure 3-59.

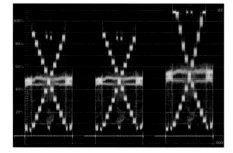

Figure 3-64 RGB Parade display of the chip chart in Figure 3-58.

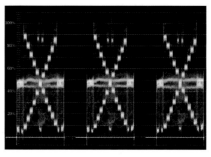

Figure 3-65 RGB Parade display of the chip chart in Figure 3-59.

Figure 3-62 shows a regular Flat Pass waveform. The trace shows a huge amount of excursion in the highlight chips (the top part of the trace has thick lines), while the midtones and the shadows show very little excursion from chroma information (which displays thinner lines). Figure 3-63 shows the Flat Pass waveform of the neutral image for comparison.

Figure 3-64 shows an RGB Parade of the same chip chart with the bluish highlights. Because there should be no chroma information in this chart, all three portions of the parade should be identical. Because only the highlights were moved toward blue, note that all three portions are almost identical at the midtone line and below. But above the midtones, the red channel is very low, the green channel is close to being correct, and the blue channel is well above the other two channels. Figure 3-65 shows the way the neutral chip chart should look.

Parade displays are as important in obtaining chroma information as luminance information.

For many colorists, these parade displays are as important in obtaining chroma information as luminance information. But the most obvious evaluator of chroma information is the vectorscope.

Vectorscope

The vectorscope helps analyze hue and chroma levels, keeping colors legal and helping to eliminate unwanted color casts. We will get into some detail in this section of the book on how the vectorscope works. For more in-depth descriptions, see the bibliography of this book for other resources to explore. With the gain, setup, and gamma corrections done while monitoring the waveform

TIP

With a good hardware or hybrid scope, it is possible to zoom in on a specific part of the waveform for a closer look. Bob Sliga, a veteran Chicago colorist who also worked as part of the Apple Color software team, often uses this feature to check for compression when he is raising whites or lowering blacks. This allows him to keep a closer eye on any clipping or crushing of detail. Neal Kassner, the colorist for *48 Hours* on CBS, also uses this trick, zooming in vertically and horizontally sometimes to isolate the exact part of the image that he is trying to balance.

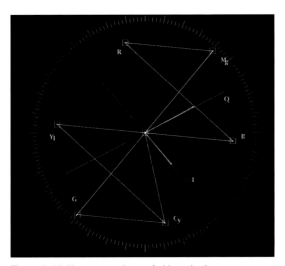

Figure 3-66 Vectorscope image fed by color bars.

monitor primarily, the colorist's attention focuses more on the vectorscope for the hue and chroma work. The chroma strength of the signal is indicated by its distance from the center of the vectorscope. The closer the trace is to the outer edge of the vectorscope, the greater the chrominance or the more vivid the color. The hue of the image is indicated by its rotational position around the circle. The easiest way to imagine these relationships is to picture a color wheel superimposed over the face of the vectorscope, as in Figure 3-67.

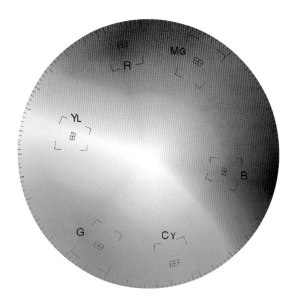

Figure 3-67 The graticule of a vectorscope superimposed with a color wheel. This helps explain the relationships of the colors on a vectorscope.

We already touched on this a little bit in Chapter 1, but one of the important relationships to understand is the position of the various colors around the periphery of the vectorscope (see Figure 3-67). The targets for red, blue, and green form a triangle. In between each of these primary colors are the colors formed by mixing those primaries. So the color between red and blue is magenta. The color between blue and green is cyan, and the color between red and green is yellow. These secondary colors form another triangle. The other interesting relationship that is formed on the vectorscope is that complementary colors are directly opposite each other. Red is opposite cyan, magenta is opposite green, and yellow is opposite blue. These relationships will play a pivotal role as you begin to manipulate colors.

For example, if you are trying to eliminate a magenta cast in an image, a glance at the vectorscope will tell you that you need to add green, which is opposite magenta. Or you could reduce red and blue in equal amounts (the two colors that make magenta). If an image has yellows that are too cyan, then adding red will begin to solve the problem. Eventually, you should not even need the graticule (the graphic part of the vectorscope that identifies color targets) to know where the colors lie on the face of the vectorscope.

The chroma information presented on the vectorscope is instrumental in trying to eliminate color casts in images. As stated earlier, chroma strength is represented by its distance from the center of the vectorscope. Because white, black, and pure grays are devoid of chroma information, they all should sit neatly in the center of the vectorscope. While most video images will have a range of colors, they also usually have some amount of whites, blacks, and neutral grays. The key is to be able to see where these parts of the picture sit on the vectorscope and then use the color correction tools at your disposal to move them toward the center of the vectorscope.

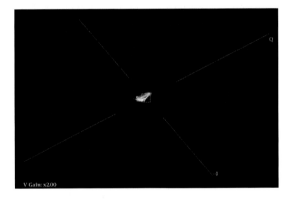

Figure 3-68 Vector display of a white signal on a Tektronix WFM7120. The display has been zoomed in to magnify the center of the vectorscope 2x. This helps to center the white dot more accurately in the center of the vectorscope, assuring proper white balance.

One useful tip in trying to accomplish this task is to use the vectorscope's chroma gain controls to zoom in on the center of the signal. Increasing the gain allows you to better see exactly where the neutral chroma information is sitting. Many software-based scopes do not allow you to take this setting out of calibration like this. Many external scopes, such the Tektronix WFM7120 (see Figure 3-68), have magnifying functions that allow for this important function. In Figure 3-68 the vectorscope was set to Gain in order to better examine the very center of the vectorscope display. Some scopes will call this function Magnify. As you may guess by the clean trace with very little chroma, the vectorscope was being fed a nearly perfect white signal. (A black signal would be indistinguishable from a white signal, by the way.)

Let's take a look at some example images to see how these images appear on the vectorscope. Remember, luminance is not displayed on the vectorscope, so we only need to consider how the chroma and hue of an image are displayed.

Figure 3-69 White sheet of paper with reddish cast.

Figure 3-70 White sheet of paper with a bluish cast.

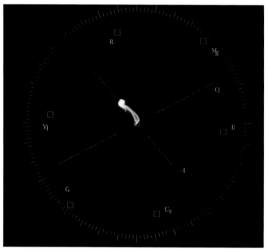

Figure 3-71 Vectorscope image of Figure 3-69.

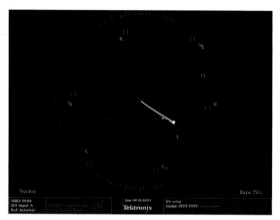

Figure 3-72 Vectorscope image of Figure 3-70.

Let's start with a white sheet of paper. If you want, you can load file properwhitebalance.tif into your favorite color correction application that allows still images, or convert the .tif into a video file. Figure 3-68 shows the vectorscope displaying the same white sheet of paper we saw earlier in the chapter. This white sheet of paper has had a proper white balance. Notice how all of the trace is limited to a fairly tight circle around the center of the vectorscope. Figures 3-69 and 3-70 show a white piece of paper that is not white balanced. You can load these files from the DVD as well. They are warmwhitebalance.tif and bluewhitebalancepaper.tif. Notice that the trace has begun to extend outward from the center, toward the yellow and red targets in Figure 3-71. This is the indication of the reddish cast of the image. In Figure 3-70, the white paper has a bluish cast, and Figure 3-72 indicates the cast of the color with a trace that descends down toward the blue target on the vectorscope.

Masking Again

To simplify the task of understanding how a vectorscope displays a more complex image, we will use the same masking technique that we used in the waveform examples. We already analyzed this image in the waveform section (see Figures 3-43 through 3-45). Figure 3-73 is the image from Artbeats' Kids of Summer Collection. Figure 3-74 is the resulting vectorscope display. Notice the large amounts of trace extending toward yellow, green, and blue. With this image, this trace is simply showing the natural colors that are in the image, not "color casts" like the ones that we were trying to get rid of in the other images in the chapter.

Figure 3-75 shows the Artbeats' image with a small rectangular mask over the blue blanket in the background and a small corner of the girl's shoulder. Notice the difference between Figure 3-74 and Figure 3-76. In Figure 3-76, the small tangent of blue that was closer to the center of the vectorscope (a less intense blue) is missing. So is a small hook on the top of the tangent extending toward red. That hook was the highest chroma value of skin tone, coming from a highlight of skin on the girl's shoulder. The rest of the vectorscope is unchanged.

Figure 3-77 has the image with the mask over the intense blue of the dress. Figure 3-78 is the vectorscope reading for Figure 3-77. Notice that the large tangent that is just to the cyan side of the blue target is missing, while the smaller, less intense blue near the center is back. Compare Figure 3-74 and Figure 3-78. The portion of the trace that indicates the blue dress becomes very apparent.

Flesh Tones on a Vectorscope

The most critical colors to reproduce accurately are flesh tones. Because everyone knows instinctively how these should look, there is little room for error. Regardless of the racial background of the subject, flesh tones are always indicated on the vectorscope within a few degrees of one another. There are, however, trends in reproducing skin tones and even a geographic bias toward certain skin tone hues depending on where the colorist works, according to some colorists. Veteran Chicago colorist Bob Sliga believes that West Coasters like more golden skin tones; the East Coasters like pinker skin tones; Midwesterners like something in between. Many other colorists that I have interviewed from both coasts— and all the cities in between—agree that regional biases toward certain skin, sky, water, and grass tones exist.

Figure 3-73 From Artbeats' Kids of Summer Collection, shot 109.

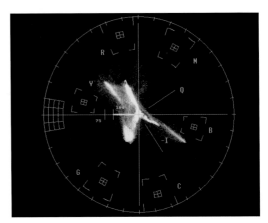

Figure 3-74 Vectorscope display of Figure 3-73.

Figure 3-75 Mask over blue blanket.

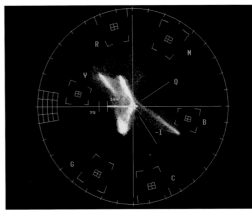

Figure 3-76 Vectorscope display of Figure 3-75.

Figure 3-77 Mask over blue dress.

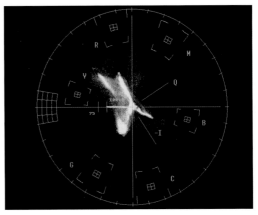

Figure 3-78 Vectorscope display of Figure 3-77.

Regardless of this, positioning skin tones is actually a fairly easy thing to do. The same instinctive understanding that allows everyone else to know a bad skin tone when they see it is the same instinct that helps you place it correctly in the first place. In addition to pure instinct, you are aided technically by the I-line on the vectorscope. This line, which runs from about the eleven o'clock position to about the five o'clock position, is widely accepted as the line where skin tones should fall. The color correction guide for FCP goes so far as to call this "the flesh-tone line." While this is not technically accurate, it is certainly a good rule of thumb.

The I-line is indicated on the vectorscope shown in Figure 3-79. Not all software scopes label this line. The I-line runs perpendicular to the Q-line.

Like any creative rule, this flesh tone line is to be used as a guide, not an absolute dictate. Randy Starnes, the colorist for *Grey's Anatomy, Desperate Housewives, NYPD Blue*, and *Northern Exposure*, among other high-profile productions, explains:

> *Generally people think that skin tones fall within 10° or 20° of the IQ vector, which lies somewhere between red and yellow. I've had engineers tell me that my job was not done correctly because it's obvious by looking at the scope that my skin tones were not on the IQ. So I lined up everybody and showed that everybody's skin tones were not the same, so they couldn't fall on the same vector. But it does generally fall within that vector.*

The entire shot of Figure 3-80 is monochromatic except for the man's skin tones, which provide some warmth to the image.

As a test, check some of your own flesh tone video on a vectorscope to get a feel for where the pleasing skin tones land. Part of

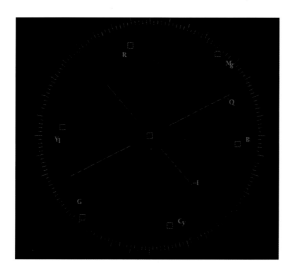

Figure 3-79 I-line on a Tektronix WFM7120. The top part of the I-line, which runs from the center of the scope up to about the 10 or 11 o'clock mark, is generally accepted as the "flesh tone line," though that's not the reason why it exists on the vectorscope.

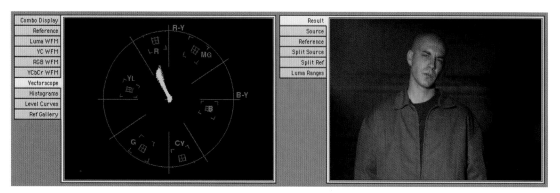

Figure 3-80 Screen capture from Synthetic Aperture's Color Finesse running in FCP. The video image is from Artbeats' Mixed Cuts Collection, shot LM113.

increasing your experience as a colorist is to develop an understanding of where certain colors should land. If you can, look at unusual, affected skin tones in spots or TV shows that you like and see where they land in comparison to the flesh tone line. Try downloading spots or trailers and importing them. The colors that were intended for broadcast probably won't be quite the same as these imported files, but if you view them on a broadcast monitor, you can at least see where a professional colorist was able to take a certain skin tone to create a certain look.

Figure 3-81 shows a fairly one-sided vectorscope trace. There is virtually no magenta, blue, or cyan. The largest portion of the trace lands in the yellow/red vector. This is mostly from the pile of hay and the hay between the cobblestones. The spike that just misses the red target is the rooster's cowl and the red of the wheel. The green is coming from the trees, the grass in the cobblestone, and the green of the farm machine. The reds are a bit on the illegal side. It would be a good use of secondary color correction to define that particularly strong red component and draw it back into the legal zone without affecting the farm machine or the hay.

In Figure 3-82 the black, gray, and white tones, which vary from the bluish cast of the paper towel to the subdued warmth of the rocks, create the bulk of the middle of the trace. There are spikes toward yellow, orange, and red from the colors in the watercolor palette. The intense spike to blue is coming from the fold of blue cloth in the upper left. The whites are running a little cool, which may be appropriate for this shot, or it could be easily warmed up for a different feel.

The vectorscope in Figure 3-83 shows lots of blue from the life vests and the sky. The red life vest is almost hitting the red target perfectly. The trace extending between red and yellow is the yellow oars and gunwales of the boat. Yellow in real life is rarely the yellow of the yellow vectorscope target.

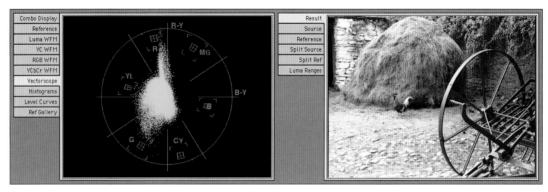

Figure 3-81 This one-sided trace gets most of its yellow-red tones from the hay.

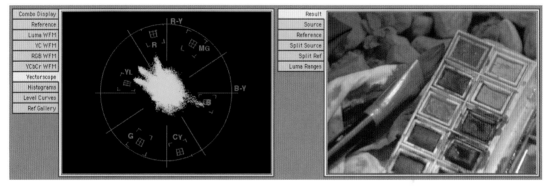

Figure 3-82 From Artbeats' Recreation and Leisure Collection, shot RL123. The black, gray, and white tones create the bulk in the middle of the trace.

The specific hue of yellow that is indicated by the yellow target on the vectorscope is not the most pleasing yellow color. It is the yellow of color bars. Most people prefer their yellows to be a bit more golden. And a golden yellow is a yellow with more red in it.

Randy Starnes says the yellow of the vectorscope's yellow target is a color most colorists avoid:

> I think most colorists will turn the yellow vector a little bit away from green to compensate for what television does to yellow. The yellow of color bars is not the yellow of print art, so we turn that a little. Most people do. An example: In longform telecine, if you're doing an hour or 2-hour story, quite often a lot of us will take the yellow secondary and move it 2 or 3 degrees away from green and then load the list, so the yellow is a little less green in your whole show.

The colorful shot in Figure 3-84 is like a good break in a game of pool. The yellows are going close to the yellow target but are a few degrees toward red. The blue sky is heading toward cyan. And the red balloons are pretty close to hitting the red target exactly.

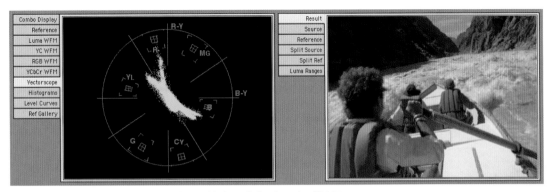

Figure 3-83 Courtesy Artbeats' Recreation and Leisure Collection, shot RL117.

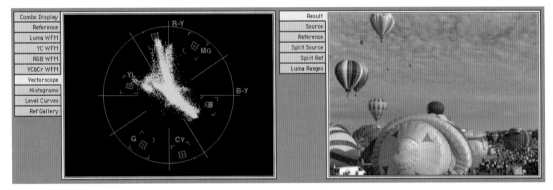

Figure 3-84 Courtesy Artbeats' Recreation and Leisure Collection, shot RL101.

A Diamond in the Rough

If you still want more scopes to play with, you can try the split diamond scope. This is a proprietary display that is only on Tektronix scopes, but it is worth a quick mention because it helps with two important tasks. One is that it can easily identify gamut errors. These are illegal colors that can get your projects kicked back by the QC department at a broadcaster or can at the very least give your images unexpected viewing results further down in the transmission chain when they are altered to create legal colors.

The other thing that the split diamond display can do is help you balance colors.

The way that the split diamond display works is fairly simple. Any colors that are out of gamut show up outside of the two diamonds that make up the split diamond display. The top diamond shows a square where the difference between blue and green is displayed, so gray images (or at least images that have the same green to blue ratio) go right up the middle, with the darkest images at the bottom of the diamond. The bottom diamond shows a

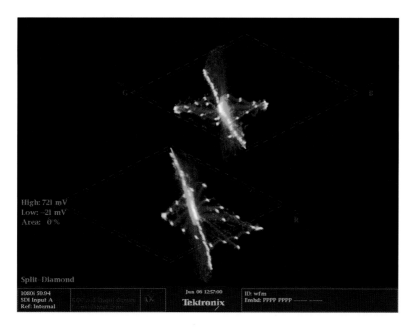

Figure 3-85 Split Diamond gamut display of ChromaDuMonde camera chart with a warm (red) cast to it.

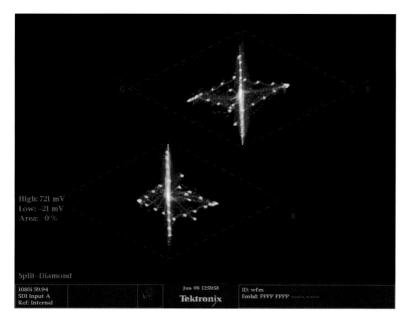

Figure 3-86 Split Diamond gamut display of ChromaDuMonde camera chart corrected to neutral.

square where the difference between red and green is displayed, so gray images (or at least images that have the same red to green ratio) go right up the middle, with the darkest images at the top.

So a balanced black will show up perfectly at the crux of the two diamonds. Balanced whites are at the very top and bottom of the two diamonds. And balanced gray runs straight up the middle of the two diamonds. If there is a red cast, the trace of the bottom diamond skews to the right. (Figure 3-85) If there is a blue cast, the trace in the top diamond skews to the right. If there is a green cast the trace in both diamonds would skew to the left.

Summary

For nearly all professional colorists, the various waveform displays—Flat Pass, Luma only, RGB Parade, and YCbCr Parade—plus the vectorscope are the main methods for analyzing your image. While experienced colorists often rely on their eyes, they use these scopes to provide an unchanging reference to guide them as they spend hours color correcting. Without them, their eyes and grades would eventually drift off course. Spend time becoming comfortable with these scopes and knowing what part of the video image corresponds to the images on the scopes.

In the next chapter, we will discuss two additional means for analyzing your images. Neither of them is widely accepted by professional colorists, but part of that is because they really haven't had these tools to work with until recently. The two tools we will explore are the eyedropper and the histogram. Both of these tools have relatively long histories of success with photo retouchers, who are the "print brethren" to the colorist.

4

OTHER METHODS TO ANALYZE FOOTAGE

Although the methods described in this chapter may not have the blessing or respect of "big iron" colorists, they are still valid ways to envision your footage and to have the footage show you what you need to do to fix or improve it.

Info Palettes and Other Numeric RGB Readouts

In addition to scopes, another useful tool for color and tonal analysis is provided in the form of an eyedropper or Info Palette in many programs. Most imaging applications have them. Figures 4-1 through 4-3 show a variety of Info Palettes from various manufacturers. The feature allows you to sample specific pixels and see what their RGB makeup is. This is very similar to using an RGB Parade waveform monitor, but instead of looking at the whole picture, you're examining specific pixels.

This is very similar to using an RGB Parade waveform monitor.

This feature allows you to click on various areas of the picture and see a readout of the RGB values of a specific pixel (or small group of pixels) on the screen. Using this feature on pixels that you believe should be white, black, or neutral gives a great deal of information about color casts in those areas. Just as the vectorscope displays the absence of chroma by placing the signal in the middle of the monitor, it is possible to detect the absence of chroma with numerical RGB information. The absence of chroma with the eyedropper is indicated by the numerical similarity of the three channels to each other.

The absence of chroma with the eyedropper is indicated by the numerical similarity of the three channels.

Pure white in RGB 8-bit color space is R255, G255, B255. Pure black is R0, G0, B0. Fifty percent gray is indicated by R128, G128, B128. If the balance of red, green, and blue values are not identical

Big Iron

This is casual postproduction industry lingo for big, expensive, dedicated hardware. In this context, it means "the guys who operate the million dollar color correction suites." Big iron is a term meant to separate the men from the boys, but it really separates the men's bosses from their wallets.

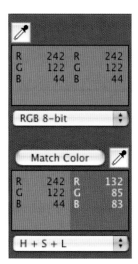

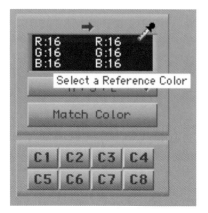

Figure 4-1 Info Palettes and eyedroppers in Color Finesse. Color Finesse's eyedropper tool is available on the right hand side in all of the tabs. The information can be represented as 8-bit RGB, 8 bit, 10 bit, 16 bit, Floating Point, or RGB percentage. It can also be displayed as HSL or Hex.

Figure 4-3 Info Palettes and eyedroppers in Avid Media Composer. The eyedropper tool is available in all of the color correction tabs. The eyedropper information in Avid can be displayed as 8-bit or 10-bit RGB values. Also, all sampled colors can be named and saved in Avid bins for future recall and comparison, even between projects.

Figure 4-2 Info Palettes and eyedroppers in Apple Color. The Info Palette numbers are only available at the bottom of the 3D scope display. Note that Color represents the RGB values on a scale from 0.000–1.000, instead of the more traditional 8-bit RGB values from 0–255. Color can also represent a number of values in the HSL, YPbPr, and IPT color spaces.

or nearly identical, you have information that can help you eliminate the difference.

For example, use the eyedropper to sample an area of the screen that should be neutral gray. If the numerical RGB readout for this sample reads R60, G62, B94, then you know that your image is too blue. The difference between the red number and the green number is insignificant on a scale of over 200, but the blue number is about 50% higher than the red and green numbers.

If the readout indicated R200, G200, B100, then the image would be too yellow. Yellow is the secondary color between red and green on a vectorscope or color wheel. Instead of saying the image is too yellow, we could also describe it as not being blue enough. Blue is the complementary color opposite yellow on a vectorscope or color wheel. Until you have memorized the relationships between the primary colors of red, green, and blue and the secondary colors of cyan, magenta, and yellow, refer to your vectorscope or a color wheel. If you are trying to use RGB controls to reduce magenta, then decreasing red and blue will solve the problem. To reduce yellow, decrease red and green, or increase the complementary color, which is blue.

RGB Color Flash Cards

Although the relationships between RGB colors have been discussed elsewhere in the book, it can't be stressed enough that having a thorough and complete understanding of these relationships is crucial to your ability to use any color correction software. All these relationships can be visually compared—and better understood—on the graticule of a vectorscope.

So make up the following flash cards and study them. Put the part of the line before the colon (:) on one side of the card and the part after the colon on the other side.

Red is the opposite of: cyan

Magenta is the opposite of: green

Blue is the opposite of: yellow

Cyan is the opposite of: red

Green is the opposite of: magenta

Yellow is the opposite of: blue

Magenta is made up of: red and blue

Cyan is made up of: blue and green

Yellow is made up of: red and green

Red and green makes: yellow

Blue and green makes: cyan

Red and blue makes: magenta

The other important concept to remember is that adding a color that you need or subtracting a color that you don't want affects the picture in two different ways. Consider the previous example. If you decrease the amount of red and green to make a picture less yellow, then you are also *decreasing* the overall brightness or tone of the image. By increasing the amount of blue to make the picture less yellow, you are also *increasing* the overall brightness of the picture.

> *Adding a color that you need or subtracting a color that you don't want affects the picture in two different ways.*

Let's see how this actually works. To simplify, we'll take a yellowish green color and attempt to make it more pure green. Analyzing the color as RGB numbers, it is R104, G194, B0. But let's also look at this color as hue, saturation, and brightness, which is H88, S100, B76. If we attempt to swing the hue more toward green, we could simply eliminate the red in the image. What does that do to our RGB numbers, though? For a pure green hue, this means that we get R0, G194, B0. The trick is that even though the hue is now perfectly on green (120), the saturation and brightness have also

TIP

To follow along with the examples in the book, create a color using Apple's Color Picker or the Color Palette on a PC in any application, (Adobe Photoshop would be a natural, but even Microsoft Word would work), and adjust the color while watching the RGB numbers.

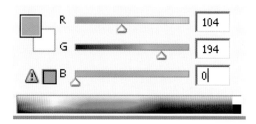

remained the same in the HSB numbers, but if you look at the two colors, the first looks brighter than the second.

You could also try to increase the greenness by simply cranking up the green channel. Starting from our original example of R104, G194, B0, we would increase the green channel to its maximum, which manages to swing the hue around to 96. Dropping the amount of red gradually swings the hue closer to our green destination of 120, but it isn't until we get red back down to 0 that the hue gets all of the way to 120. Our final color here is much more saturated than our result in the first example because we've cranked the green channel to its maximum number. The apparent brightness still does not match the original example.

Now let's try to swing the hue by looking at our color wheel and using complementary colors. If we want to reduce yellow, we add its complementary color, which is blue. If we are trying to compensate for the amount of red in the image, we could simply match the intensity of the red with the same intensity of blue. So an image of R104, G194, B104 does actually swing the hue right where we want it: 120. However, now our green is a pretty pale shade of light green.

Our final attempt is to split the difference between red and blue instead of simply adding blue. Because our original example was R104, G194, B0, we'll cut the red amount in half and add that amount to the blue, giving us R52, G194, B52. This gives us a much more saturated image and maintains the hue at 120. If we were trying to maintain the look of a certain brightness or contrast of the image, we could now raise the amount of green either up to its maximum of 255 or lower it. But if we want to maintain the hue, we can only lower the amount of green down to one level above the red and blue numbers. In the current example, this would be R52, G53, B52. When the values of all of the channels match, remember, we have no hue at all because there is no chrominance. And if green drops below the red and blue numbers, we are left with the complementary color of green, which is magenta.

Averaged Color Sampling

Rudimentary implementation of RGB sampling tools—or *eye-droppers*—sample a single pixel as a reference. However, selecting an individual pixel in an area may not actually be representative

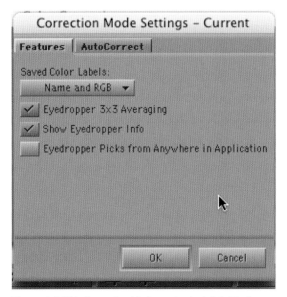

Figure 4-5 This is the Info Tab in After Effects. Clicking or dragging on a pixel shows the RGB numbers for the sample. If you want to see a 5 × 5 average, hold down control on a PC or command on a Mac.

Figure 4-4 This Correction Mode setting in Avid's Media Composer color correction engine allows the selection of 3 × 3 averaged color sampling instead of single pixel color sampling.

of the actual color in the general area of the pixel. In most recent applications it is possible to define the size of the sample that is taken. That RGB sample is then averaged over a small area of pixels; for example, a 3 × 3 grid of pixels (see Figure 4-4) or a 5 × 5 grid of pixels. Depending on the area you are sampling, this averaging is much more useful than sampling individual pixels due to the possibility of noise in the image or subtle color variations from one adjacent pixel to the next.

Averaging is much more useful than sampling individual pixels.

Sampling RGB information with single pixel samples does have its uses. It can help you analyze areas that you think may be clipped. Areas of pure white or pure black can be a telltale sign that clipping or crushing has occurred. This test can be performed by watching the RGB numbers as you slowly drag the eyedropper inside an area of deep shadow or bright highlight. Minor fluctuations mean that the areas sampled have not been clipped. They can also mean that there may be some noise in the signal that can be addressed by the noise reduction tools that may exist in your arsenal of color correction or effects filter tools.

Not all random noise is a bad thing. With highly overexposed or underexposed portions of a film image, many colorists point to the fact that the film grain still creates "life" or "texture" in these portions of the image, while on video, an overexposed highlight merely results in lost detail, making it much less interesting.

Numeric RGB samples can also assist you in creating reference points for matching shots in a scene. You can compare skin tones, product colors, or even the depth and contrast of shadows. When using RGB sampling for this purpose, it is wise to use an averaged sampling to reduce the possible randomness.

One interesting use for these numerical readings could be in determining the strength of contrast between the shadows and highlights of shots that are in the same sequence and should match. You can quantitatively measure the ratio between the darkness of a shadow and the brightness of a highlight and compare that ratio with the same areas of another shot. This is similar to a technique used by professional photographers and cinematographers. They often measure the brightness values of their subject's highlights and skin tones and shadows with a spot meter to properly light them with the desired contrast.

> **You can measure the ratio between the darkness of a shadow and the brightness of a highlight.**

Even shots created with meticulous quality control and the highest level of professionalism are subject to noticeable variations in levels and color. Peter Mavromates, postproduction supervisor for David Fincher's *Panic Room*, explains the scope of issues that can cause these changes:

> *When you think about the making of a movie, movies are, at minimum, shot on really short schedules of 15 days and most long schedules [are] 80 or 90 days, and there are schedules that are even longer than that. Maintaining consistent lighting, quality control, etc., over that amount of time is impossible. If you're shooting on location outside during the day, the light changes minute by minute if it's a weather situation where there are clouds coming in. And if you're on a set and you actually manage to maintain consistent lighting over a number of weeks, you've got other issues that come in; you've got photochemical processes that drift, telecine scanners that drift. A number of different issues make it different: Actors, who despite their professional training, will go out and go to the beach over the weekend, and they come in on Monday in the middle of the same scene, and they've got a suntan. Stuff like that. You could make a list of a thousand things that affect how something looks.*
>
> *Now on Panic Room, what I just described was particularly difficult because it was one set for a large number of days. We're on one set day after day after day, and the inconsistencies creep in there. They creep in there a lot of times even though the lighting is all the same on the same set. What happens is that you move the camera and you're shooting an actor a certain way. Well, by shooting that way you suddenly find that the light kicks very strongly on the*

wall behind them. And what that means is that their side has become bright even though none of the lighting has changed, but just by the fact that the light is being bounced more directly into the lens, that angle is brighter. The wall in the background is brighter and so now [it] no longer matches the reverse angle of the other actor.

Let's examine some images using RGB sampling. The following are RGB samples taken from various portions of the image in Figure 4-6. As a shorthand, I'm just listing the RGB numbers in that order, separated by commas. All of these images are available in the "Tutorial Footage" folder on the DVD. Load them and follow along.

Figure 4-6 Frame grab from Artbeats' Kids of Summer Collection, shot KS109.

- Yellow hat: 222, 155, 43. This really nice hue of yellow has a lot of red in it.
- Blue dress: 14, 63, 237.
- Bluish/white blanket: 238, 244, 252. While the blanket looks fairly white on video, this sample gives away its bluish cast.
- Flesh tones, girl in blue dress: 125, 69, 46. Flesh tones, girl in yellow: 121, 55, 30 and 151, 82, 49. Race does not change the basic hue of flesh tones.
- Grass: 43, 110, 30. A very nice grass color.
- White color on blue dress: 183, 197, 235. Fairly blue.
- Highlight on yellow flower: 252, 250, 237. If this were a straight highlight, the blue would be a little deficient. On a yellow flower, though, this is an appropriate highlight.
- Pigtails: 2, 2, 2 and 11, 4, 5. Pretty good numbers here. The 11, 4, 5 numbers are a little high on the red side, but sampling numerous points on the pigtails shows a wide spectrum of subtle colors in the blacks. Averaged out, these numbers are appropriate.

Figure 4-7 A nice day for a row in Ireland. This image is in the Tutorial Footage folder on the DVD as "Irishrowboat.tif."

The following are RGB samples taken from various portions of the image in Figure 4-7:

- Shadows: 4, 10, 9. Many shadow samples came back with a similar red deficiency that we may want to correct.
- Skin tones: 197, 144, 157. He's Irish, so we may forgive the pink skin tones, but maybe we can pull down some of the blue. Notice the flesh tone numbers in the previous example. They all descend smoothly. But not our ruddy friend here. Pulling some blue out will reduce the magenta cast to his skin.
- Bright water reflections: 204, 235, 240 and 236, 246, 246. All's in order here.
- Sky: 253, 253, 253. Sampling of the sky showed there was still detail there, and the white is about as white as it gets.
- Boatman's coat: 133, 147, 163. Similar to the flesh tones, if we want this coat to be truly gray, we'll need to notch down the blue in the midtones. Our blacks and whites have the right amount of blue, so be careful to isolate the blue reduction to the midtones.

The image in Figure 4-8 is a little dark. We'll fix that in one of the tutorials. What else can the Info Palette reveal about where we should start? RGB samples are:

Figure 4-8 Dark fence. This image is in the Tutorial Footage folder on the DVD as "fence.tif."

- Several fence readings: 30, 44, 34 and 32, 55, 38 and 22, 39, 28. All show this to be a little cyan. We are looking for a nice weathered gray. That means pulling down the green and a little notch down on blue.
- The blacks of the post: 8, 9, 10 and 5, 5, 4 and 9, 13, 12. This shows that blacks are in good shape. These good blacks are a warning that any color casts we attempt to fix will need to be limited to the midtones.

The image in Figure 4-9 looks a little blue. What do the numbers tell us?

Figure 4-9 Blue boats. This image is in the Tutorial Footage folder on the DVD as "boatsatdock.tif."

- Wood on front boat: 95, 41, 22. This doesn't tell us much, since we don't know what these numbers should be. Wood can be many hues.
- Red kayak paddle: 187, 47, 78. This seems a little blue if we want a red that's right on target.
- White from various outboard motors: 187, 221, 196 and 202, 237, 215. Now we're learning something. Reds are deficient and greens are a bit high.
- Green from trees: 20, 54, 44. This seems blue as well.
- Sky blue: 146, 209, 223. Seems very green for a blue sky.
- Gray of second boat: 122, 180, 195. Another revealing number. Red is deficient. Because this is very close to that center number for 24-bit color images, we know that to balance this, we need to work on midtones.

Histograms

Another powerful tool for analyzing video images is the histogram. A histogram is a graph that breaks the video signal down into individual pixels and distributes them on a graph where the x defines the luminance of the pixels—with the darkest pixels to the left and the brightest pixels to the right—and the y displays the number of pixels at each luminance level.

A histogram is a graph where x defines the luminance of the pixels and y displays the number of pixels at each level.

In addition to showing the overall brightness levels of the pixels, the histogram can also display the individual red, green, and blue channels graphed in the same way. This information can be very valuable in figuring out whether a given color channel has problems in the shadows, midtones, or highlights.

Analysis

Let's take a look at some sample images to see how they appear when analyzed using a histogram. These images are available in the "Tutorial Footage" folder on the DVD.

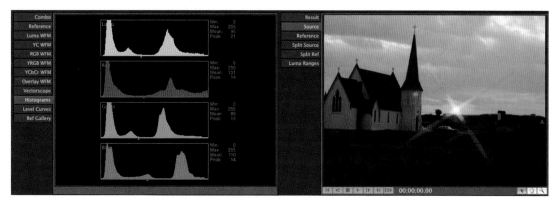

Figure 4-10 No surprises in this histogram. This image is in the Tutorial Footage folder on the DVD as "church with cross of light.tif."

The histograms in Figure 4-10 show pretty much what you'd expect from this image: lots of shadows and some bright midtones. The only bright element is in the red channel. Nothing looks like it's clipped or crushed.

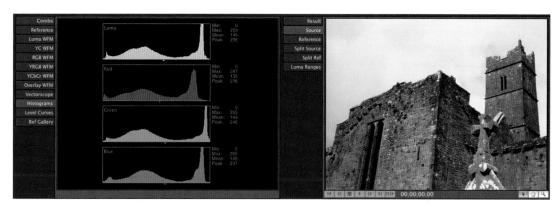

Figure 4-11 Good histogram, little correction needed. This image is in the Tutorial Footage folder on the DVD as "closecastle.tif."

Figure 4-11 shows nice histograms. There is no clipping or crushing of the signal. The sky may be going a little green. You can see this by the fact that the green spike on the right side (bright side) of the histogram is further to the right than the blue spike. We might want to pull those blacks down a bit to add some richness. The spike of luminance at the top is definitely sky. There might be enough detail there that we can make the sky more interesting.

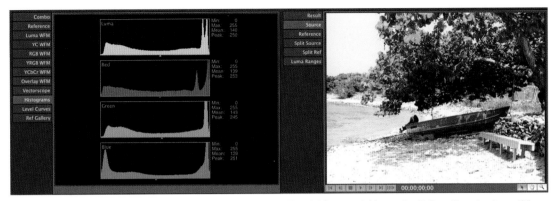

Figure 4-12 Not many blacks to work with. This image is in the Tutorial Footage folder on the DVD as "jamaicanboat.tif."

There are not a lot of blacks in Figure 4-12. We can pull down the shadows to create some richness. It looks like the red channel clipped a bit on the high end. Rolling down the highlights a little will help this look less washed out. The sharp spikes on the high end of the histograms is definitely indicative of a problem with the highlights.

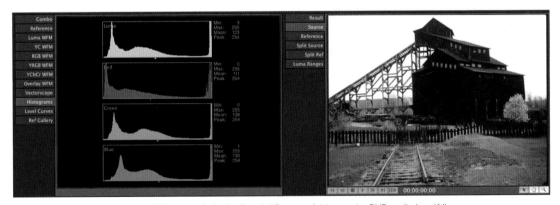

Figure 4-13 Plenty of shadows. This image is in the Tutorial Footage folder on the DVD as "mine.tif."

In Figure 4-13, there seems to be plenty of room to work with the shadow detail. The blacks could come down a little because there's some space at the low end of the luma histogram. Also, the black levels (to the left) of the green and blue histograms are not as far over to the left as the red histogram, showing elevated levels of cyan in the blacks. The large spike of dark in the luma histogram can probably be spread out a little, improving detail in the blacks of the mine structure. It does seem from the bright spikes on the right of all the histograms that the sky has been clipped rather severely. There is not much we can do to salvage that. You could pull the entire bright highlight level down. This wouldn't bring back the highlight detail, but it would make it easier to see the detail in the blacks because your eye wouldn't be so flooded with light. This is a careful balance, though, because you don't want the sky to look too dreary, unless that is the intent. Some skilled compositors might pull a key from the luma of the sky and simply replace it with something more interesting.

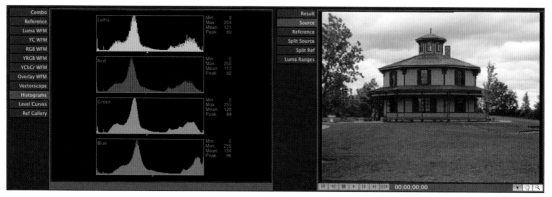

Figure 4-14 Faded blacks and elevated greens. Some of the green is coming from the grass and the color of the building, but there also is a general green cast to the image. This image is in the Tutorial Footage folder on the DVD as "octagonal building.tif."

The blacks of Figure 4-14 seem very washed out, as indicated by the distance from the left side before the histogram starts to have any significant number of pixels. The low end of the histogram can definitely be pulled down to create some nice, solid blacks. There is still some highlight detail in the bright whites.

Figure 4-15 shows some surprising histograms. The amount of blue and green in the low end of the histograms is unusual. There is the expected peak in the red channel histogram, but it is not clipped. Also, the luma histogram shows most of the picture sitting in the shadows, but the overall impression is of a fairly bright image. There is very little bright highlight, but that is as it should be. Other than the highlight of the ring sitting on the skull, very little else should be bright white. Correcting the red would be possible because nothing's clipped, but the red adds a lot to the image.

Figure 4-16 is a beautiful histogram. The blacks could be pulled down to give some definition to the picture, but there's not much in this picture that should be pure black, and lowering the blacks would definitely lose some detail. It's the same with the whites. They could be pulled up some to add some punch and sparkle, but there's no definite bright white in the image. The large spike of blue in the highlights gives us a reason to look at pulling down

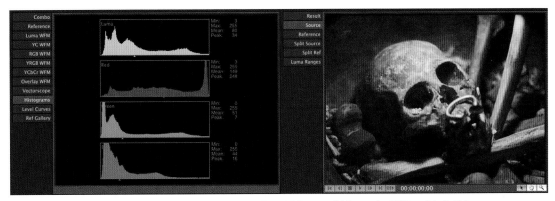

Figure 4-15 Green and blue surprise. This image is in the Tutorial Footage folder on the DVD as "skull.tif."

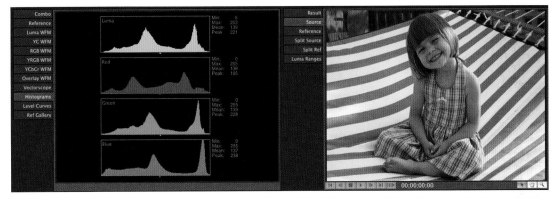

Figure 4-16 This is an excellent histogram, but note the midtone spikes. The green and blue spikes are probably caused by the stripes in the hammock. This image is in the Tutorial Footage folder on the DVD as "haleyhammock.tif."

some blue in the highlights. The skin tones appear very nice, so any blue correction would need to either improve the skin tones or at least not make them worse. The green of the hammock and the warm colors of the girl's dress are evident in their respective histograms. The large spike of midtones in the luma histogram is a possible clue that midtones could be moved down to create a richer picture.

Clues

Like looking at a waveform monitor, there is no way to tell just by looking at a histogram that the image is good, but the histogram can give you some definite indications that something may be wrong.

Some things to look for are:

- Posterization, which can be seen as bands of pixels with similar levels

- Clipping, with large, sharp peaks of pixels at either far end of the spectrum
- An overly large percentage of pixels in the middle of the spectrum, with none on the ends, indicating that your blacks and highlights are not well defined
- Missing levels of luminance—called *combing*—that indicates data loss, probably due to some color space conversion (this is pretty rare to see in video color correction, but it can happen with imported images)

The Zone

Although there is no "correct" histogram, the famous photographer Ansel Adams developed his Zone System for properly exposing and printing photographs. This system could give you an indication of what to shoot for. The goal of the Zone System was to match the exposure of the negative with the ability of the final print paper to reproduce that image. This created a series of zones that certain tones of the scene were supposed to fall into. The main point was to figure out in which zone you wanted to place a certain element (like the skin tone of your subject) and to properly expose and then develop so that the particular element ended up in the intended zone of the final print. The Zone System also helps photographers predict how the other elements will print in comparison to the main subject's zone. The other goal was not to lose important detail in the highlights and shadows. Adams didn't have histograms to analyze his photographs, so he broke each image into 10 zones based on their tonal range and attempted to distribute the exposure of the film so that the darkest and brightest zones usually had some exposure, but there were very few spots on any prints that went pure white or pure black to the point where detail was lost.

Most critics consider Ansel Adams to be a master of tonal range. He knew how to control it and what to do with it to provoke an emotional response. Yet, Adams's perspective on the importance of this skill was not that it was used to perfectly portray the *reality* of any given scene but that it portrayed *the way the scene felt*. This is a critical distinction for an aspiring colorist. Adams provides the important clue that the goal is not reality, but mood. He used tone to tell story. Another interesting note on the subject of Adams is that even in the 1960s, 1970s, and 1980s, he was still making prints of negatives he had taken back in the 1930s. As he aged, his prints changed to become much more bold and contrasty in comparison to his earlier prints of the same negative. This should make a clear statement that picking the "correct" tonal range for an image is very much a subjective undertaking and one that can and should be interpreted using more than just technical terms, but also emotion and feeling.

Many people who are unfamiliar with Adams's processes may place the entire weight of his artistic ability on his skill with a camera, but most photographic enthusiasts know that his skill in the darkroom—which is very analogous to the art of color correction for video—was just as crucial to the success of his prints.

For more information about Ansel Adams's Zone System, see the bibliography of this book.

5

COLORISTS' TOOLS—PRIMARY COLOR CORRECTION

The previous two chapters explored the tools you have to *analyze* your image, and the next two chapters will explore the tools you have to *manipulate* your image. These tools are broken down by work flow. Colorists generally break their work flow down to Primary corrections and Secondary corrections.

Primary color corrections are the corrections that apply to the entire image. They are overall, general corrections. Secondary color corrections are the corrections that are specifically applied to only a portion of the image. These corrections are applied to areas of the image that the colorist chooses and isolates from the rest of the image through a number of means, including mattes pulled on certain luma ranges or color vectors or by means of drawing mattes—sometimes called vignetting or spot color correction.

This chapter will explore the first part of the work flow: Primary color correction. The two main tasks of the colorist in Primary color correction are setting the tonal ranges and balancing the colors. You'd think that because colorists are called colorists, the most important of these manipulations involves color. However, the thing that really transforms most images from mundane to marvelous resides in the tonal correction tools.

Tonality Rules! (Or Colors Drool)

The tonality of an image is basically expressed in the range of luminance levels from black to white and where they fall in relationship to one another. The basic color correction tools have the ability to expand or compress the overall tonal range and to adjust the balance of how that range is weighted. To do this, the color correction engine basically remaps the levels of the incoming footage to new final output levels. The two main levels to remap are the highlights and the shadows. These define the limits of the tonal range of the image.

The two main levels to remap are the highlights and the shadows. These define the limits of the tonal range of the image.

The other important element in manipulating the tone of the image is to decide on where the center tones of the image will be remapped. This is called the gamma or midtones. Some programs or tools will offer very basic controls over gamma, and others allow you to create complex gamma corrections, similar to parametric EQ in audio instead of simple bass and treble controls. The advanced tools allow you to determine multiple gamma ranges and to determine the slopes of each gamma curve and how they blend into and out of one another.

Before delving too deeply into gamma, let's take a look at manipulating the extremes of the tonal range. These corrections are very standard. At their root, they are the basic controls that editors have almost always had with the time base correctors or TBC controls of gain and setup. One of the first things you will want to manipulate when doing a correction is to set the upper and lower limits of your image. To turn this into a highly generalized statement, you would want your blacks to be black and your whites to be white, without violating the legal limits. To simplify this discussion, we will set these limits at 100IRE on a waveform monitor for the top end and 0IRE for the bottom. (Also see page 58 for a discussion of legal limits with various scopes, formats, and video standards.)

Hammer and Saw of Color Correction

As you experiment with the following tonal corrections, use the basic Master HSL sliders for now. Each graphical user interface for each product will call this something a little different, and new versions of software will rename the old tools as they go. The tools we want to use now are the most basic color correction tools at your disposal: master black level, gain, and gamma.

If you are using Final Cut, follow along by using the Highlight, Mids, and Blacks sliders in the Level Controls of the simple Color Corrector filter (see Figure 5-1). In Color Finesse, use the RGB Gain, Gamma, and Pedestal sliders at the bottom of the HSL > Controls > Master tab (see Figure 5-2). In Apple Color, use the Master Lift, Master Gain, and Master Gamma controls in the Basic Tab in the Primary room (see Figure 5-3). In Avid, open the Color Correction mode or Toolset and use the Gain, Gamma, and Setup sliders in the HSL > Hue Offsets tab (see Figure 5-4). In Adobe Premiere or After Effects, drop a Color Correction > Levels effect on and use the Gamma, Output Black, and Output White sliders (see Figure 5-5).

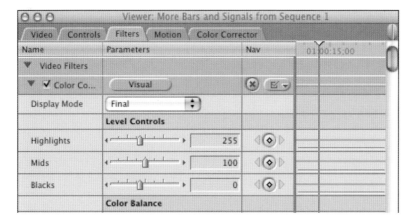

Figure 5-1 Basic tonal range controls in Final Cut Pro.

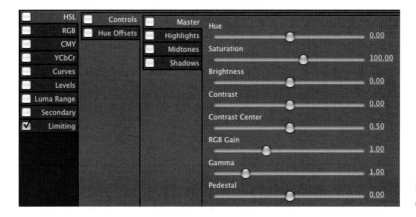

Figure 5-2 Basic tonal range controls in Color Finesse.

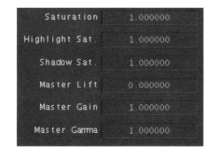

Figure 5-3 Basic tonal range controls in Apple Color.

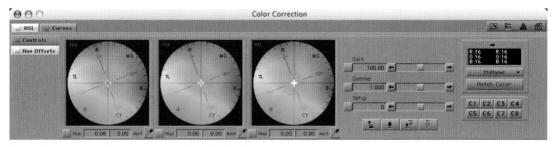

Figure 5-4 Basic tonal range controls in Avid Media Composer.

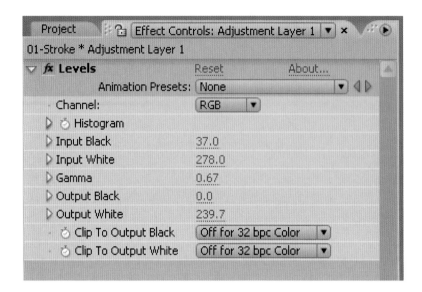

Figure 5-5 Basic tonal range controls in Adobe Premiere or After Effects.

Basic Black

The first thing you should adjust in any correction is the black level, which is sometimes also referred to as *pedestal, lift*, or *setup*. The reason for this is that in most color engines, all of the other computations are based on this level. It gives you a strong "base" to build the rest of your correction on. Normally if your picture looks a little washed out or there is not much detail in the blacks, you need to look at this level and get it to around 0IRE. The exception to this rule is if there is nothing in your image that *should* be black. If your image is:

- Shot through a fog or smoke
- Is mostly snow
- Is a long focal length shot of some distant skyscrapers
- Has a subject that is entirely midtones and highlights

then there probably isn't anything that needs to be pure black. In cases like these, you should rely on your subjective judgment.

The first thing you should adjust in any correction is the black level.

One of the primary tools for setting luminance or black levels is the waveform monitor. The specific position of the deepest black or the brightest white is not as important as watching how compressed the waveform is at the top and bottom. If you lower the setup to get it down to 0IRE but notice that the lower levels of the waveform are starting to compress into a single, thick line at the bottom, you know you're losing detail down in the shadows. Sometimes this means compromise. Usually you want that black point to be all the way to 0IRE, but if you start compressing the shadow details before you reach 0IRE, then you may need to use

Watch the "Spreading_the_ tonal_range" video tutorial in the Video tutorial folder on the DVD.

your eye to tell you when the blacks are rich enough. You can also bring the blacks all the way down to 0IRE and then use your gamma control to "uncrush" the details in the shadow by lifting the gamma.

So the clue that you are clipping or crushing is not really the *position* of the waveform but the overall *shape* of the waveform. Examine it carefully as you move the shadows toward 0IRE and the highlights toward 100IRE. When the shape—or excursion—starts to compress into a single, tight line, then you know you are killing detail.

There was a good example of this in Chapter 3 on page 75. Re-examine Figures 3-39 and 3-40 and notice how Figure 3-39 has a certain shape to the brightest picture potions. When that level passes a certain point, the shape of the excursions change. That is the point where you start to really focus your adjustments. Just like scrubbing a piece of audio to find the very first bit of sound, you can increase and decrease the level while watching for that crucial point when the black level is low enough but the shape of the wave is maintained.

> **Another analogy for controlling your adjustments is that it is similar to focusing a camera.**

Another analogy for controlling your adjustments is that it is similar to focusing a camera. To make sure you are in perfect focus, you have to go a little bit beyond your focus point then come back to the sharpest focus. Color correction is similar. The only way to know if you have taken the image far enough is to take it too far, then come back to the place where it belongs.

 Some NTSC scopes may show black at 7.5IRE. For a thorough understanding of where black should be placed, see page 4 of Chapter 1, *How to Determine the Proper Black Level.*

Throw Caution to the Wind

Randy Starnes warns about allowing these adjustments to become too detailed:

> *The more a person grades film, the more quickly they can recognize the perfect exposure of the film. That process can take 5 minutes; it can take 15 minutes. If it starts to take longer than 15 minutes, you'll start to lose your audience. Make the moves bold. Don't be constrained by technical limits. See what you can do. You can always come back. One of the most frustrating things for a client to participate in is a slow, deliberate manipulation of the image. You lose track of where you are and where you want to go.*
> **"Make big sweeping moves [to] provoke more feedback from your client."—Randy Starnes**
> *If you make big sweeping moves, you can do the same thing quicker. And you provoke more feedback from your client. They see it and you see it. One of the things that we have to watch out for is that our brain compensates for a*

lot of what we see. If you move too slowly—if you're too cautious—your brain may tell you that the image is right. But following a plan or a philosophy of making large changes keeps your brain from catching up or from convincing you that you've gone as far as you can. You make multiple changes. You go in three or four different directions, you save those and you compare them, and you quickly winnow out the ones that are not pleasing to you or your client. You narrow down your choices.

Back to Black

Getting the blacks low without deforming the shape of the waveform near the bottom helps preserve shadow detail. There are certainly times when you may want to intentionally eliminate shadow detail in your pictures, but this is rarely a good thing. Keep an eye on your waveform monitor when doing these first steps to ensure that you are exploiting as much of the picture information as you can.

To better understand this, let's look at three waveform images in Figures 5-6 through 5-8 as we attempt to find the proper setup for an image. The image we're trying to correct here should have a full range of luma values from black to bright white.

The waveform image in Figure 5-6 indicates that the picture probably looks a little washed out. No part of the waveform is sitting on the 0IRE line. The image in Figure 5-7 has black that is at the proper level. Notice the way the shadow area of the waveform looks. Now compare it to the third waveform image, Figure 5-8. In the third image, the shadows have started to compress into a tight line on the 0IRE line. The broad, open excursions of shadow detail are compressing. This indicates that shadow detail is being crushed. If we are trying for an optimal image, there is a lot of detail being lost in this lower range in Figure 5-8.

When the setup has been properly tuned, we can look to adjust the bright end of the image. If your waveform shows that you don't have any parts of the image that extend all the way up to 100IRE

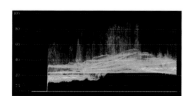

Figure 5-6 Blacks are a little high, indicating a washed out image.

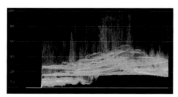

Figure 5-7 Blacks are set correctly on the 0IRE line with no crushing.

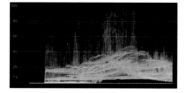

Figure 5-8 Crushed blacks and loss of detail are indicated by the thin, bright line at the bottom of the trace.

(the highest luminance), you may want to raise your luminance levels so that things that *should* be very bright hit that mark. If your image doesn't have anything that *should* be completely bright, then use your eye to determine the maximum luminance level.

Value of 100IRE

While all colorists agree that not every image should be brought all the way to 100IRE, Randy Starnes pointed out that nearly every image should reach the extremes in terms of tonal range:

> *Not every image should hit 100, but the majority of the time you will find in any image rich blacks and bright whites. We broke the rule a long time ago that whites had to be 100%. They don't need to go there, but you'll have a better image if you have a full volt of video somewhere in your picture.*

(One *volt* of video refers to the full 700 mV of video signal that is equal to 100IRE, plus the 300 mV of sync.) Figure 5-9 shows a waveform with the graticule set to display in millivolts instead of IRE. Notice the orange numbers from 100 to 800 along the left side of the image. Compare them to the numbers on the left side of Figure 5-7. This is actually the same trace as in Figure 5-7, just using a different scale to do the measurement.

Starnes continues:

> *Since you're dealing with a television image that is transmitted, a low signal is going to give you more noise to signal, vision image that is transmitand your goal is less noise to signal. Transmission introduces noise inherently. Our equipment has gotten better and better, so the post process—*

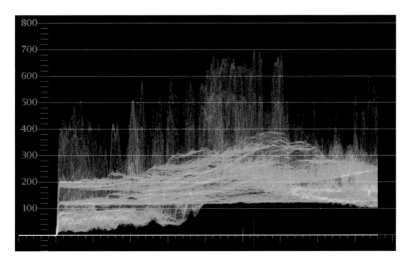

Figure 5-9 A waveform display with the graticule measuring in millivolts.

editing and color correction—is not introducing noise; transmission is introducing it. So in order to preserve that image with the lowest signal-to-noise ratio, you want to be able to build in a volt of video.

If you have a night scene, you're not going to have bright whites, but if you have a night scene with a practical inside a window, you're going to have an opportunity to have a volt of video. That carries over well. You're not going to see a lot of commercial images that don't have the full range or at least a volt of video. Most of the time, you push it to 100% and past so it jumps out at you, so it carries across better. Obviously, a white that is less than 100% is going to be a duller white.

Beyond the basic question of correcting images so that some point reaches 100IRE is another question of exceeding that range. Most broadcast specs actually allow temporary specular highlights to reach as high as 108IRE. Most professional camcorders do not clip images until around the 110IRE mark. Check with your dub house or broadcast client for specifics, but if you have an extra 8IRE of range to make chrome bumpers and sparkling water pop a little more, then use it.

How to Get to 100

When adjusting the upper range of your image, there are many tools that you can use. For now, let's discuss the Brightness and Gain controls. You may only have one of these controls. You may also be provided with *both* of these options. If you only have a single option, then you would follow a similar procedure to the one outlined for setup. You need to bring the brightest portion of the waveform up or down to create the brightest possible legal limit, assuming that your image has something that should actually be pure white.

You want to look out for the same kind of compression in the waveform trace up in the highlights that you were on the lookout for in the shadows. Don't take the brightness up so high that you lose detail in your highlights. Just as with the crushing of shadows, the loss of highlight detail is seen as a squeezing or compressing of the excursions in the upper portion of the waveform. On a monitor, an experienced colorist sees that the highlights begin to flatten out and lose texture. When your highlight levels have been set, revisit your black levels. Depending on how your Brightness or Gain control works, you may have slightly altered your setup (black) level, so you may need to make several small adjustments back and forth to the setup and brightness controls because they interact with each other. If you only have a Brightness control, instead of a Gain control, then you will

Practical

A light on set that is seen in the frame of the film or video. In an interior shot, this could be a table or floor lamp. In an exterior shot, it could be a street light or flashlight. The practical may seem to light the set.

have to perform an annoying little "Texas two-step" as you move back and forth between brightness and black until both levels are where they belong.

If you have a color correction console, like those by Tangent Devices or JLCooper, then you can be spared this issue because the consoles allow you to simultaneously manipulate as many controllers as your fingers can move. Experienced colorists are skilled at bringing blacks down simultaneously with bringing whites up, or pulling gammas down, while at the same time adjusting blacks or highlights. Trying to do color correction with a single track ball is one of the complaints that "real" colorists often make about "desktop" systems. However, almost all desktop color solutions can be operated with manual user interfaces, like Tangent Devices' Wave controller or JLCooper's Eclipse.

Math Class

If your color correction controls provide for both gain and brightness, then you'll need to understand how they differ from each other. Inside the brain of your color correction engine, many of the controls work like a basic spreadsheet. You simply take every digitized pixel in the image, assign it a number, and run it through the spreadsheet, which has a simple formula. The finished equation becomes the output image value.

For brightness control, the equation is additive. If you increase brightness by 2, you are simply adding 2 to the master RGB value of every pixel. The bad thing about this simple process is that it means that if you have already set your blacks at 0IRE and you add 2 to every value, your blacks are now at 2IRE. Brightness takes the entire waveform and moves it, lock, stock, and barrel, up by the same amount. Sometimes that may be just what you want, but usually you want more control than that.

That's where the Gain control comes in. Gain is usually done multiplicatively. That means that if you make an adjustment of 10 to Gain, your carefully set 0IRE black level is unaffected because 0 times 10% is still 0. If you increase a pixel with a value of 10 by 10%, it only goes up 1 value, while a pixel with a 90 value will go up 9 values.

Other color correction programs use different formulas to alter brightness. You don't need to know the specifics, but sometimes it does help to understand exactly what's happening under the hood.

The other complex equations that come into play involve luma ranges. When you do a gain adjustment to highlights, midtones, or shadows only, the multiplier that you choose with the slider also has to take into account an additional factor of where in the range each pixel resides. The multiplier is then modified by the percentage determined by its position in the specific luma range you are correcting. That's how you are able to control very specific tonal ranges of the image. So if you adjust your shadows, it *mostly* affects the shadows, but it also *slightly* affects your midtones. The amount of the correction is ramped. A correction in the midtones will also slightly affect the pixels in both your highlights and shadows.

Enough math. Let's move on.

Gamma Quadrant

With the top and bottom range of your image set, your image may still appear too dark or too light. The solution to this comes from the Gamma control or midtones. Gamma correction is one of the notable improvements over the basic TBC controls that editors were accustomed to back in the linear editing days. It is one of the secret weapons in many colorists' arsenals because it seems to solve a lot of difficult problems. Gamma correction allows you to maintain essentially fixed levels in your shadows and highlights while adjusting the midtones up or down independently. This allows you to keep your image legal while still altering the perceived overall brightness of the scene.

Gamma is one of the secret weapons in many colorists' arsenals.

Another change that gamma correction makes is that the image is perceived to increase in contrast as gamma is lowered and decrease with increased gamma level. Often when a picture is a little washed out despite having proper black levels, dropping the gamma will give it a nice, rich feeling.

Lowering gamma, or even blacks, also usually increases chroma, so that is something to watch out for while setting black and gamma levels.

In or Out

If you just tried out the previous little gamma experiment using your color correction tools and got exactly opposite results, this may be time to explain a confusing aspect of altering gamma. Mainly this has to do with whether your color correction engine is making the gamma corrections on the incoming image or the outgoing image. After Effects' Levels control gives you gamma control of the incoming image, so this is one of the tools that may react the opposite of what you might expect. The reason this behavior seems backward is that if you watch a waveform monitor while adjusting the gamma in a program that does the remapping based on the incoming gamma, then as you move the gamma down, the midrange values go *up*! Most video people will feel that the tools that control the outgoing gamma are more intuitive because moving the gamma down will move the middle values on the waveform down as well.

The explanation of why incoming or outgoing gamma corrections behave in opposite ways means more math. We'll keep it brief, though. Let's assume that to the computer, gamma means 50. This number is the same whether it is incoming gamma or outgoing gamma. Remember, these corrections are usually just based on doing an equation to an incoming number to get an outgoing number. Well, if your color corrector affects the *incoming* signal, that means it sees 50 and, by default, wants to map it to 50 for the outgoing image. When you move the gamma down by 10, you're telling the computer, "Now I want the gamma of 40—which is darker than 50—to be mapped *up* to 50," so decreasing gamma in this situation means *raising* the level. This is fairly counterintuitive, but there are a lot of color correction engines that use this model.

For other engines, it sees a default of 50 for gamma on the incoming side and a 50 on the outgoing side. Now, when you raise gamma, if you are raising the *outgoing* gamma by 10, you are saying that you want the digitized value of 50 to be remapped *up* to 60. This provides the behavior most people would expect.

The other thing to think about is that these gamma corrections are like a rubber band. As you compress the values on one side of gamma, you are stretching the values on the other. This can result in banding in gradients as a finite number of brightness values are spread out. Imagine if you were to draw vertical lines as tightly as possible on a rubber band that was stretched evenly between two points. Now, if you were to grab the center of that rubber band and pull it straight toward one of the end points, the lines on the side that is being pulled tight start to spread apart. The lines on the side you are pulling toward start to compress.

As you compress the values on one side of gamma, you are stretching the values on the other.

This can also be visualized by doing gamma corrections on a horizontally gradated image, as shown in Figures 5-10 through 5-12.

To further refine gamma adjustments, some programs provide controls for gamma knee adjustments. This parameter allows you to control the position of a secondary range within the gamma. You can think of it as upper gamma and/or lower gamma. The controls allow you to control the center position or the target luminance and the width of the secondary range, which defines the spread of the luminance values. It then allows you to alter this second gamma range by increasing or decreasing the values in the specified area.

TIP

 A word of caution: When you create computer files— such as QuickTime—you need to understand that PCs and Macs have different gamma mapping. Macs generally display gamma much higher than PCs. It may be necessary to run some cross-platform tests and possibly specific platform adjustments of your output to ensure a quality image across the board.

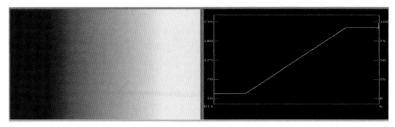

Figure 5-10 Source BWRamp test signal with no correction. Note that the waveform next to the ramp displays a straight line from black to white.

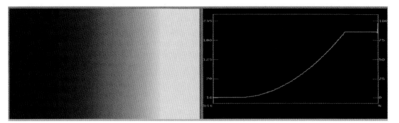

Figure 5-11 The same signal after lowering the gamma. Note that the waveform trace from black to white curves downward, with more levels closer to black.

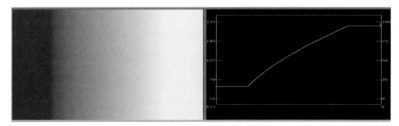

Figure 5-12 The same signal after raising the gamma. Note that the waveform trace curves upward, with brighter levels earlier in the ramp, and that the black levels are slightly washed out.

Most color correction plug-ins or built-in color correction engines have many ways to accomplish the same task. Sometimes it is because a certain tool offers an easier way to approach certain problems, and sometimes it is because different editors prefer to think about their images in different ways and are more comfortable with certain tools. By adding many different ways to approach the same corrections, they make everybody happy.

Tool Time

Setup, gain, and gamma controls have the widest range of tools to do the same basic job. You can use the basic TBC-like sliders or you can use Curves or even Histograms (sometimes known as Levels).

So far, we've discussed using slider controls to alter Setup, Gain, and Gamma controls. But there are more intuitive tools available that provide more precise control. One of those is the Histogram or Levels control.

Level Playing Field

To use the Levels tool, you must understand the histogram display as described in the previous chapter on page 103. To review briefly, the histogram shows the brightness of pixels as plotted on a simple x-y graph. The brightness is plotted horizontally, along the x axis, while the y axis shows the number of pixels at each luminance level. Additionally, most histograms have pulldown menus that give you access to the level controls of the individual red, green, and blue color channels. This can be very useful for fixing color problems, but for now let's stick to the overall combined brightness levels of all of the color channels. This is known by several different names, depending on your software, including RGB, Master, Composite, and RGB Master levels.

Although it looks like the histograms we used to evaluate our images in the last chapter, Figure 5-13 is really a Levels control in disguise. A histogram doesn't give you control over your image, but the Levels control provides control, usually by way of two

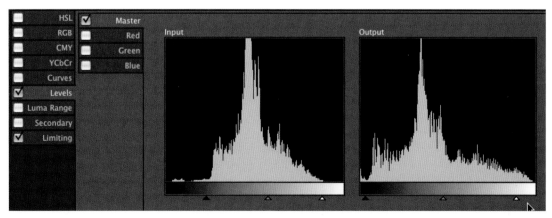

Figure 5-13 Levels control (histogram) from Color Finesse. Note that both input and output histograms can be adjusted. The Master Level is active in this view, but the red, green, and blue channels can also be activated and manipulated separately using the tabs on the left, below the Master Level.

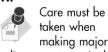

TIP

Care must be taken when making major adjustments to a single range of the picture because you can end up creating a solarized look. In an extreme example, you could lower the highlights to black. Be careful to check the new adjustments you've made against the uncorrected image. This can help spot areas that have become clipped.

small triangles placed at either end of the histogram/level interface and a third triangle in the middle to adjust gamma.

Some programs only provide you with a single Histogram/Level control. Others provide histograms for both the incoming levels (as digitized) and the outgoing levels (as corrected), like the Color Finesse UI in Figure 5-13. Some provide a histogram for the incoming levels and just a slider for the outgoing corrections. Sometimes you can only adjust one side of the histogram, either incoming or outgoing. You have to do a little experimenting with these controls while keeping in mind the discussion on the difference between affecting the incoming or outgoing gamma and how the results of these two different adjustments affect the appearance of the image.

To gain a better understanding of what is going on with Levels controls, check out the difference between the input side and the output side of the histograms in Figure 5-13. Before the Levels were manipulated, the two sides were identical. Note the positions of the black and white triangles at the bottom of the input side. They have been moved in significantly from their original positions at the extreme ends of the histogram. When these parameters were adjusted, it spread out the histogram on the output side. A histogram with "space" on either end usually indicates a low contrast image. Spreading out the range—as was done in Figure 5-13—increases the contrast.

The main attraction of using this Levels tool is that you have graphic feedback as you make your level adjustments.

Color Balance with Levels

Color balance can also be manipulated using Levels, though it's a bit tricky. Much more attention should be paid to the video monitor while doing this because the individual histograms don't really present a full picture of what's going on.

To affect color balance using Levels, you have to look at all three individual color histograms to see if the levels are spread evenly in all three channels. Figure 5-14 shows the three color channels (plus luma) for an image that is very cyan. You can see from the red channel histogram that the red channel is very low compared to blue and green (which make cyan). Also, there is hardly any blue or green in the shadows. This can be confirmed by looking at the RGB Parade waveform (Figure 5-15) and vectorscope (Figure 5-16) for the same shot. To correct this shot, I moved the black and white triangles on the input side to spread the range of each channel so that they matched more closely from color to color (Figures 5-17 through 5-19), then I recentered the gamma of each. The resulting histogram of the corrected shot shows that the levels are a closer match (Figure 5-20).

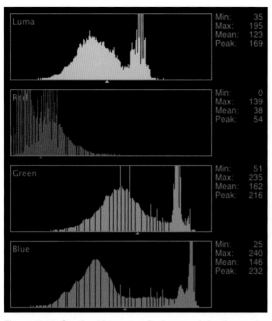

Figure 5-14 Starting histograms for luma and the three color channels.

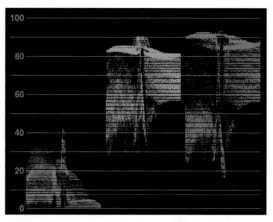

Figure 5-15 Starting RGB Parade waveform for the same image.

Figure 5-16 Starting vectorscope for the same image.

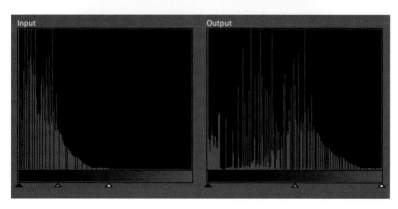

Figure 5-17 Red Level shown as adjusted to fix cyan color cast.

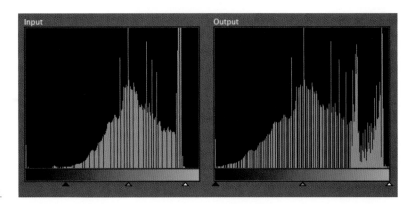

Figure 5-18 Green Level shown as adjusted to fix cyan color cast.

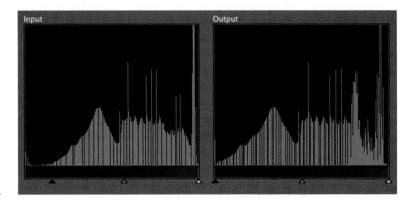

Figure 5-19 Blue Level shown as adjusted to fix cyan color cast.

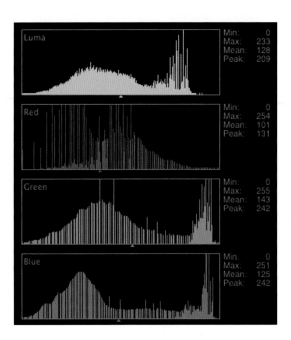

Figure 5-20 Resulting histogram for the corrected image.

Hue and Hue Offset

Hue, as applied to the entire range of the picture, should really be set with color bars. It is rarely suitable for fixing color casts, like poor white balancing. All the hue control—sometimes called the *phase control*—does is rotate the hue of all of the colors the same amount.

Some color correction engines are capable of offsetting hue in specific luma ranges of the picture by specific strengths, and this is a great way to correct color casts. This is what was added to Final Cut Pro's interface with the transition to version 3. FCP users know this feature as the 3-way Color Corrector.

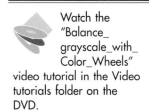

Watch the "Balance_ grayscale_with_ Color_Wheels" video tutorial in the Video tutorials folder on the DVD.

Figure 5-21 Apple Final Cut Pro Color Corrector 3-way color correction filter.

Figure 5-21 is a screenshot from Final Cut Pro 3's 3-way Color Corrector. This tool allows specific hues and saturations in specific tonal ranges to be balanced intuitively. Figure 5-22 is the Hue Offset control for Avid Symphony. Figure 5-23 shows the Color Balance wheels in Apple Color. Figure 5-24 shows the Hue Balance wheels in Adobe Premiere and After Effects, which are accessed through Effects > Color Correction > Three-Way Color Corrector menu. All of these controls work similarly to the trackballs that da Vinci and other "big iron" colorists use to balance their colors.

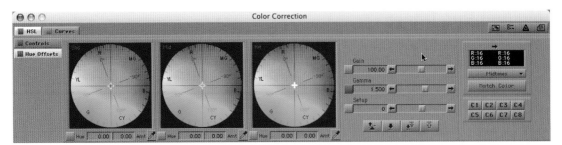

Figure 5-22 Avid Hue Offset wheels.

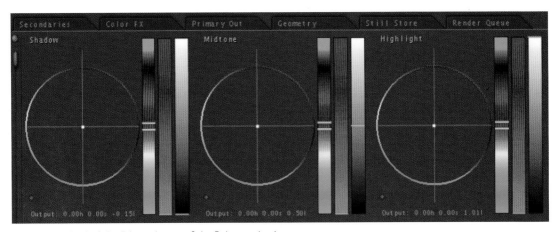

Figure 5-23 Apple Color Primary In room Color Balance wheels.

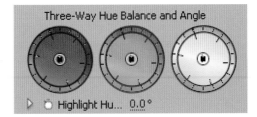

Figure 5-24 Adobe Three Way
Hue Balance and Angle wheels.

To use the 3-way Color Corrector, you analyze the picture—primarily with the vectorscope and RGB Parade waveform monitor—and determine the specific color of the cast. One way to do this is to locate an area of the vectorscope that appears to indicate a white, black, or gray area of the picture. This area should be near the center of the vectorscope. If the vectorscope is displaying a portion of the image that is truly white, black, or gray, it would be perfectly centered on the crosshairs of the vectorscope. For an image with a color cast, that center position will be slightly offset. You can then use the Hue Offset controls to try to center that color cast. You can also use this feature while monitoring an Info Palette-type display that shows the RGB values numerically. By selecting a portion of the image that should have no chroma, the Hue Offset controls can be used to dial in the correct color balance. For example, if you use the Info Palette to analyze a piece of gray asphalt in a road and see that the blue values are higher than the red and green values, you can use the shadow or midtone wheel to pull those tones toward yellow, which is the opposite direction—the complementary color—to blue.

Isolating a Color Cast

One of the hard things to do, especially for a beginning colorist, is to figure out which part of the vectorscope should really be centered. Certainly in most full color images, there are portions of the picture that *should* extend out toward reds or blues or greens.

To figure out what should go in the middle, try masking off everything except the specific neutral tone you are aiming to balance. In a traditional color correction suite this is an easy task because most have video switchers (vision mixers for our British readers) and can quickly make a wipe to isolate the area.

In software it's a little harder to do. One of the easiest pieces of software to accomplish this in is Apple Color. All you have to do is go in to the Geometry room and zoom in all the way to your selected neutral tone, whether that's black, white, or gray. This will fill the vectorscope with just that color, and you can balance it perfectly in the center (see Figures 5-25 through 5-30).

Watch the "Geometry_ Room_trick" video tutorial in the video tutorial folder on the DVD.

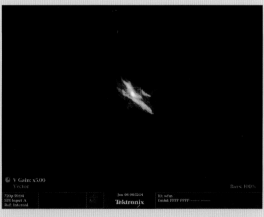

Figure 5-26 Vectorscope reading of full image. The image is close to being balanced and has a fairly low saturation, so it is mostly centered. The vectorscope is set to a 5x gain to better see the center of the vectorscope.

Figure 5-25 Full image.

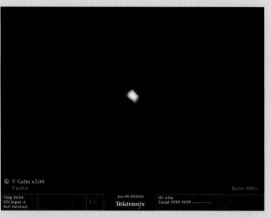

Figure 5-27 Color's Geometry room zoomed in on (isolating) the black area to the right of the steering wheel.

Figure 5-28 Vectorscope reading of just the isolated black area. Note the tight dot in the center of the vectorscope, which has a 5x gain to better see the center of the vectorscope. The black area forms a nice, tight dot, indicating that the blacks are well balanced.

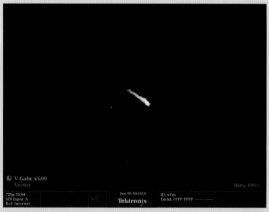

Figure 5-29 Color's Geometry room zoomed in on (isolating) the white clouds in the sky. Clouds are not the best choice for a white point because even in a perfectly balanced image, they usually have a blue cast (or a warm cast at sunset). The picture doesn't present us with any other white point choice. Specular highlights (bright shiny things) definitely shouldn't be used for white balancing.

Figure 5-30 Vectorscope reading of the isolated white area. The image is fairly well centered, but it extends out a short way toward the blue vector, probably indicating some sky instead of an actual blue cast.

Be careful to understand what tonal range the color cast is affecting. If it is the whole image, then use the master Hue Offset wheel, if your software has one. If it is only in the highlights, then only adjust the Highlights wheel. Despite what your eyes may tell you, color casts are rarely the same strength in all tonal ranges. Oftentimes, color casts can go in opposite directions in each tonal range, so adjusting the individual Color wheels is usually the best practice anyway. Hue Offset can also be used to great effect to create moods and special looks. Adding blue to the shadows, red to the midtones, or yellow to highlights, for example, may give emotional context that is not present in the "correct" white balance. Remember that color provides you with many important emotional clues that you can use to steer your audience.

If you intentionally decide to create a color cast, consider leaving one of the tonal ranges in perfect balance. Many colorists will balance blacks almost no matter what they do with the rest of the signal. This can actually help to emphasize the color cast even more in some instances because if the whole image is blue, for example, then your eyes can compensate for that cast and trick your brain into balancing the color automatically. However, if whites or blacks are balanced and the rest of the image has a cast, then your brain "locks on" to the balanced portion of the image and doesn't compensate for the intentional color cast.

Color casts are rarely the same strength in all tonal ranges.

Most current color correctors have a kind of automated version of Hue Offsets built in to their plug-in that works pretty much like using the white and black balance buttons on a video camera. You click on an area of the picture that should be black and "black balance" it; then you do the same with white. If there are no white or black areas of the image, you can select any neutral gray area of the image and click on the Color Balance button. This doesn't offer a whole lot of control, but it is very quick and intuitive.

There is also the old urban legend of a colorist who balanced his blacks on the black suit the talent was wearing and white balanced on his white shirt. Despite this, the colors did not look right. The problem was that the suit was really dark blue and the white shirt was really a light pink. So the shadows went yellow and the highlights went cyan. Of course, the important moral of the story is that you need to be sure that the colors you are trying to balance are actually supposed to be neutral in the first place.

Be sure that the colors you are trying to balance are actually supposed to be neutral.

It is possible for the Hue Offset wheels to introduce some fairly saturated chroma levels. High levels of chroma introduce bleed and noise pretty quickly. Use your eyes to tell you what's right, and keep an eye on your vectorscope to see what's legal and what's not. Dropping chroma below what's "normal" is often done for effect. It can also reduce noise or chroma bleed and can sometimes

TIP

Make the problem obvious. Sometimes it's helpful to crank up the chroma quite a bit when adjusting hue or fixing color casts so that the problems are actually accentuated. Or if you have an external vectorscope, you can take it out of its detente—also called the unity or neutral—position and crank up the gain on the vectorscope to get the same clues to hue and color casts. Some vectorscopes also have a Magnify option that allows you to zoom in on the center of the vectorscope or on specific quadrants. Because the center position of the vectorscope is the absence of color and the outside edges are maximum chroma, increasing the gain makes it more apparent where subtle colors lie in relationship to one another. It also makes subtle adjustments in hue and RGB balance much more noticeable.

eliminate moiré in fine lines. Two schools of thought are available on making chroma adjustments. One is to make these at the beginning, using only color bars to set the levels. The other thought is to make them near the end to ensure that other adjustments that have been made have not seriously affected the chroma. For example, changing gain or gammas or even black levels will also change chroma levels, and some RGB balancing could also raise or lower overall chroma levels significantly. Leaving chroma until the end lets you compensate for these adjustments, but you are essentially left doing this by eye. My rule of thumb for chroma adjustments is to err on the side of being desaturated.

Hue Offset can be very beneficial in maintaining the look of a nice picture that happens to have some illegal levels. Instead of pulling down the saturation of your entire image until the offending color hits the legal target, you can specifically hunt down the offending color and wrangle it into place without affecting any of the other colors.

Luma Ranges

Watch the "Luma_Ranges_in_Color_Finesse" video tutorial in the Video tutorials folder on the DVD.

As we touched upon earlier, when trying to adjust luminance and gamma controls or trying to eliminate color casts, one of the valuable features in a color correction package is to be able to isolate those adjustments so that they only affect certain luma ranges (or tonal ranges). For example, correcting a blue color cast across the entire picture to fix a skin tone may introduce a yellow cast that exists only in the highlights or blacks. With the ability to adjust the colors of highlights, midtones, and shadows individually, you can solve this issue easily.

In addition to making these corrections on the factory preset values for the descriptions of shadows, midtones, and highlights, many programs offer you the opportunity to carefully craft these descriptions using curves, as shown in Figures 5-31 through 5-34.

Figure 5-31 Full color image of Susannah from the short film *Susannah,* courtesy of director Evan Nicholas.

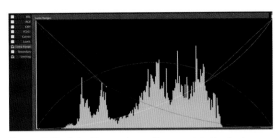

Figure 5-32 Color Finesse Luma Curves set to the factory default. Note the position of the Bezier curves.

Figure 5-33 Image of Susannah in the Color Finesse Luma Range UI with the factory preset.

Figure 5-31 shows the full color image. In Color Finesse and the higher end Avid products, it is possible to call up a view of the image that shows exactly which parts of the image are considered to be shadows, midtones, and highlights. The shadows are displayed as black. The midtones are displayed as gray, and the highlights are displayed as white. It is also possible to change the portion of the picture that is considered to be a shadow, midtone, or highlight. This is important because when you begin to adjust highlights, midtones, and shadows, you can now adjust very specific portions of the picture instead of just general "factory preset" tones.

Figure 5-32 shows Color Finesse's Luma Range view. This is displaying the Luma Range curves as they display the factory preset ranges for shadows, midtones, and highlights. Notice that most of the picture is considered to be a midtone (gray). In the case of this image (Figure 5-31), affecting gamma will affect nearly the entire image, while adjustments to shadows and highlights will affect very little of the image.

Figure 5-33 shows what the factory preset luma ranges look like. The gray domelike curve indicates the portion of the image (represented by a histogram) that the factory considers to be midtones. Note that the dome covers nearly all of the histogram. The black curve that swoops down from the upper left to the lower right indicates what the factory considers to be shadows. And the white curve swooping from the opposite direction is what the factory considers to be highlights. You'll notice that these curves all overlap. They have to or any corrections you applied would "cut off" at some point, leaving you with banding or solarization, depending on how far you took the correction. The curve of these luma ranges indicates the strength of the corrections you apply. So the high part of the shadow curve shows that the deepest blacks will be affected the most by any correction you make to shadows, and it will have a small affect on the midtones and almost no affect on the highlights.

Figure 5-34 shows how I chose to reset the factory definitions for shadows, midtones, and highlights. Note that the curves are

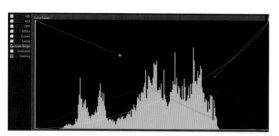

Figure 5-34 Color Finesse Luma Curves set specifically for this shot. Note the revised position of the Bezier curves.

Figure 5-35 Image of Susannah in the Color Finesse Luma Range UI with the luma curves set specifically for this shot. Compare this to Figure 5-32.

much shallower. The resulting Luma Range display (Figure 5-35) shows the new definitions of shadows, gammas, and highlights. Note that it will now be easier to affect just the colors or tonal range of the sky because it is now defined as a highlight. Also, more of the car is defined as a shadow, so if you wanted to affect the car as a whole, it would now be easier.

The image itself hasn't actually been changed at all in this step. All we have done is change what the color corrector considers to be a shadow, midtone, and highlight for this particular shot. This ability provides the colorist with a considerable amount of power.

Will you use this power for good or evil? Only the shadow knows.

The ability to radically change the luma ranges can also help when trying to isolate problem areas of a picture. If you're faced with mixed lighting, with a subject lit with tungsten or halogen and a bright blue window visible in the background, you can use luma ranges to isolate the bright window. Using Luma Ranges to isolate the window is a matter of describing the brightness of the window with a specific range, in this case the highlight range.

Another important reason to dig into Luma Ranges is when a large portion of your picture sits in only one of the preset ranges. For example, you may have a very dark scene, where virtually the entire picture resides in the shadows. To effectively work on this image, you can alter the ranges so that the really deep shadows are represented by one range—shadows—while the middle shadows are represented by the next range—midtones—and the midtones and highlights are all represented by the highlight range. The object is to determine what you need to be able to change independently of the rest of the image. In the previous example, if you believed that the shadows were fine and there were really no midtones to worry about, you could isolate the highlight levels into midhighlights and bright highlights by adjusting the luma ranges.

Despite the great benefits of controlling luma range, generally you will not have to manipulate luma ranges much unless you find

Thinking about the Budget

One consideration before you start to play with the luma range editing capabilities is that, like most things, color correction is usually done on a deadline and with a budget.

To stay on budget or deadline with your corrections, you should stick with the "main" or "primary" color correction capabilities of your application. A sure way to kill that budget is to define the specific luma range of every shot or to add color effects or secondary color correction to every shot. Secondary color corrections and luma range definition are fantastic tools that help you accomplish specific tasks, but you need to consider how long you have to grade the entire project and how much time you can devote to each shot. Hopefully, you can make each shot of a longer form project look pretty good in under a minute. I typically had about 2 days to grade a 600 shot, 48 minute documentary. That works out to about a minute and a half per shot or 20 minutes of color correction work for each finished minute of programming. American dramatic prime time shows are usually in the range of 1000 shots in a 1-hour show and are usually graded in 12–16 hours, averaging a bit better than a shot a minute. Reality shows are closer to 1200 shots in an hour long show and only usually budget for a single day, including laying it off to tape, which works out to about 170 shots an hour or close to three shots a minute. Color correction for digital intermediates can vary greatly, but they can average about 20 minutes (about two reels) per day.

Neal Kassner, a colorist for CBS' *48 Hours*, estimates that he has about 16 hours to color correct that show's 1200–1500 shots per episode. That's 75–90 shots an hour. Other colorists I've spoken to have mentioned averages for a nationally telecast documentary as 6–8 minutes to correct one minute of finished program time. On spots, the average is 3–8 hours for a single 30 second spot or a series of spots based on the same material. Some facilities expect certain "output" from their colorists, such as 100 shots an hour.

Craig Leffel, of Chicago's Optimus, says that it depends if the corrections are from tape or server or if the OCN has to actually be racked on the telecine. For film negative, the average is four to six shots an hour if there are only a few shots per reel.

Some of these numbers have changed somewhat over the years as colorists are transitioning from a work flow that was originally almost entirely "straight off the telecine" to a current work flow where telecine transfers get transferred "flat" to either a digital disk recorder, some kind of a server as a file, or to a tape format like D5, then the colorist basically does a tape-to-tape color correction or color corrects from a file. Back in the day, a rule of thumb for telecine transfers was 1 hour to grade 11 minutes (one 1000-foot 35 mm reel).

The trick to grading an entire project on budget is to leave enough extra time to work on the shots that really need the additional attention.

Until you get more experienced at estimating how long you need to really tweak an entire project, try to get a first pass at all the shots done in half of your budgeted time. Then use the second half of the time to polish the overall corrections and devote extra time to trouble shots or those that have high emotional significance or importance to the story.

Also, don't forget to leave time for revisions, especially if you don't have absolutely every single decision maker in the session.

OCN

Original camera negative.

Racked

Physically placing the spool or reel of film on the telecine and threading it.

Telecine

This is the machine—or sometimes used as a description of the process—that transfers film to video in realtime. The telecine feeds the image to the color correction hardware. I've heard at least three different pronunciations, and everyone will tell you that the way they pronounce it is correct. TELL-uh-sin-ee. Tell-uh-SEEN. TELL-uh-sin-uh. The other way to transfer film to video (or data, actually) is with a film scanner which, as of the writing of this book, is not realtime, but it is getting close.

you are not able to control the specific tonal ranges of the image as precisely as you want. Changing luma ranges also takes a considerable amount of time, when you consider that you still have to actually make the corrections after you set the ranges. You definitely need to consider the amount of time you are taking for each shot when you are working under a deadline.

How fast you color correct depends a lot on various criteria, but in a survey I took of professional colorists, longform colorists generally have under 30 seconds per shot to complete a correction, and shortform colorists only have a couple of minutes per shot. Check out the sidebar on budgets that originally appeared in the book *The Art and Technique of Digital Color Correction*.

Curves

Figure 5-36 makes the name *Curves* seem like a bit of a misnomer. These are the default positions for the Curves controls, showing no change between input and output levels.

Figure 5-37 demonstrates the amount of control that is possible with Curves. Each color correction engine has limits to the number of points that you can put on a given line, but even with only four or five, the amount of control is much more specific than what is available with basic levels adjustments and luma ranges. The curves in this figure simply indicate the possibilities for control, not an actual correction.

Curves are a powerful way to deal with color levels, although in some situations they are less intuitive than other methods. When adjusting levels in this type of graphical user interface, you are normally presented with four boxes with diagonal lines, one for each color channel (red, green, and blue) and another box representing overall composite level. Each box is merely a graph with the input (source) level charted on the x axis of the graph and the output along the y axis. The default of a 45° angle shows that the input and output are equal. So if you grab the diagonal line in the middle (the gamma) and drag it upward, you are remapping the luminance of the middle pixels to be brighter. Similarly, dragging the same middle point backward will brighten the image as well because you are asking to map a darker input value to the middle output value.

While these two adjustments seem to be having the same affect on the picture, they are actually doing two very different things. You can see the difference numerically in some programs by watching the starting point of the adjustment. If you select the true center point mathematically, it will be 128x and 128y. Dragging this point straight up to, say, 168 means that all of the input values from 128 and below are being stretched up to a maximum level of 168 on output, and the levels above 128 input are being

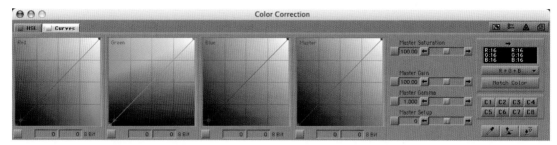

Figure 5-36 The Curves Controls in Avid Media Composer. Several applications have Curves controls, but Avid's are the "sexiest." Apple Color added Curves controls to its arsenal as part of its update from Silicon Color's FinalTouch.

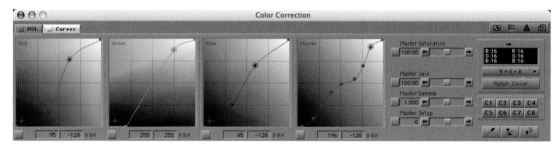

Figure 5-37 Numerous points adjusted on all four Curves in Avid Media Composer.

compressed between 168 and 255. By dragging the same point backward to, say, 100, you are mapping all of the input levels below 100 to spread out to a maximum value of 128, and all of the values from 100 and above are compressed into the range of 128–255. Dragging the lower left corner to the right remaps the shadows so that the blacks are clipped. Dragging the same point upward remaps the blacks so that the darkest input pixels now are much brighter.

The Basics of Curves

Let's take some basic examples and see what curves would provide the intended result.

In Figure 5-38 notice the look and levels of the waveform with the Curves in their unity, or default, position. Every input value matches every output value. This is taken from a screen shot of Avid Media Composer. The other feature provided by Media Composer from within the Curves tab is the ability to "eyedropper" blacks, whites, and grays. This provides an automatic white balance. It is an excellent tutorial in Curves to use these eyedroppers and see how it affects the curves. When you eyedropper colors, you can see where the point of color displays in relation

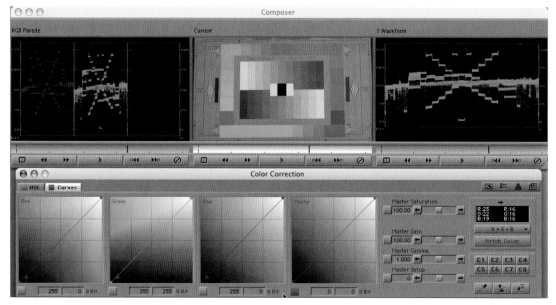

Figure 5-38 Avid Media Composer Curves interface with DSC Labs ChromaDuMonde camera chart.

Unity

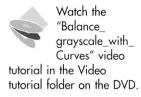 This describes the default position of any control setting. In a video facility, unity levels are engineered to maintain consistent output throughout the facility.

Watch the "Balance_ grayscale_with_ Curves" video tutorial in the Video tutorial folder on the DVD.

to the Curve. The small crosshairs in Figure 5-38 represent the sample taken from the middle black chip.

The Curves in Avid's Media Composer are really nicely designed to provide color-based clues as to what will happen by moving the curve in one direction or the other. For example, pulling the blue curve up will add blue, while pulling it down will add yellow.

In Figure 5-39 we've dragged the lower left corner of the Master Curve (representing black) and pulled it up, raising the black level so that what had been 0 on a scale of 0–255 is now 20. This moves the waveform monitor up from 0IRE to about 10IRE. Notice the numerical input and output values under the Master Curve.

The opposite move is made in Figure 5-40. We've taken the 0 point of the Master Curve and moved it 20 levels to the right. This crushes all the pixels that had a luminance level of 20 and below down to 0.

In Figure 5-41 the highest point in the Master curve, 255, was moved backward by 20. This moves all pixels with a value of 235 and above up to 255. The other tonal move that's happening with all these moves that is not as apparent is that when all of the values above 235 move up to 255, all of the values below 235 also move somewhat, spreading the 20 point move across all the values from 0 to 234.

In Figure 5-42 the highest point on the Master curve was moved down to 235. This remaps all of the pixels between 235 and 255 down to 235, effectively clipping whites at 235.

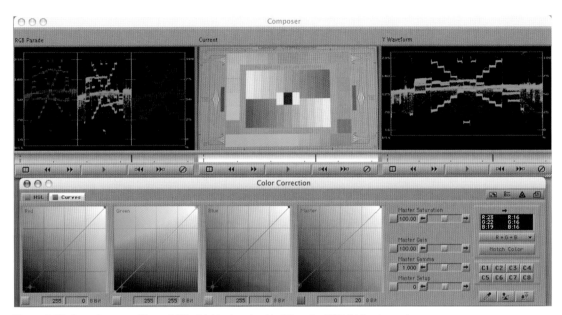

Figure 5-39 Same image as Figure 5-38 with blacks raised to 20 on the RGB 8-bit color scale.

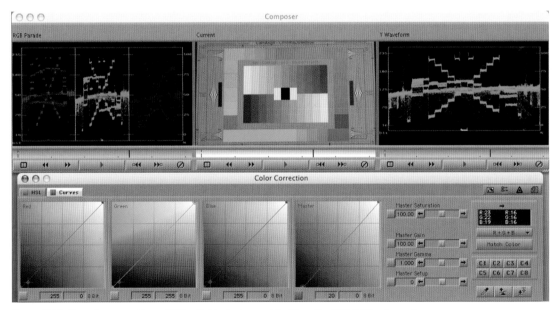

Figure 5-40 Same image as Figure 5-38 with blacks lowered to 20 on the RGB 8-bit color scale.

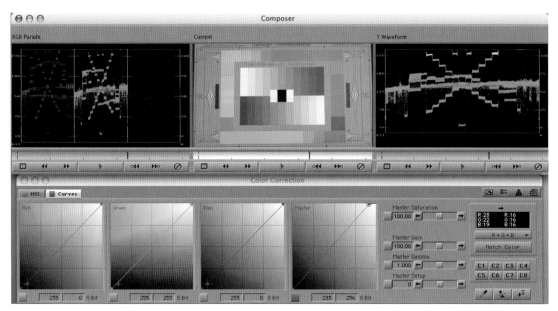

Figure 5-41 Same image as Figure 5-38 with highlights raised.

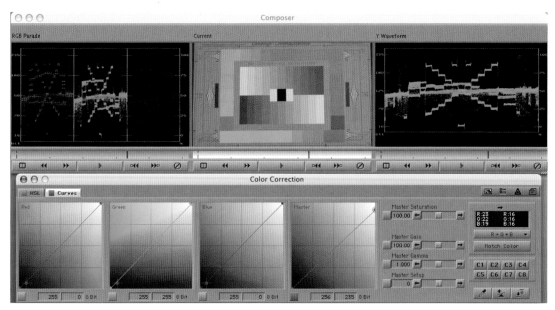

Figure 5-42 Same image as Figure 5-38 with highlights lowered.

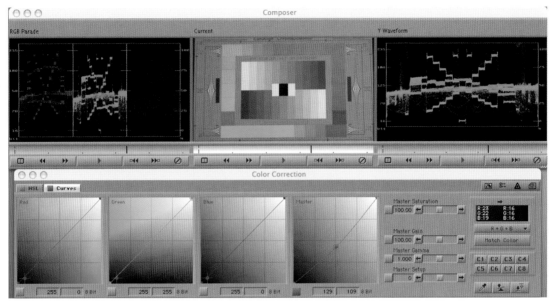

Figure 5-43 Same image as Figure 5-38 with midtones lowered by lowering the middle point on the graph.

Figures 5-42 and 5-43 show two midrange moves with very similar end results. Figure 5-42 takes the input value of 129 and moves it down by 20, mapping pixels around the 129 level down to 109, darkening the midtones of the picture. Figure 5-43 shows the 129 midtone level pulled forward by about 20, mapping the levels at 129 up to 150. Another variation of this move that would be even more similar would be pulling the point at 108 forward to 128. All of these moves would darken the midtones.

Again, two similar sets of moves have similar end results: Figure 5-44 shows the midrange point of 128 brought back 20 points to 108, brightening the midtones, by mapping 108 input values to 128 output values. Figure 5-45 shows the midpoint of 128 being brought up by 20. This also brightens the image by remapping 128 input values to 148 output values. If the input and output numbers are not what you'd expect, remember that the original point on the graph is *not* the input value. The *direction* of the move indicates input or output changes. Any move that is vertical changes the *output* number, while horizontal moves change the *input* value. Try some moves in Curves while viewing the input and output numbers.

If you have curves for each of the RGB channels, you can easily fix different color casts in the highlights, midtones, and

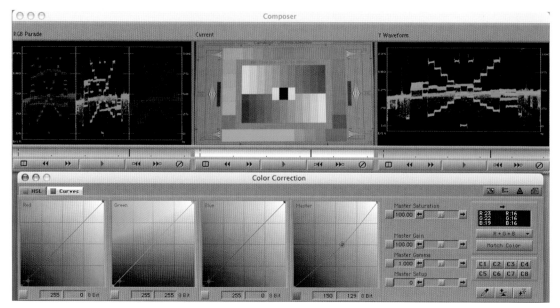

Figure 5-44 Same image as Figure 5-38 with midtones lowered by moving the middle point on the graph to the right.

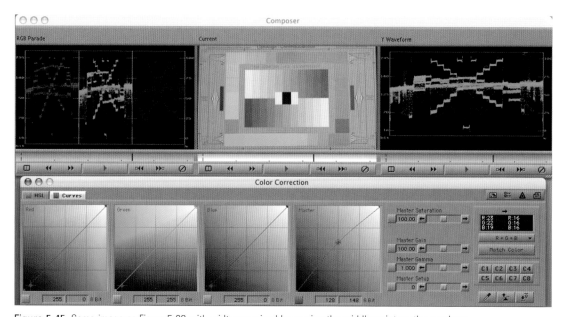

Figure 5-45 Same image as Figure 5-38 with midtones raised by moving the middle point on the graph up.

shadows. If the midtones are too blue, but the highlights go green, pull the middle of the blue curve down and then adjust the top of the green curve down. You may need to make additional luminance and gamma changes after color fixes because the individual color adjustments will affect overall levels. You should experiment with different ways to correct bad color casts before locking in to one. Hue Offsets is much easier for most casts than Curves, but many people prefer the control they have with Curves.

In my book *The Art and Technique of Digital Color Correction*, colorist Terry Curren explains that he uses Curves almost exclusively for most of his basic corrections. To deliver these corrections with speed, he monitors the RGB Parade waveform monitor. By adjusting specific points along the Curves for red, green, and blue while monitoring the respective color "cell" in the RGB Parade waveform, you'll find that you have very direct control of the waveform monitor with the Curves. This is similar to the kind of direct control you have by using the Color Wheels and viewing a vectorscope.

The benefit of Curves is to gain very precise control over specific luma ranges. If you only need general control inside a luma range—highlight, midtone, or shadow—then another tool may be faster and more intuitive. But of all the tools, the Curves tool gives you the most specific control when you really need it.

Precision Control When You Need It Most

The Master Curve levels can solve very specific problems with difficult images. Figures 5-46 though 5-48 are from a tutorial

Figure 5-46 This is the original image. A very dark image that appears to be unusable.

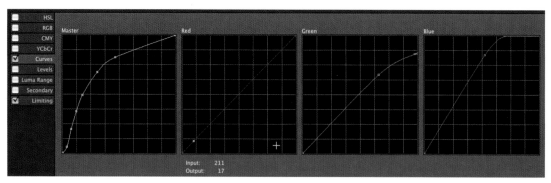

Figure 5-47 Radical correction in Curves to spread tonal values in the shadows and correct color balance.

Figure 5-48 Before and after image of Curves correction.

that will be fully explored in a later chapter, but even a quick examination of the difficulties of correcting this image show where Curves really shine. It's all about control.

Figure 5-47 shows the amount of manipulation needed to control all of the fine levels of shadow to create a pleasing silhouette from a muddy, dark mess. To do this, it was necessary to hold some of the darkest shadows where they were, so there would be some definition in the blacks, but then add several points to the curve to begin spreading or stretching the shadow detail out. Also, curves were added in the blues, greens, and reds to manipulate the color of the sky, giving it a more natural color than the greenish hue of the original sky.

Tal, a veteran editor at Chainsaw in Santa Monica, California, color corrects on an Avid Symphony. For him, the Curves tab is one of the main staples of his color correction diet. He says:

If you go to the Curves and you add a point about a quarter of the way down the luminance curve line and curve it up a little, and add another point a quarter of the way up from the bottom and push it down a little, you'll have a shallow S. That is the most effective, most immediate, helpful way to make a picture look better in 90% of the cases. Just that little S curve makes things look a lot more like what you want them to look like (see Figure 5-49).

The way that Tal's trick works is by slightly crushing the blacks, making them appear richer and brightening the highest highlights. Also, the midtones in between the two points have a steeper curve. The steeper the curve, the higher its contrast.

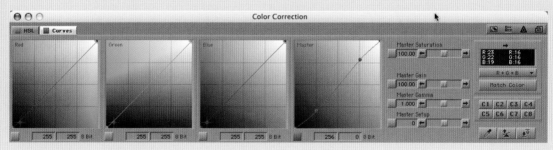

Figure 5-49 S Curve trick in Curves.

6

SECONDARY COLOR CORRECTION

The previous chapter discussed the tools available to do Primary corrections, in other words, those that affect the overall balance and tone of the entire image or raster. Oftentimes it is necessary for even further control of specific regions of the picture. Color corrections that affect only a specific region or vector of an image are called Secondary corrections. There are two parts to making a Secondary color correction. The first is to qualify the area you want to affect and the second is to affect it in some way. There are a number of ways to qualify an area of the image to work on:

- Selected based on a specific luminance by creating a luma matte, (Figure 6-2)
- Selected based on a color vector by creating a vector-based matte, (Figure 6-3)
- Selected with a geometric shape or hand-drawn mask, (Figure 6-4)
- Selected by any combination of these three methods, (Figure 6-5)

Raster

This is computer terminology that has crossed over to video to represent an image created from horizontal lines of individual pixels. The raster refers to the entire video image.

Qualify

This term means that an area of the picture is specifically isolated for a correction by any number of methods. You could qualify something for correction using its hue, chroma strength, or tonal value. You could also qualify an area of the image using a "window" or garbage matte. For example: "I qualified the brightest highlights by making a matte of everything over 90IRE."

Figure 6-1 Original full color image, courtesy Artbeats' Sports 1 HD Collection (clip SP105H2).

Figure 6-2 Matte created based on luminance, selecting only the whites.

Figure 6-3 Matte created based on vector (HSL) information (blue jerseys).

Figure 6-4 Hand-drawn Bezier shape in the Geometry room of Apple Color. The mask itself would be a white area within the outlined shape, qualifying the infield grass.

Figure 6-5 Matte created using a vector and an oval garbage mask. The vector qualification selects the blue jersey color, and the yellow outline of the oval garbage mask selects only the blue of the baserunner, while masking away the blue of the batter's jersey.

The most obvious example of secondary qualifications include:

- The vignette, or spot color correction, which uses a user-defined shape to define a location on the screen and then allows you to alter the correction inside or outside of that defined area. These are often created to darken the outside edges of the picture, though there are much more sophisticated reasons to use a vignette or spot correction.
- The vector qualification, which selects a specific color on the screen and allows you to change just that color or to leave that color and change everything else. A well-known "demo" example of this is taking a shot of a car and select only the specific color of the car body and change it to a totally different color while leaving all of the other colors in

the picture—like skin tones, grass, and sky—untouched. For our example (Figure 6-7), we've used the qualification in Figure 6-3 and corrected only the colors inside the matte from their original blue to red.

Figure 6-6 Original image from Artbeats.

Figure 6-7 A vignette has been added to the image, darkening the edges to focus attention on the central action, adding depth and making the image more cinematic. The runner and catcher are the same brightness as in Figure 6-6, but the outside edges of the image are darker.

Figure 6-8 Blue uniforms have been changed to red using the qualification from Figure 6-3 and turning the pixels within the qualification red.

Vector

Basically "vector" is just a fancy way to say "a specific color." More technically, it is a position or coordinate in space or a direction between two coordinates. On a vectorscope, the vector is the specific position of a color in the two-dimensional circle defined by the vectorscope. The "targeted" vectors on the vectorscope are the three primary colors—red, green, and blue—and the secondary colors between them—magenta, cyan, and yellow. A colorist might say, "I'm trying to keep the yellow from drifting into that green vector."

Vignette

The standard dictionary meaning for this word is a photograph or other image with edges that shade off gradually. To a colorist, vignette is both a noun and a verb. The noun describes a shape placed in the picture to allow a different correction inside and out. Usually this correction is used to create the effect of fading out (usually darkening) the edges of the image. As a verb it is simply the action of making the vignette.

Garbage Matte

A shape that is drawn to exclude or reinclude portions of an image that have been selected by some other procedure, such as a color vector isolation. Garbage mattes effectively clean up the "garbage" left by other procedures or processes. They tend to be fairly rough and are drawn clear of whatever boundary the other process is trying to select. So in the case of a color vector selection, the garbage matte selects a rough area around the color vector to deselect any unwanted portions of the image that had been selected by the color vector isolation.

Secondaries

Shorthand for Secondary color corrections. The plural is often used because most applications allow you to have multiple Secondary color corrections—secondaries—on a single image.

Vector-Based Secondaries

For vector-based qualifications, each system works a little differently, but the basic operational method is to define the specific color that you wish to change. Usually this is done with some kind of eyedropper method. When this initial gross selection is made, then you refine the selection by increasing or decreasing the luma range, saturation range, hue range, and softness of the matte. Then you select the new target color. Any pixels that are within your selected and refined range are then remapped to the new color. In Apple Color, vector-based secondaries are accomplished in the Secondary room using the controls at the top right (Figure 6-9). In Avid Symphony, they are done with the vectorscope-like display in the Secondary tab (Figure 6-10). In Final Cut Pro, they can be attempted with the Color Corrector 3-Way filter by spinning down the triangle at the bottom (under the Blacks wheel) to reveal a set of controls called "Limit Effect." (Figure 6-11) In Color Finesse, use the Secondary Tab near the bottom left corner (Figure 6-12).

One of the things that differentiates the high-end color correctors from the lower end tools is the ability to define the affected secondary range and to soften the effect of the color change between affected and unaffected colors. Otherwise, the Secondary corrections look very electronic and noisy because there are harsh cut-off points between the colors. Be aware of this difference when choosing a color correction application if Secondary color correction is important to your work.

Secondary color correction does not have to be limited to special effects like changing the color of a car. Sometimes it is an important tool in dealing with color gamut issues. For example, if

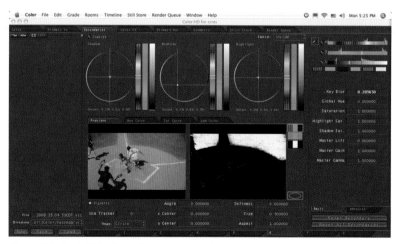

Figure 6-9 Apple Color Secondary room controls.

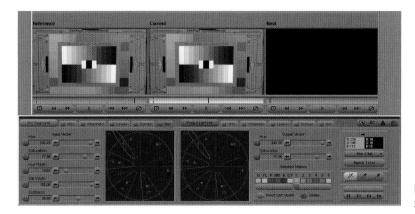

Figure 6-10 Avid Symphony Secondary Tab controls.

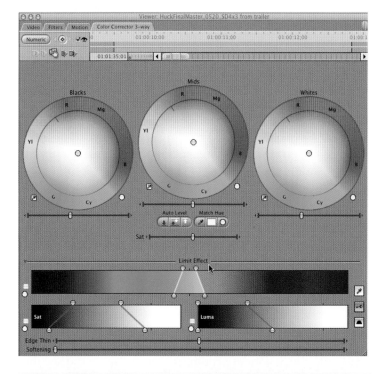

Figure 6-11 Final Cut Pro "Limit Effect" in Color Corrector 3-Way.

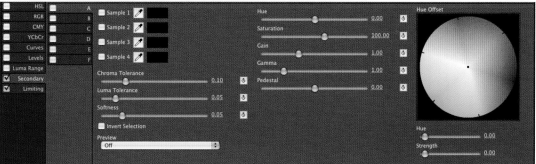

Figure 6-12 Color Finesse Secondary Tab controls.

your image has one specific color that is violating legal gamut, instead of desaturating the entire image until the one offending color has been brought inside of gamut, you can select the color with a secondary qualification and reduce the saturation of just the one color.

Also, certain colors cannot be very accurately captured on video. Kelly green is one that comes to mind. Many shades of yellow and red are also not reproducible on video. This can be a problem if one of those colors happens to be crucial to your client's brand identity. In this case, you can isolate the problem color and attempt to make it more closely resemble your client's vision, while not polluting the other colors with the correction to the specific vector you needed to change.

Similarly, skin tones can be crucial to the look and feel of a project. Secondary corrections are often used to isolate skin tones, pulling the green out of black skin, or changing yellowish skin tones toward pink or pinkish skin tones toward golden while leaving the rest of the image's color palette intact.

> *In addition to skin tones, humans have an innate connection to a few other specific colors, including grass and sky.*

In addition to skin tones, humans have an innate connection to a few other specific colors, including grass and sky. These colors are often targets for experienced colorists who are trying to improve a shot because all viewers know what these colors should look like. We all have preferences for how those colors should look that are not necessarily based on the reality of the actual color or the truth of the way that those colors—skin tones, sky, and grass—are captured on film or tape. So colorists often do Secondary color corrections on these colors.

Let's create a Secondary color correction to punch up the grass in the baseball footage we've been examining in this chapter. I did this correction using Apple Color.

Load the SP105H2 footage from the Artbeats folder in the Tutorial Footage folder on the DVD into Color or some other application that allows for Secondary color correction.

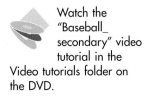

Watch the "Baseball_secondary" video tutorial in the Video tutorials folder on the DVD.

1. Go to the Secondary room (tab) and enable the secondary using the check box in the upper left corner (Figure 6-13).
2. In the upper left corner, click on the eyedropper (Figure 6-14). That will enable a red crosshairs overlay on your main image (Figure 6-15). Center the crosshairs on some portion of the grass and click. Then click on the eyedropper icon again to turn off the crosshair overlay.
3. The selected color from the eyedropper/crosshairs creates an HSL selection in the secondary HSL Qualifiers area to the right of the eyedropper (Figure 6-16). It also displays the matte that is created that identifies the selected area of your image (Figure 6-17). The grass is pretty well isolated, but

Figure 6-13 Enable check box in Secondary room.

Figure 6-14 Secondary qualifier eyedropper.

Figure 6-15 Crosshairs overlay on image to select secondary color vector.

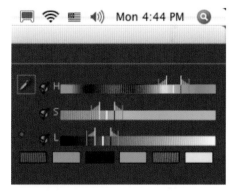

Figure 6-16 HSL Qualifier sliders indicating the range of the initial selection.

there is quite a bit of green grass color that is not properly selected.

4. Use the HSL Qualifier sliders to widen the selections for hue, saturation, and luminance. Holding down the shift key while moving either end of the range will allow you to just move that one end of the range, otherwise moving the white line at one end of the range moves the other end of the range in the opposite direction by an equal amount. "Focus" the ends of the range so that you get the best selection of grass with the least selection of any other color. This takes some experimentation. Figure 6-18 shows what the HSL Qualification sliders looked like when I was done with my qualification. This resulted in the matte seen in Figure 6-19, which has a much stronger selection of the grass than in the original selection (Figure 6-17).

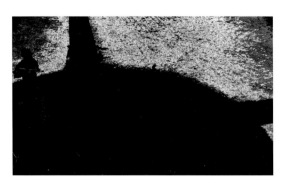

Figure 6-17 Matte shows white areas where image has been selected or qualified.

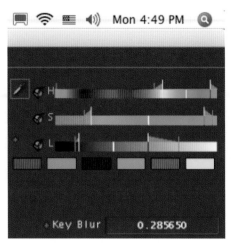

Figure 6-18 HSL Qualifiers with new ranges tweaked from initial eyedropper selection.

Figure 6-19 Matte shows stronger selection of grassy areas due to tweaked HSL Qualifier sliders.

5. Add some key blur to the mask to make your correction blend in better. That completes the "qualification" part of the Secondary correction.

6. Now that we have an area of the image that is well-defined as "grass," we now use the familiar tools in Color to adjust just the area inside of the white mask. (You can also choose Control menu near the top left of the Secondary room to alter the colors outside of the mask instead of the inside of the mask if you want.)

7. You can use the color wheels to make the grass more pure green and/or add saturation (Figure 6-20). My correction goes a little beyond what would be normal for a TV image, but I wanted it to stand out (Figure 6-21). Compare the grass to the original image in Figure 6-22. Notice that none of the other colors changed except the grass. The skin

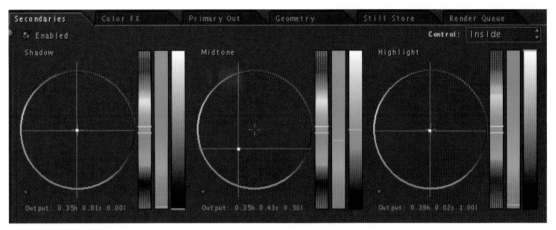

Figure 6-20 Color Wheel adjustments to make grass greener, mostly in midtones.

Figure 6-21 Final image with Secondary correction of grass.

Figure 6-22 Original image without Secondary correction of grass.

tones, earth tones, whites, and uniform colors all stayed the same.

Randy Starnes explained his use of secondary as he was correcting shots for an episode of MTV's *Making the Video*:

I like my skin tone on this show not to be too red, and I like to have green grass and green screen shots to be cool green and a lot of green. So for green grass I take the green secondary. Of the six-vector color corrector, I take the green element only and turn it to cyan, away from yellow. I'll boost the saturation just of that green, and that always makes grass look better. If you take the green grass and move it away from yellow, it makes the difference between a springtime green and a fall green that's close to dead.

Skies: take a sky and keep it consistent by rolling the blue either down toward the cyan side or up toward a process blue or up farther toward magenta if I want it to be there for the time of day.

Mike Most was the visual effects supervisor for *Ally McBeal*. Before that, he was a sought-after colorist for prime-time episodics and worked on such signature shows as *LA Law* and *NYPD Blue*. Most explains that this is a world where the main skill is maintaining continuity:

> *Secondary correction for me was a way of fixing what I couldn't get quite right with the basic primary controls because Secondary correction basically acts as a keyer. It keys whatever color you tell it you want to select or whatever range of colors you tell it you want to select and lets you change just those colors. That can be a great help when you're trying to make, say, a very green tree into a very fall, golden-leaf tree. And I used to have to do that quite often, especially on NY[PD Blue]. Short of that, it doesn't have a whole lot of use.*

Secondary correction basically acts as a keyer.—Mike Most

> *If a cameraman has shot his film right—and let's face it, most professional cameramen shoot beautiful film—so given a decently shot piece of film, you should be able to get what the cameraman was seeing without having to do anything fancy with it: ripping the colors out of it and recoloring them to something else.*
>
> *I used to use Secondary correction sometimes to change my flesh tones a little bit because that tends to get a little out of hand with certain stocks, but generally I think that Secondary color correction is way, way, way overused. Unless you're trying to achieve something totally unique, as in a commercial, there's very little need for it in most cases. And I think a lot of colorists go to it far too quickly. That's one of the things that I train people not to do.*

Secondary Limitations

There are several things that Secondary color correction *cannot* do. These are important to note, especially if you have any kind of prepro contact with clients that are considering using Secondary color correction.

Some Secondary color correction tools can only alter hue and saturation, yet clients often request to alter the color in a way that requires a change in luminance. Also, the lower the saturation level of a color that needs to be altered, the more difficult it is to isolate that color shift from others around it. Think of it like a game of darts played on a vectorscope. The lower saturation images are in the middle, and the higher ones are near the outside. If you toss a dart at a color near the outside, you'll either hit the one you were aiming for, or at least one that's adjacent to it. In the center of the dartboard, a near miss can still mean you've selected an image 180° from the one you aimed at.

In addition to the difficulty of isolating the color, lower saturation colors also offer less information to be able to increase the saturation because increasing saturation means increasing noise.

Alex Scudiero, a colorist and principal at I³ in Chicago, was one of several colorists who cautioned against the use of secondary until later in the correction process:

> Some inexperienced colorists will go right for the secondary to change something specific, but then they'll get further into the correction and realize they need that secondary for something else, so they've painted themselves into a box. Try to correct using the basics first.

As color correction technology advances, this advice becomes a little less relevant because many color correction systems offer dozens of "secondaries" so even an inexperienced colorist won't "paint themselves into a box" very easily. With the original da Vinci systems that were delivered, extra secondaries cost extra money to purchase. But Color has eight secondaries, each of which can be corrected inside *and* outside of the qualification, making it more like 16 secondaries.

However, this is still valuable advice to heed because each secondary correction will take a significant amount of time to perform, and all jobs are done on some kind of deadline, so Secondary color correction should be used judiciously if for no other reason than time.

Vignettes or Spot Color Corrections

Another widely used type of qualification for Secondary color correction is the vignette or spot color correction. This is the ability to select a specific geographic area in the picture and adjust levels within that area without affecting the other areas of the picture. da Vinci colorists know this feature as Power Windows. In Apple Color it is known as Vignette in the Secondary room. In Avid Symphony it is called Spot Color Correction.

The terminology is a bit confusing because Apple's Color calls any spot correction or shaped mask a vignette, but the term "vignette" also means an image that fades out or darkens at the edges.

When creating these vignettes or spot corrections, some color correctors are limited to a handful of geometric shapes, like circles, ellipses, and squares. In skilled hands, though, this is more than enough control. Some of the more recent high-end color correc-

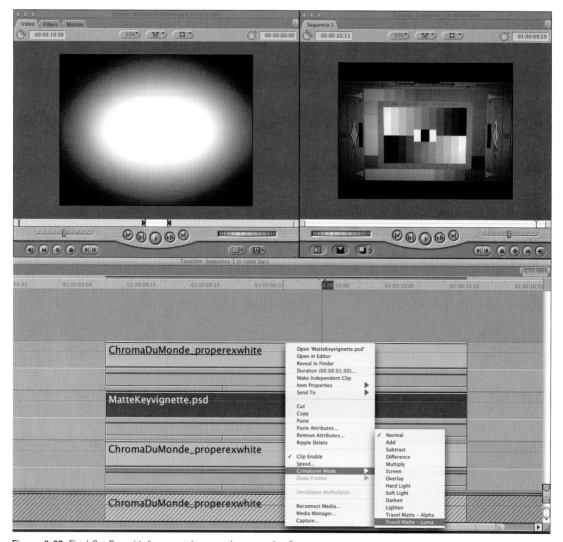

Figure 6-23 Final Cut Pro with "poor man's spot color correction."

tion engines have the ability to create a larger number of organic, hand-drawn shapes. Plus, many color correctors, like Color, can track these vignettes as portions of the image move within the frame. This is incredibly valuable.

Although vignettes and spot color correction are a fairly rare feature *in name*, it can be accomplished by almost all NLEs using simple wipes and mattes. To do a vignette in Final Cut Pro, simply sync a corrected shot on one track with an uncorrected shot on a lower track and use a wipe or matte to reveal the correction in only a specific geographic area (Figure 6-23). This obviously takes a bit more effort than a one-step solution, but the capability is certainly available to almost anyone.

Figure 6-24 Original image (RED footage) from the short film *Susannah*, courtesy of director Evan Nicholas.

Figure 6-25 Same image as Figure 6-24 with vignette added.

Spot correction is useful for many reasons. One of the most common is to create a true vignette, darkening the edges of the image to focus attention on the subject. This technique is used a lot in TV spots. When applied by a skilled colorist, you should never really notice that a vignette has been applied, but you should be able to look for vignettes by focusing your eyes on the corners of the TV image instead of on the center. When you do this, it becomes more apparent that the edges or corners have been darkened. Figure 6-24 and Figure 6-25 show a before and after image with a vignette applied. I used a fairly strong vignette to make sure the image could be seen properly on the printed page, but vignettes are typically much more subtle.

Another common use for spot color correction is to *dodge* or *burn* the image, in much the same way that photographers do with prints in the darkroom. A specific area is selected—say, a blown-out sky—in an otherwise nicely exposed image, and the levels are brought down in just that portion of the image. This is one of the things that can assist colorists doing film transfers to translate the higher latitude of film to the lower contrast range of video. In an image where the sky might have held detail in the bright areas on the negative as well as in the shadows of the landscape, on video the only way to properly hold detail in both areas is to spot correct the sky and the landscape separately.

Another use of spot color correction is to add the look of gradient filters to an image, for example, coloring a plain-looking sky to a rich sunset. In a film-to-tape transfer session, this is often done by actually using photographic filters in the filter gate. But spot color correction can also help you fix it in post without a full telecine session. This is usually easiest to accomplish by pulling a luminance mask on the sky and adding a large, horizontal, very, very soft-edged mask. The softness of the mask creates a gradation similar to what many directors of photography add "in camera" with a gradated filter on the sky. This effect can also be done with just the soft-edged mask, without the use of the luma key.

Vignettes or spot corrections can really add the finishing touches to a correction. Randy Starnes, a colorist for many prime-time TV shows, says da Vinci's spot correction—Power Windows—allowed him to add just a little more glamor to your favorite stars and to subliminally focus the audience's attention to specific parts of the screen.

Watch the video tutorial "Susannah_vignette_glow_face" in the Video tutorials folder on the DVD.

I use Power Windows quite often to give a person a glow to his or her face. Separate the person by putting an oval soft-edged window on the face. Bring the luminance of the face up. If you include the face and a little bit over the top of the head, behind the person a little bit, it almost has the effect of a backlight or a halo. Make somebody look subtly a little special, kind, angelic.

I used Power Windows quite a bit on Dr. Quinn, Medicine Woman *to separate the star and make her look even more beautiful, more radiant. A lot of people use them for vignettes. They can bring your attention to the center of the screen or wherever you want that attention. Place an oval window with a center where you want the eye to go and then soft edge so you don't see it.*

Another use is to add punch to lighting. To amplify the effect of a light—let's say a window and light that's streaming in—I'll often put in a Power Window, make it a long oval aspect, and rotate it from the direction that the sun would be falling in the window and soft edge that. Inside that Power Window I'd increase the luminance, and probably outside I'd bring the blacks down, and that just makes the light more powerful.

I'm doing skies right now. I've got a sky where I want to keep the bottom of the image bright. I want to keep the blue in the sky, so I'm going to make a circular Power Window, and I'm going to change the aspect ratio so it's horizontal lines, take the sky, separate the sky, and then bring the luminance down inside the window. I'll add some blue to the sky and then soft edge the window, and that will keep the lower end of the frame where all my talent is bright, and it won't blow out the sky.

Figures 6-26, 6-27, and 6-28 show a spot color correction or vignette similar to that described by Randy Starnes to give the stars of the show a special glow. A soft-edged oval was drawn around the face, and the levels inside were increased and warmed up slightly. The levels outside the oval were brought down a little as well. This served to separate the talent from the background a little and make her visually more special.

Figure 6-26 Original image from the short film *Susannah*, courtesy of director Evan Nicholas.

Figure 6-27 Shot with a vignette around the actress's face, darkening the background and warming her skin tones.

Figure 6-28 This is part of the Apple Color UI showing the mask that qualified the face. The two ovals indicate the inside and outside softness of the mask.

Unqualified Use of Secondaries

With so many secondaries available—at least in Apple's Color—one of the "off prescription" uses for secondaries is simply to use them like Photoshop Adjustment Layers.

Basically, just do the most general color balancing and level adjustment in Primaries, then use successive secondaries—without qualifying any specific portion of the image—to continue to refine the original correction. That way, if you want to back off or eliminate part of your correction, you can simply disable the secondary tab for that portion, leaving all of your other work intact.

This method of using secondaries in Apple Color was developed by Bob Sliga while he worked for the Color development team at Apple:

> You can go back to the days when we didn't really have Secondary color correction, when we could only grab the six vectors and change saturation and hue and maybe luminance a little bit. That was the typical Secondary color correction where you could isolate a color. Up until da Vinci changed the game by Secondary color correction isolating

a color by using a luminance key or an HSL key or by putting a window around something which wasn't traditionally called a secondary, but they called that Power Tiers. Color's Primary In room is where you do all your balancing, and the Secondary room is not just picking colors. We can use it as eight separate levels of color correction, full up RGB. It's not selectable color correction, it's full up RGB color correction. We're creating a color as opposed to just enhancing it, and that is how the game has changed. Having eight secondaries, I think I've filled one up once, where I've run out of room. If you're that far down, either (a) the shot was totally mis-shot, or (b) the effect you're trying to create was "you better be paying big money per hour," because if you're using all eight windows and secondaries per scene on a feature or on a commercial, that's a long time color correction. This can be as basic as you want it or as complex as you want it. Does every job need all the complexity? No. But it's good to have the headroom if you need to be able to take something or push something a different way or a different color. I think the colorist that learns these tools and is more flexible and thinks "outside the bun" will be effective longer.

The colorist that learns these tools and thinks "outside the bun" will be effective longer.—Bob Sliga

Summary

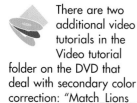

There are two additional video tutorials in the Video tutorial folder on the DVD that deal with secondary color correction: "Match_Lions_including_Secondary" and "Color_Secondaries."

Secondary color correction is really a step that can take an ordinary color correction and make it extraordinary. The skill that needs to be developed to use it most effectively is to have an understanding of how to isolate—qualify—the part of the picture that you want to change. After that, it is using your "artist's eye" to know when to leave the image alone.

It is very possible with secondaries to make the image look unnatural because you are essentially breaking the image down. One way to maintain a natural look is to continually compare the original image to the correction you're working on. (In Apple Color, you do this by clicking on control-G.) If you see that even a small part of your correction is worse than the original, find a new way to qualify the image or back off your correction until the problem is resolved.

7

TUTORIALS

You've got the tools, so let's run them through their paces and make bad video look decent and give good video some real pop.

In the Dark—Improperly Exposed Video

One of the most common problems is video that has been improperly exposed. The basic TBC-type controls—hue, saturation, luminance, and black level—give just enough control to make the picture viewable. But with the addition of just a few color correction tools, we can really salvage a pretty decent picture.

I did this correction in Color Finesse. You can do it in any color correction application that you have access to or with which you feel comfortable. Load the still image file called Sue.tiff from the tutorials section of the DVD for this chapter.

Figure 7-1 Image starting point: a very dark image that appears to be unusable.

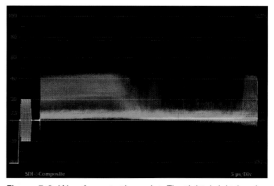

Figure 7-2 Waveform starting point. The tight, bright band along the line that indicates black on the right side of the waveform indicates that the blacks are crushed a little on the artist. No part of the waveform is much above 40IRE. The waveform is in FLAT mode, showing chroma information, so the portion of the trace that is below 0IRE is legal.

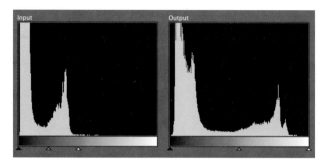

Figure 7-3 Initial Levels correction.

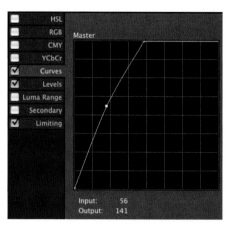

Figure 7-4 Initial Curves correction. This is an alternative method to the Levels correction.

1. Start by analyzing the image. Generally speaking we're looking for a full range of luminance values, from nice, rich shadows through a full range of midtones, all the way up to bright, sparkling highlights.

Our first example, Figure 7-1, is far too dark to be usable. Notice where the image "sits" on the composite Flat waveform monitor (Figure 7-2). We will bring it up to a nice, fairly bright look, but examining the picture, there are clues that this image should not look really bright. We'll discuss those clues shortly.

Let's bring up the overall levels to get a better idea about what we want to do.

2. As an experiment, let's use the Levels to do an initial adjustment. I did the correction on the Input side of the Levels control, but you can use either the input or output side. Pull the white point triangle on the Input side to the left all the way to the first semilarge bump in the histogram until the Output side of the histogram spreads out nicely with blacks going all the way to the right, like in Figure 7-3. Be careful to watch the image itself, though. If you go too far, the drawings on the yellow pad of paper start to get noisy. Also experiment with moving the gray midtone triangle on either the input or the output side to try to see into some of the midrange shadows. This midtone adjustment needs to be done while watching the image itself, not the histograms. Set this level by "feel." Also, be careful not to introduce too much noise into the image as you make these adjustments. If you don't have a Levels (histogram-type) controller in your application, then you can accomplish this with Curves or basic Master Levels controls (Figures 7-4 or 7-5).

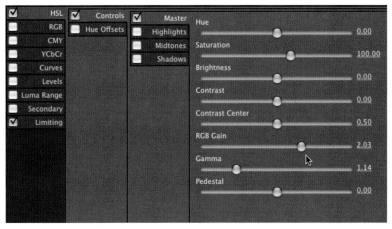

Figure 7-5 Initial Master HSL correction. This is another alternative method to the Levels correction.

Figure 7-6 Image with initial corrections applied.

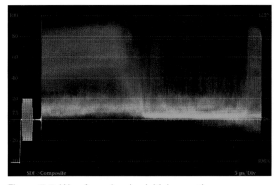

Figure 7-7 Waveform showing initial correction.

TIP

Blur is another tool that the big boys have in their color correction arsenals. It is not included specifically in the color correction capabilities of most desktop systems, but it is usually available elsewhere on the system. (Apple Color does offer this function in the Color Effects room.) The ability to blur a specific luminance range, especially highlights, is a powerful color correction capability because the sharpness of an image is a visual clue that our brains decipher as affecting contrast. Blurring blown-out highlights is sometimes helpful in solving the electronic look that the clipping of the signal induces.

If you go too far, the drawings on the yellow pad of paper start to get noisy.

Now the image is viewable.

Black is pretty much as low as it can go in this instance. The highlights of this image are not going to reach 100. The main thing that will limit you—however you decide to set your main levels—is noise and grain. When you have an image this dark, bringing it up high enough will definitely begin to introduce a lot of noise in the image. Maybe this is acceptable to you or your client, but chances are that you will introduce unacceptable amounts of grain as you move your gain.

Some color correction plug-ins and all of the serious dedicated color correction boxes are equipped with noise reducers that could help in an instance like this. (Apple Color can do noise reduction in the Color Effects room with plug-ins from Graeme Nattress.) Noise reduction may not seem like it belongs in a color correction tool, but it is instances like this—where you are limited in making a correction because of noise—that it becomes obvious why it is included in some color correction packages.

The main thing to look for in an image like this is shadows.

The main thing to look for in an image like this is shadows. Not luminance level shadows, but the type of shadows that are cast during daylight by the sun. With this image there really aren't any, and the ones that do exist are very soft. What does that tell us? It tells us the image was taken under either very overcast skies or it was taken at dusk, just after the sun went down, with only the evening sky as illumination. So when we try to settle on luminance values for this picture, we are not going to take the levels up too high because they will conflict with the information provided by the shadows.

What will bring this picture out of the mud more than anything else is not how much the highlights are raised but where we put the shadows and gamma. Because so much of the picture is in deep shadows, using controls that only offer us control of shadow, midtone, and highlight will only take us so far. We can use the added control of the Curves tab to stretch out our deep shadows and provide some detail in the lower range. The reason that Curves will help us more than any other tools is because we can mark multiple points in the Master Luma curve to manipulate. Most other tools only give us three points (Master, Gamma, Setup).

We can use the added control of the Curves tab to stretch out our deep shadows.

3. Try several attempts at correcting each of these images starting from scratch. Use different tools.

4. Correcting midtones will also add some definition to the image. How much is too much? With the shadows, you definitely want to anchor some of the nice rich blacks so that there is a healthy bottom to the image. Watch the image on

the monitor and keep an eye on the waveform to make sure that blacks don't ride up too high. From then on, keep your eye on just your monitor to watch for encroaching noise as you bring up the shadows and midtones.

Because we have spread the luma values so much from their original position, we risk posterizing the image. This never looks natural, so when you start to see posterization—look at the sky around the wisps of hair and in the gradation in the piece of paper—you need to back off. It's better to leave the picture a little dark than to introduce noise and artifacts. Remember: First, do no harm.

When you start to see posterization you need to back off.

Skin tones are a clue to latch on to for color balance. The face must remain dark, or the colors will become artificial and unnatural, but the skin tone in the hands should look right. Make sure the hands don't look dirty because that indicates that the levels have spread too much and the skin tones are posterizing.

You can use Secondary color correction to attempt to turn the sky dark blue or even orange to hint at a late evening sky. That will help sell the luminance of the image.

5. Without resorting to Secondary color correction, you can pull a lot of the green out of the sky and put in quite a bit of blue. I did this in the blue and green curves. Try to find where on the green and blue curve the "sky" begins.

Most colorists will warn about the danger of focusing your attention on *just* the scopes or *just* the monitor. You must keep your eye on both. The scopes will keep you honest. They will warn you that something's not right with the monitor. Sometimes a monitor will drift or be accidentally set up wrong, and you'll find yourself fighting against the information that the scopes are telling you if you're really watching your monitor. They provide a check

TIP: David Fincher Tutorial

 If you're interested in a detailed look at how a professional colorist approaches this, buy or rent the DVD collector's edition of the movie Seven, directed by David Fincher. Stephen Nakamura was the colorist for the home video release. One of the special features on the disk shows Mr. Nakamura color correcting the climactic last scene. As you watch the output of the da Vinci 2K color corrector that he's using, he narrates what he's doing and—more importantly—why. It's a superb tutorial in itself.

Figure 7-8 The before and after of this image. You can see that even though the picture is still relatively dark, the image is now viewable and pleasing.

Posterizing (posterization)

 Posterization is the breakdown of a natural, continual gradation to the point where there is visible banding between levels. Posterization can be an artistic effect that is applied to an image, but in color correction, it describes image artifacts that occur when attempting to spread the tonal range beyond the scope of the bit depth of the image. For example, in a sky, the image may have recorded 30 distinct levels of blue in a nice, fine gradation, but if you spread those 30 distinct levels out to a range of 300 levels, the sky will exhibit banding from one level to the next.

and balance to each other. If you feel there is a discrepancy between what your scopes say and what the monitor says, then check them both. Is the monitor set up correctly? Is everything terminated properly? Are the scopes properly calibrated?

The scopes will keep you honest.

If the scopes and monitor are in agreement, then you need to keep shifting your attention back and forth between them. However, with an image like this, we aren't going to need the scopes quite as much because nothing is going to get even close to the legal limit. Also, when correcting an image that needs this much work, you are going to be seeing more important clues in the monitor than on the scopes because the artifacts that this severe correction will create are only going to show up on the monitor.

6. Watch for:
   - Banding or posterizing in the piece of yellow paper
   - Strange shades of gray blocking up the fine detail of the wisps of hair
   - Banding and clipping in the sky

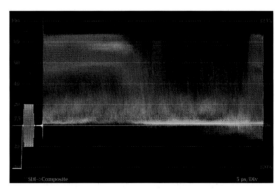

Figure 7-9 Waveform showing final correction. Note the spread of the waveform compared to Figure 7-2. Also, note that the tight, bright line at black is opened up quite a bit compared to the original, indicating that the darkest shadows now have more detail.

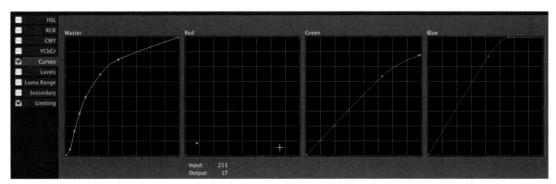

Figure 7-10 These are the final Curves corrections that resulted in Figures 7-9 and 7-10.

- Grain in the face
- Hands becoming contrasty and noisy
- Too much level or chroma turning the grass or the red shirt "electric"

7. Because this is a tutorial, you should take the image too far. Make big moves so that you can see the errors on the monitor. Crank the levels up until you start to see banding in the paper or grain in the face or until you lose detail in the wisps of hair, then slowly notch it down until you can no longer see the artifacts. As with so many things, the best way to learn is to make mistakes. So try for the mistakes.

   Make big moves so that you can see the errors on the monitor.

8. Save various corrections and then compare them to each other. Also, compare a few of your favorites in the context of the shots around them. Saving is another important learning tool. On a da Vinci, this would be done by saving stills or scratch pad memories. These are reference frames. They can help by providing you with a base correction that you can return to keep things consistent. They can also just be various corrections on the same frame so that you can quickly toggle back and forth to determine which correction is best.

Bright and Flat

Let's take a look at an example that kind of comes from the opposite end of the spectrum: This image is fairly low contrast. Increasing contrast should help focus our attention on the central figure in the image: the car.

I will work on this image in Apple Color. Call up the file Susannah_carturn.mov from the Tutorials folder on the DVD.

Bit Depth

The number of bits (the smallest data amount) used to describe a color. Eight bits of color depth gives you 256 shades of gray. Then you multiply those 256 shades of gray times the three color channels (256 × 256 × 256) to show how many colors you can describe in that color space (16.7 million colors). While 10-bit video doesn't sound much better than 8-bit video, it actually has 1024 shades of gray instead of 256, or a total of over a billion colors. Obviously, 10-bit video is going to be preferable for color correction. The preceding bit depth computations generate numbers that are on the theoretical limits.

Figure 7-11 This is a fairly low contrast shot (an HD down-convert of raw RED camera footage) from the short film *Susannah*, courtesy of director Evan Nicholas.

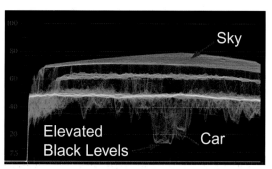

Figure 7-12 Luma waveform of the image in Figure 7-11.

TIP: As Simple as Black and White

When setting tonal ranges, Chicago colorist Alex Scudiero likes to double check his corrections in black and white. He turns the chroma completely off on his monitor and looks at the image in its purely tonal form. He showed instances with high saturated colors where the vividness of the chroma was tricking the eye about the actual levels of the image. Some colorists also do this occasionally to "wash the eye" for a moment. It's sort of like cleansing your palette before tasting a fine wine.

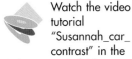

Watch the video tutorial "Susannah_car_contrast" in the Video tutorials folder on the DVD.

1. Our first step is always to set the blacks as low as we can. Pull the Master Lift (blacks) down until the part of the waveform that descends down in the middle of the trace (the part of the image that represents the car) just touches the "black" line on the waveform monitor. Notice the shape of the trace. Make sure you don't squeeze or deform the shape of the bottom of the trace as you get close to black. When the shape starts to deform, that's your cue to move the Master Lift back up a bit. Experiment with how far you can bring the blacks down. Watch the waveform monitor as the blacks start to crush, then shift your attention to the image as you pull the blacks back up a bit.

2. With the blacks set, bring up the highlights using the Master Gain control. The sky could be brought all the way up to 100IRE if you want (making sure that the subtle gradation of the sky doesn't crush into a single, thin line at the top). I chose to leave the sky a bit under 90IRE.

3. With those corrections done, play with your Master Gamma level while you watch the image itself on the video screen. Find a level that feels comfortable and that focuses as much attention as possible on the car itself.

4. When gamma is set, go back and check on the gain and lift levels; they will definitely have moved due to the changes in the other tonal ranges. Your image, waveform, and final controls should look something like they do in Figures 7-13 through 7-15.

The shot is improved, with more focus on the car. When I cut back and forth between the correction and the original (using control-G) in Color, I could actually see the focus of the shot shift from the top half of the picture to the bottom half.

We're going to work on a more severe color cast in the next tutorial, but I think that this shot could also be improved by removing the subtle blue color cast. Because this is the desert, I would prefer more of a smoky, warmish cast to convey the heat and parched

Figure 7-13 Same shot as Figure 7-11 with added contrast by lowering gamma and lift and raising gain.

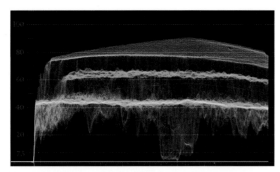

Figure 7-14 Luma waveform of the image in Figure 7-13.

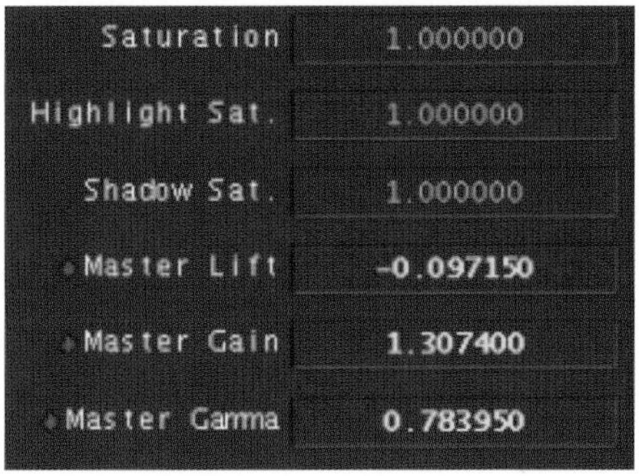

Saturation	1.000000
Highlight Sat.	1.000000
Shadow Sat.	1.000000
Master Lift	-0.097150
Master Gain	1.307400
Master Gamma	0.783950

Figure 7-15 Screen shot of the Basic Tab in Apple Color's Primary In room after the original correction to improve contrast.

texture. To do that, we'll stay in the Primary In room and use the Color Wheels.

5. Just as with tonal corrections, our color balancing will start with the blacks or shadows. To provide a reference for the eye, I want the car to have a real black, without any color cast to it. So we'll try the tip from an earlier chapter and go to the Geometry room of Color and zoom all the way in on the undercarriage of the car. You have to be a little careful because Susannah (the car) isn't black but dark green. If you balance the dark green of the car body to black, then all the shadows will go slightly magenta. Figure 7-16 shows that I zoomed in on the undercarriage, which is essentially completely shadow.

6. Now you can go back to the Primary In room and use the gain on your vectorscope. (Using the internal Color vectorscope, choose the 25% gain choice. This is actually backward of the controls on most vectorscopes that would increase in gain to zoom in.) Now you can simply move the Shadow color wheel to "focus" the blacks into the center of the vectorscope.

Figure 7-16 Apple Color Geometry room UI, showing the zoom in to the undercarriage of the car. Only the portion of the image within the red bounding box will be displayed (zoomed to full screen) on your monitor and waveform or vectorscope.

7. Reset the Geometry room so you can see all of the image, and let's set our Highlight Color wheel. I started out by trying to take the highlights in a warmer direction, but because the sky is mostly highlights, it turned the sky into a weird color. Instead of going warm, I went blue. Blue worked to get the sky to be the right color and gave the mountains a bluish cast as well. The interesting thing about this is that it plays into one of the color theory concepts that we'll talk about later in the book. Cool colors recede, and warm colors come forward. It's kind of an optical illusion. But by making the sky and mountains cool, we are creating fantastic depth to the shot that wasn't there before. Also, by creating an area of coolness in the image and another area of warmth, we are also making the image inherently more interesting instead of all being the same color palette.

   Cool colors recede, and warm colors come forward.

8. With the highlights cool, let's take the midtones Color Wheel very warm. I didn't look at the scopes at all while doing this. Just look at the image itself. I tried to get as much of a parched, hot desert look as I could get. I stopped adding warmth when the road started looking artificially red.

9. With the midtones cranked so hard toward red, recheck your blacks and highlights. They'll probably both need to go back toward blue. You can use the Geometry room and vectorscope trick to get the blacks balanced again.

10. You could possibly adjust the Master Gamma level again to bring up the overall level. My image is fairly dark and brooding. You could set your gamma higher if you're trying for a midday look.

Figures 7-17 through 7-19 show the final results of the correction. The image is definitely much stronger. Depending on the choices of the director and director of photography, the image could go in a different direction, but this is one idea.

Figure 7-17 Final correction (compare with Figure 7-11). Notice that in addition to having more overall contrast (darker darks and brighter highlights) the shot now also has color contrast (warmth contrasting with coolness).

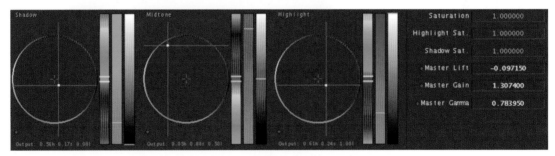

Figure 7-18 These are the final positions of the Color Wheels in Apple Color to create the effect in Figure 7-17. Notice that the blacks and highlights went cool, and the midtones went warm.

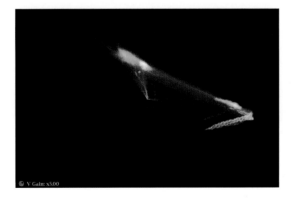

Figure 7-19 This is a Tektronix WFM7120 vectorscope, zoomed in 5x to show the final correction.

Casting for Colors

The image in Figure 7-20 has a range of problems. This is a bad film transfer from a very old 8 mm color home movie. The biggest problem is the red color cast and lack of detail on either end of the luminance range (Figure 7-21).

We'll attack this image a couple of ways. First, let's use the basic Color Corrector 3-Way filter in Final Cut Pro. Call up file "8mmracecar" from the Tutorial footage file on the DVD.

Figure 7-20 This image is dark and has strong color casts.

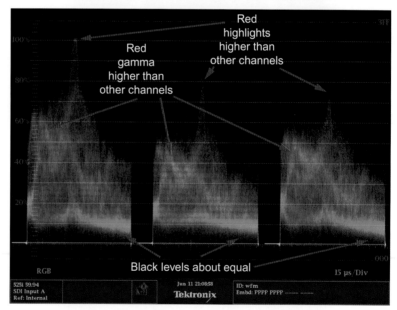

Figure 7-21 The waveform shows compressed shadows and a very low overall luminance.

1. Start by analyzing the RGB Parade waveform (see Figure 7-21).

The RGB waveform shows that black levels are pretty close to matching, though all of them are just slightly elevated. You can tell that the black levels match because the bottom of the red, blue, and green cells on the RGB Parade all are at about the same level. The highlights—basically the one bright highlight above the rear wheel—definitely show the strong red cast. The little peak in the middle of all three cells is a different height in each cell. The red cell (left side) peaks at a little over 100%. The green cell (middle)

Watch the video tutorial "FCP 3 way correction of race car" in the Video tutorials folder on the DVD.

peaks at 80%, and the blue cell (right side) peaks at about 75%. The midtones also show the strong red cast with the main part of the "white" car showing up at about 60% in the red cell, less than 50% in the green cell, and about 55% in the blue cell. This shows that each tonal range—shadows, mids, highlights—all have slightly different color casts.

2. Spread the tonal range using the three sliders under the blacks, mids, and whites color wheels. Make sure that you don't crush or clip any of the three color channels as you set the levels. I brought down the blacks a little, then I brought up the highlights just a small amount. Finally, the image still looked dark to me, so I pulled the gammas up quite a bit. When I did this, it raised the highlights past legal, so I ended up with highlights actually lowered from their original position. Instead of using the "visual" display for Color Corrector 3-Way, switch to Numeric. See the upper left corner of Figure 7-22. Figure 7-22 and Figure 7-23 are actually displaying the same data, but Figure 7-23 is providing the numeric data. Figure 7-23 shows my initial tonal range correction: blacks lowered from 0 to –13, mids raised from 100 to 113, and highlights dropped from 255 to 226.

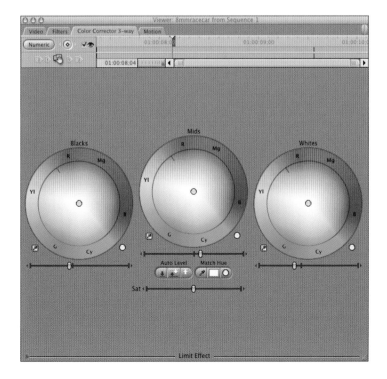

Figure 7-22 Final Cut Pro's Color Corrector 3-Way filter in Visual mode showing the preliminary tonal range correction.

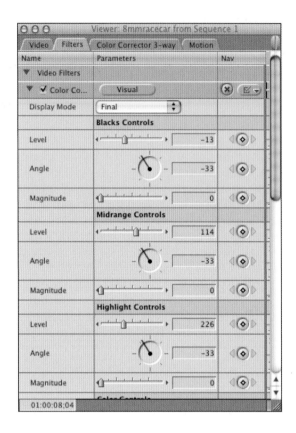

Figure 7-23 Final Cut Pro's Color Corrector 3-Way filter in Numeric mode showing the preliminary tonal range correction.

3. With the tonal range spread, use the blacks, whites, and mids Color Wheels (in that order) to balance the RGB levels in the RGB Parade waveform. Get the black levels in each cell to be equal, then get the peak highlight in the middle of each cell to be the same height, then use the mids Color Wheel to balance the main shape of the trace across all three cells. Use your eye on the image to make sure the main body of the race car looks white. Figure 7-24 shows the filter settings I ended up with to balance the image. Figure 7-25 shows the RGB Parade waveform with the balanced image.

4. Set a final tonal correction now that the highlights are balanced (Figures 7-26, 7-27, and 7-28).

Noise reduction should be used with a delicate touch. Err on the side of not enough.

There's quite a bit of noise in the image, so a pass through some sort of noise reduction filter might be a good idea. Noise reduction should be used with a delicate touch. Err on the side of not enough. If you're just working in Final Cut, try Noise Industries' FxFactory Pro set. It has a Noise Reduction plug-in among many other useful plug-ins, including a wide range of drag-and-drop color correction effects. For Color, try plug-ins by Graeme Nattress.

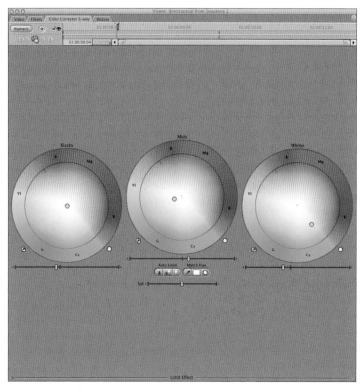

Figure 7-24 Color Corrector 3-Way screen shot showing the color balance correction. Note that each wheel was corrected in a different direction with a different strength.

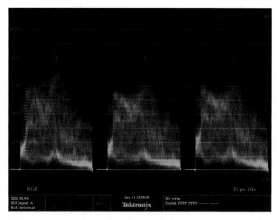

Figure 7-25 RGB Parade waveform showing the balanced image. Note that when the image was balanced, the highlight was brought down, so now we need to revisit the tonal corrections.

Figure 7-26 Final corrected image of the race car. Compare this to Figure 7-20.

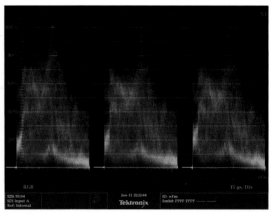

Figure 7-27 RGB Parade waveform of final image. Compare this to Figure 7-21.

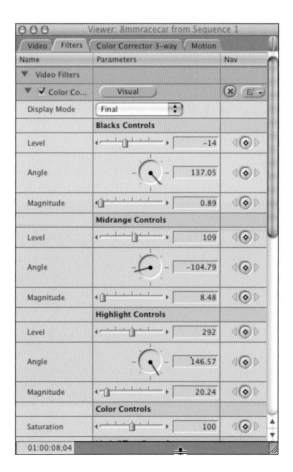

Figure 7-28 Color Corrector 3-Way with final corrections in numeric view.

On the Fence

The weathered fence image in Figure 7-29 has several problems: low luminance levels, color casts, and low contrast. Take a look at the RGB Parade waveform image in Figure 7-30, and you can see how blocked up the shadow detail is. The thick, bright lines at the bottom of each cell show how crushed all of the shadow detail is. This image has black levels down at 0IRE. Remember, you need to know whether your blacks are supposed to be at 0IRE or at 7.5IRE (see page 4 for a full explanation). The highest video levels barely reach above 50IRE. Also, the red channel is the lowest, with green highest and blue somewhere in between, indicating an image with a green-cyan cast.

Watch the video tutorial "Color Finesse correction of Fence" in the Video tutorials folder on the DVD.

Confirming these results on the histogram in Figure 7-31 shows that the blacks have been clipped drastically. The sharp, steep cliff wall at the lower end of the histogram is the clue that describes the clipped black level. It also shows that there are no pixels in the highlights range at all.

I'll tackle this correction in Color Finesse. You can use whatever software you have available. Open or import the Fence.tiff from the Tutorials footage folder on the DVD for this chapter.

1. The first step is to get those black tones in line. As usual there are a number of ways to do this, depending on your tools. The Level tool is an option, or you can work with Master HSL sliders. A few quick level changes should open the tonal range up a lot (Figures 7-32, 7-33, and 7-34).

There's a definite color cast to this image that we need to address next. The RGB Parade waveform (Figure 7-32) shows that the blacks are fairly well balanced, though the blue level may be slightly lower. The highlights are definitely higher in the greens

Figure 7-29 Fence image with problems of low luminance, color casts, and low contrast.

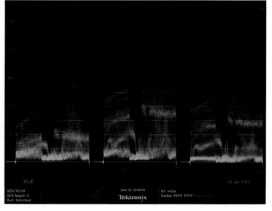

Figure 7-30 The RGB Parade waveform shows the crushed blacks and low overall levels. Note bright lines at the bottom of each cell, indicating crushing and no video signal over 60%.

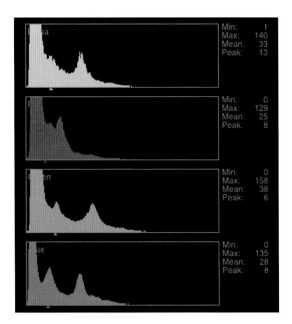

Figure 7-31 Histogram showing crushed blacks.

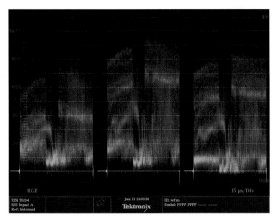

Figure 7-32 RGB Parade waveform display showing increased spread of the tonal range.

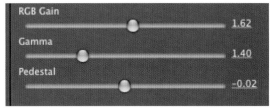

Figure 7-33 RGB Master Levels in Color Finesse showing the corrections I made to accomplish this correction.

Figure 7-34 Image of the fence with first tonal correction applied.

and lowest in the reds. The midtones are harder to see in this RGB Parade image, but if you compare the position of the thick bands of the trace in the middle of all three cells, you can see that the midtones are highest in the greens and lowest in the reds as well. This indicates a green to greenish-cyan image.

2. Let's also use the eyedropper tool to get some perspective on the color cast. Sample colors where you believe that there should be neutral tones. The fence itself is made of driftwood, which should actually be quite a neutral gray. A sample of the midtone of the fence that I took indicated R70, G94, B78, which is very similar information to what we got from the RGB Parade waveform monitor. A black shadow area on the big fence post indicated R11, G19, B7. This still indicates a greenish image, though with slightly more red than blue but not much. For highlights, there's really nothing in this image to sample.

3. Because most of the image is in the midtones, let's break our rule about balancing blacks, then whites, then midtones and start with the midtones. We'll use the individual red, green, and blue sliders in Color Finesse's RGB tab. This is similar to Apple Color's Advanced tab on the right side of the Primary In room. Watch the RGB Parade waveform as you move these sliders—midtones (gamma) first this time. You can also watch the eyedropper numbers. They will update as you correct the image.

This image cleans up fairly quickly. Things to watch for include the following:

- Try to keep the nice contrasty detail of the sea waves in the highlights.
- By pulling out as much blue and green as you will need to, there are portions of the image—like the brightest highlights on the sea at the top of the image—that could start to go very red.

The final correction is a huge improvement on the original image (Figures 7-35, 7-36, and 7-37).

Figure 7-35 Final corrected image of the fence. Compare with Figure 7-29.

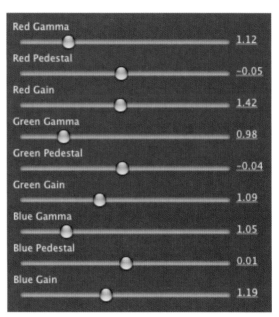

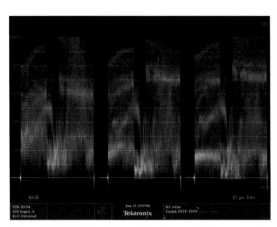

Figure 7-36 RGB Parade waveform image of the corrected fence. Compare with Figure 7-30.

Figure 7-37 RGB Tab data for the final corrections from Color Finesse UI.

That's Blue—And I'm Not Lion

Figure 7-38 was shot with the wrong filter set on the camera. Figure 7-39 has the proper white balance. Although these are both wide shots, it is common for a client to ask for two shots with mismatched white balance to be matched so that they can be intercut seamlessly. Matching shots like this is a large part of a colorist's responsibility.

This final tutorial image will address the classic daylight blue color cast. As an added twist, we'll try to match it to another shot at the same location that is correctly balanced. This is an everyday request made of many colorists. Peter Mavromates, postproduction supervisor for the movie *Panic Room*, explains the importance of matching shots:

> *You could make a list of a thousand things that affect how something looks so that when it's cut together and Joe is talking to Mary, Joe's side looks bright and green, and Mary's side looks dark and red. You've got to bring them closer together so that every cut doesn't "hurt." Another way I put it is that each cut doesn't have an "eyeblink" factor.*
>
> *It's not that the average audience member will say, "Her side is redder than his," it's that there will be a discomfort level. Their eyes will blink. It works on a subliminal level as far as I'm concerned. If there's a discomfort level with the audience, they're distracted and they don't know why. And*

*so color correction is part of that process of wrapping it in
a nice package so that you're there watching the story.*

Figure 7-38 Shot with the wrong filter.

Figure 7-39 Same shot with the correct filter, to be matched with Figure 7-38.

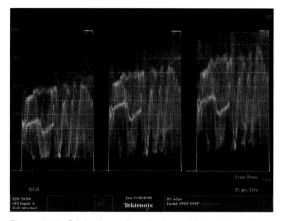

Figure 7-40 Original waveform for lion with the blue color cast (Figure 7-38).

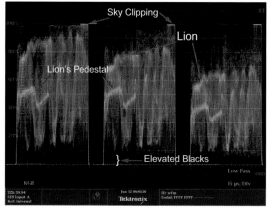

Figure 7-41 Original histogram for lion with the blue color cast (Figure 7-39).

Lions and Parades

Both images are a little washed out, as you can see in Figures 7-40 and 7-41. Let's color correct this example using Apple Color. Import or open the art_institute_lions_cool.mov and art_institute_lions_proper.mov files from the Tutorial footage folder on the DVD.

1. Use the Master Lift, Master Gain, and Master Gamma in the Primary In room to set your overall tonal range. By now you're an expert at this, so I'll just show you my final levels for both corrections. For the "neutral lion," Lift was set to

Watch the video tutorial "Match Lions including Secondary" in the Video tutorials folder on the DVD.

−0.069600 and Gain was set to 1.063800. The gamma looked good, so I left it alone.

2. For the "cool lion" I want to match the levels of the "neutral lion," so I'm going to save a still reference frame and cut rapidly back and forth between the two while trying to match the levels. You could also have a split wipe between the two and try to match them that way. To do this match, switch your waveform view to composite (or luma only). In Color, hit control-i while parked on the corrected neutral lion to save a still of it. Then hit control-u to enable the still store. The still store defaults to a split screen. If you want to do the match with a split screen, you're all set. I want to switch rapidly between the two, so I'll go in to the Still Store room and change the Transition to 1.0, as in Figure 7-42. With a still of the corrected neutral lion loaded, go to the blue lion shot in the time line. Now, when you hit control-u, the screen will toggle between the still of the corrected neutral lion and your current correction of the cool lion. Toggle back and forth very fast. You can see the jump in levels between the nice full waveform of the neutral lion and the less contrasty blue lion. Adjust the Master levels as you toggle back and forth, trying to get them to match. The levels I ended up with were Master Lift: −0.078300, Master Gain: 1.255200, and Master Gamma: 0.985500 (barely changed).

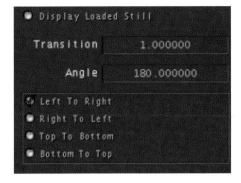

Figure 7-42 Transition control in Color's Still Store room UI. Setting this to 1.0 means there is no wipe. Setting it to 0.5 creates a wipe at the halfway mark. You can also change the angle and direction of the wipe.

3. With the tonal ranges fairly close, let's take care of the color balance differences. First, even though we're calling the neutral lion "neutral," let's balance it a little. Chicago's Art Institute (building in the background) really is a fairly warm, sandstone color, but we'll try to make it a little more neutral before we match the cool lion to it. Take a look at the RGB Parade waveform as you dial in a little less warmth, especially in the midtones and highlights. (Ignore the color of the sky for now. We'll fix that later.)

Use the red, green, and blue sliders in the Primary In room's Advanced Tab. You can use the eyedropper function in the 3D Scope of Color if you want. Try sampling a white from the tail of the shirt of the guy leaning against the handrail on the steps, a gray from the lion's pedestal, and a black from the deep shadow in the archway above the maroon banner (which happens to be for an Ansel Adams exhibit by happy coincidence!). Figure 7-43 shows the RGB Parade waveform for my color balance on the neutral lion. Notice that the scope is showing an RGB gamut error. This is from the bright sky that is clipped. I will fix that later. I set the levels (Figures 7-44 and 7-45) based on matching the colors between the red, green, and blue cells, with a little extra warmth in the highlights because the sandstone is not supposed to be completely neutral.

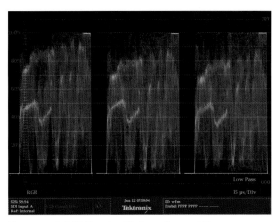

Figure 7-43 RGB Parade of balanced neutral lion.

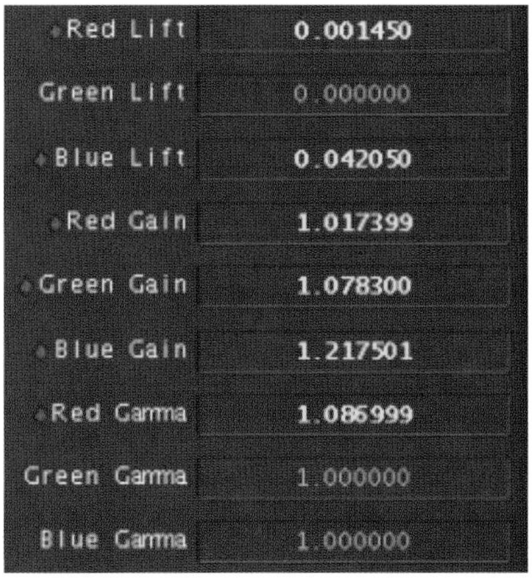

Red Lift	0.001450
Green Lift	0.000000
Blue Lift	0.042050
Red Gain	1.017399
Green Gain	1.078300
Blue Gain	1.217501
Red Gamma	1.086999
Green Gamma	1.000000
Blue Gamma	1.000000

Figure 7-44 Advanced Tab of Primary In room corrections for neutral lion.

Saturation	1.000000
Highlight Sat.	1.000000
Shadow Sat.	1.000000
Master Lift	-0.131950
Master Gain	1.120348
Master Gamma	1.000000

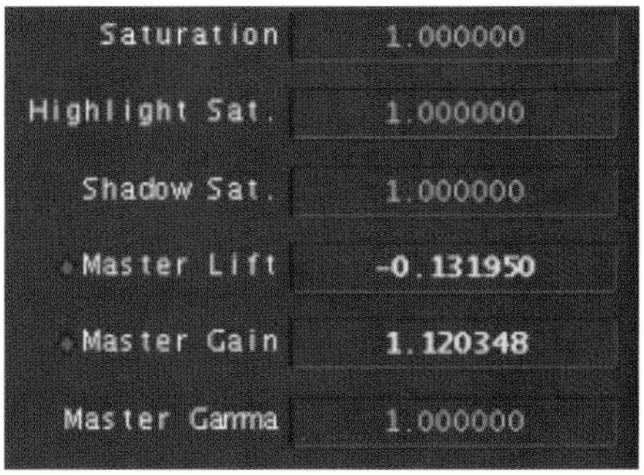

Figure 7-45 Basic Tab of Primary In room corrections for neutral lion.

4. Now match the color cast of the cool lion to the neutral lion using the method in step 2. Save a new still of the corrected neutral lion and toggle rapidly between them while balancing the color on the cool lion to match the still. The object is to try to make the various shapes in the trace match in level between the source you're correcting and the reference shot you're trying to match. Basically all of these moves involved watching the parade of RGB and figuring out which slider moved which part of the trace on the waveform. When that was established, it was a matter of trying to replicate the look of the correct image. The other analytical tool that is invaluable is using a wipe between the reference image and the blue image. Be careful not to leave the wipe in one spot. A color change may not be noticeable in the spot where your wipe is positioned, but it may have a large effect elsewhere. Figures 7-46 through 7-51 show the results of the final matching shots.

The object is to try to make the various shapes in the trace match.

The shots match fairly closely with one exception. The green color of the lions themselves do not match, even though the sandstone of the building and the gray of the pedestal all match almost perfectly. The other issue is the color of the sky, which is fairly unnatural in both images because the sky was clipped and we made some fairly radical color changes.

The answer to both of these problems is Secondary color correction. We will isolate the color of the sky and the lion from the rest of the image and grade them to match. But because our next chapter is all about Secondary color correction and other more

Red Lift	0.002900
Green Lift	0.005800
Blue Lift	-0.018850
Red Gain	1.316100
Green Gain	1.059450
Blue Gain	0.908650
Red Gamma	1.000000
Green Gamma	0.939100
Blue Gamma	1.097150

Figure 7-46 Advanced Tab of the Primary In room for the corrections to the cool lion.

Figure 7-47 Split screen between the neutral lion and the cool lion shots. The split runs from lower left to upper right.

Figure 7-48 Cool lion image corrected to match neutral lion.

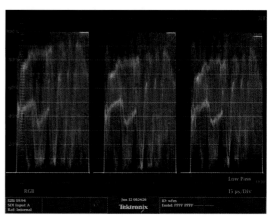

Figure 7-49 RGB Parade waveform of the balanced cool lion.

Figure 7-50 Neutral lion final balanced image.

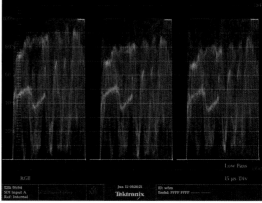

Figure 7-51 RGB Parade waveform of the final balanced neutral lion.

complex tutorials, we'll do those grades at the beginning of the next chapter.

Summary

The tutorials in this chapter walked through the practical application of a lot of the knowledge gained from previous chapters. You used numerous analytical tools, including RGB Parade waveforms, vectorscopes, histograms, eyedroppers, and judging proper video levels based on the shadows cast by the sun. You also used numerous tools to improve your image including Levels (histograms), RGB gain, gamma and lift controls, Color Wheels, and Curves. And you learned some in-depth colorist secrets, like matching to a still reference file while toggling back and forth during the correction.

8

ADVANCED COLOR CORRECTION TUTORIALS

We have already discussed Secondary color correction at length in the chapter on Secondary color correction. In this chapter, we'll practice a little bit of what we've already learned, plus attempt some other advanced color correction techniques.

Matching Colors at the Art Institute

The first tutorial we'll run though is to finish matching our two shots of the lions in front of the Art Institute of Chicago. If you're following along, reading the book in order (linearly), then you're all set to begin your correction. If you decided to skip ahead and landed here, you might want to go back and do the last tutorial from the previous chapter. Otherwise, open up the movie files art_institute_lions_proper.mov and art_institute_lions_cool.mov from the Tutorials folder on the DVD for Chapter 7.

We'll continue to work in Apple Color. Of the lower-cost desktop solutions, it is without question the one with the best Secondary color correction tools.

At the end of the previous chapter, we balanced the majority of these two movies and actually got them to match each other pretty well with the exception of the sky and the lion.

'Scuse Me While I Grade the Sky

Let's start with the easiest of the two secondary qualifications: the sky.

1. Click on the Secondary room in Color and enable the secondary with the check box at the top, near the left side (see Figure 8-1). Let's work on the neutral lion first. There are eight different secondary grade tabs in the Secondary room. Let's go in order, so make sure you're grading with the first Secondary tab (see Figure 8-2).

Watch the video tutorial "Match_ Lions_including_ Secondary" in the Video tutorials folder on the DVD.

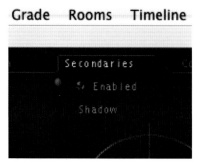

Figure 8-1 Secondary has been enabled by checking the "enabled" box.

Figure 8-2 This figure shows that the 1st of 8 Secondary tabs has been selected. The "1" tab is highlighted.

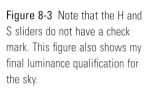

Figure 8-3 Note that the H and S sliders do not have a check mark. This figure also shows my final luminance qualification for the sky.

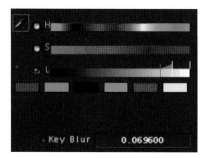

2. To qualify the area of the sky, you can start with the eye-dropper, clicking on a portion of the blown-out sky with the red crosshairs overlay that appears over your image.

That sets the starting parameters in the HSL Qualification area. Because the video level of the sky is so much higher than anything else, there's really no reason to try to qualify the hue or saturation, so uncheck those sliders and just set the Luminance slider to fully select the sky and nothing but the sky (see Figure 8-3). Remember that holding down the shift button while dragging either end of the range only moves that side of the range, instead of the default behavior or moving both sides of the range in opposite directions.

3. If you are not able to get a clean isolation using just the luminance values, you can enable the vignette portion of the secondary and draw a large window (a circle or a square) around the sky area. That will eliminate the selection in any unwanted areas of the picture that were qualified other than the sky.

4. With the sky qualified, there are a number of ways you could fix the color. Obviously, the sky is blown-out and very bright. To eliminate any strange color cast, you could simply go to the Highlight Saturation control and pull saturation completely down. If you wanted to actually balance the color, you could use any of the traditional Primary controls

to balance out the highlights, like the Color Wheels or the Advanced Tab RGB sliders or even Curves.

5. When the sky is balanced for the neutral lion shot, do the same correction to the cool lion shot. You can actually drag and drop or copy and paste your correction from the neutral lion shot to the cool lion shot. The grade won't work, but the qualification of the sky from the neutral lion shot should work on the cool lion shot.

Lion Eyes

The second qualification and grade will be a little trickier. We'll need to select the lion based on a range of hue, saturation, and luminance characteristics. The good news is that there isn't much else in the frame that is the same color as the lion. The other good news is that because the shot is a locked-off shot and nothing crosses in front of the lion, we can always "cheat" and use a garbage matte (vignette) to help us further qualify the lion. Let's start with the neutral lion and go to a second secondary tab (see Figure 8-4).

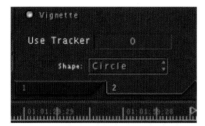

Figure 8-4 Note the cyan number "2" indicates the selection of a second secondary.

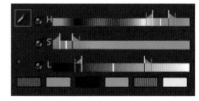

Figure 8-5 Data for my qualification of the lion's coppery color.

1. First, use the eyedropper to select a representative pixel from the lion's coppery body, or command-drag to select multiple pixels. Use the HSL Qualifying sliders in the top right corner of the Secondary room to broaden the selection to include the entire lion, tightening the qualification when it expands to include portions of the picture you don't want to affect. Remember the focusing analogy. Always take things too far and then come back. See Figures 8-5 and 8-6 for my final HSL qualification. Note that some other areas of the image are also qualified. Nearly all of the lion is qualified except for the very brightest highlights and the darkest shadows.

Always take things too far and then come back.

Colorists have different attitudes about how tight or "qualified" to make their selections before they begin correcting. Janet Falcon, a noted colorist at Philadelphia's Shooters Post and Transfer, who has worked on feature film DIs, national TV spots, and music videos, gives us a glimpse into her thought process:

Figure 8-6 Matte generated from the qualification of the coppery color.

I like to get the window [qualification] the way I think I'm going to want it, and then I go back and forth. For me they all go together. The amount of color correction, the shape of the window, the softness of the window. All those things play together. I know a lot of other people do it the other way. They'll put the color correction in first and then do the luminance key. I know Kevin Shaw does that. [Kevin Shaw is a prominent color correction trainer and consultant.] If he wants a luminance key of the sky, he'll make a color correction in a circle, then create a luminance key and bring that correction into the luminance key. I create the key as close as I think I can get it and then I color correct it. Then I go back and touch up the softness and the positioning. I do a lot of back and forth. I like to be very, very, very specific about what I affect and what I don't affect. Some people aren't that specific. I'm kind of neurotic about it.

I like to be very, very, very specific about what I affect and what I don't affect.—Janet Falcon

2. If you aren't able to create a really clean isolation with just the HSL controls, let the isolation include some areas outside of the lion, like I did, then add a soft window or vignette around the lion to "contain" your HSL correction as in Figure 8-7. Although I don't usually use square vignettes, I did in this example because the pedestal under the lion was qualified and the cutoff between the copper of the lion and the neutral stone color of the pedestal is a straight line.

3. With your lion qualified, use the Color Wheels to dial in a nice green copper look. You can keep it natural or really pump up the color to make the lion stand out in the shot, like it would in a TV spot (Figure 8-8). Save a still of the new neutral lion shot (Figure 8-9) or control-I when parked on a representative frame to save the still in the Still Store room so that we can match the cool lion to this shot.

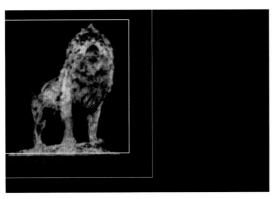

Figure 8-7 Square vignette added around lion to further isolate the qualification.

Figure 8-8 Final image of the neutral lion shot.

Figure 8-9 Still store pulldown menu. Control-I grabs a still of the current frame.

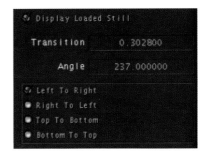

Figure 8-10 Data for wipe in Still Store room.

4. Switch over in the time line to the cool lion and run through steps 1 through 3 to select the lion. Because the color of the lion is so different between the two shots, you probably can't drag and drop the qualification like you did for the qualification of the sky, but you can try it if you want.

5. Call up the Still store and enable it, using the transition controls to place a wipe through the middle of the lion. Figure 8-10 shows the data for the wipe I used. Figure 8-11 shows part of the image with the wipe between the corrected neutral lion and the uncorrected cool lion.

6. Now use the same controls you used in step 4 to match the color of the lions. If you want to make it easier on yourself, use the Geometry room to zoom in on just the lion and then do your matching grade while watching the vectorscope or RGB Parade waveform monitor. Figure 8-12 is the final correction of the cool lion, and Figure 8-13 is a wipe between the final corrections matching the neutral lion with the cool lion.

With the initial primary grade that matched the building and most of the rest of the image, and now the secondary grades of the

Figure 8-11 Partial image of wipe between the corrected neutral and uncorrected cool lion shots.

Figure 8-12 Final image for the cool lion shot.

Figure 8-13 Split between the final, corrected versions of the neutral and cool lion shots.

lion and the sky, you have a perfectly matched shot—plus both shots look much better than the originals.

Rosy Cheeks

The next tutorial is a similar qualification, only instead of using it to match two shots, we're going to fix just a small part of an otherwise good correction. As I've mentioned before, fixing skin tones is a common use for secondary color corrections. In this shot from Artbeats' Kids of Summer Collection, we're going to leave everything alone except for the skin tones on the kids, which I think is a little cool (Figure 8-14). The shot is very well graded in its original form, but I just want to pump up the warm, summery skin tones of the kids. Previously in the book, we discussed how the color grading of skin tones actually has regional differences between colorists. I want to take the skin tones from a "New York colorist" to an "LA colorist."

Fixing skin tones is a common use for Secondary color corrections.

Figure 8-14 Original shot courtesy of Artbeats' Kids of Summer Collection, shot KS114.

Load up the KS114 clip from the Artbeats folder on the DVD. I'll be using Apple Color to walk through this grade, but you can use any software that allows you to select a secondary. You can even use Final Cut Pro's Limit Effect (which is the same as a basic Secondary color correction) inside of the Color Corrector 3-Way effect.

Because we have determined that the only thing we're going to change is the skin tones, we can skip the primary color correction altogether and go straight to our Secondary correction. Earlier in this chapter there was an interesting interview with Janet Falcon where she mentions that some people prefer to color correct the entire image in the secondary before doing their qualification. You can try that if you want, but we will do the qualification first, then we'll change the color only in the qualified area.

1. To start with the qualification, enable the Secondary correction using the check box, and use the eyedropper in the top right hand corner to select a skin tone—probably from the face of one of the kids. I used a spot on the cheek of the girl.

TIP

You can also use the shift or command key when using the eyedropper to sample and select numerous pixels by dragging over an area of the image. To do this, click on the image first, then click and hold on the shift key while dragging.

Qualifying a secondary is all about getting the cleanest matte you can get. You can view the matte that you are creating in three different ways using the Matte Preview Mode buttons (Figure 8-15). The top multicolored button delivers the Final Image display option. It basically shows your final image exactly as it will be seen, except, if you have a vignette, you'll see the outline of the vignette in yellow. The middle, gray-green button is called the Desaturated Preview (Figure 8-16). This shows your selected (qualified) areas in color, while the nonselected areas are desaturated (black and white). The bottom black and white button is the Matte Only button and presents the actual matte for the Secondary correction (Figure 8-17). Your qualified areas of the image are white, and the rest is black. This display is similar to the small matte preview display to the left of the buttons, except that it shows the effect of the blur parameters and a yellow outline for

Figure 8-15 Matte Preview mode buttons, Apple Color user interface.

Figure 8-16 Desaturated Preview mode in Apple Color.

Figure 8-17 Matte Only Preview mode in Apple Color.

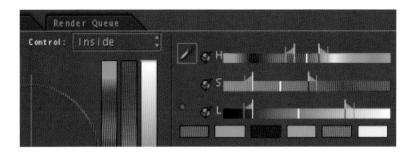

Figure 8-18 These are the final settings for the qualification of the skin tones.

Figure 8-19 Final correction of Artbeats' Kids of Summer watermelon shot. The skin tones were moved toward a more golden tone with nothing else changed.

any vignettes if the outline display button is activated (as it is in the bottom right corner of Figure 8-15).

> **Qualifying a secondary is all about getting the cleanest matte you can get.**

Whether you apply the Secondary correction to the black area or the white area of the matte is determined by the Control menu pulldown just to the left of the HSL Qualifier sliders (Figure 8-18). The default for this pulldown is "Inside." If you are correcting "Inside" you will affect the white areas, and if you are correcting "Outside" you will affect the black areas. For this correction, we want to correct the inside.

2. After the selection with the eyedropper, use the HSL Qualifier sliders in the top right corner of the Secondary room to continue refining your selection. Play with both sides of each range. You can even try unchecking the check marks to the left of each slider range to see the qualification without that particular qualifier. In some images, the qualification may not depend much on the specific luminance or chrominance, for example. My qualification can be seen in Figures 8-18 and 8-19.

3. When the skin tones have been qualified, you can use the Color Wheels to dial in a skin tone that is pleasing to you. Most of the correction will be done with the Midtone color

wheel. I did very minor corrections using the Shadow and Highlight wheels (Figure 8-19).

Day for Night

Day for night is a standard request made of colorists. Due to budget restrictions or technical limitations, oftentimes it is necessary to shoot a shot during the day that is supposed to happen at night. Selling this illusion is often a collaboration between the colorist and the director of photography.

Several things factor into the look of footage that needs to look like night. Many people believe that simply making the image blue will deliver the nighttime look. Really, the issue is that the biology and anatomy of our eyes work different at night. The receptors that pick up color differences do not operate as well in low-light situations as the receptors that pick up luminance differences. Our eyes have a harder time detecting any colors at night, but we are mainly insensitive to red in low light, so to be true to the reality of the situation, we need a very desaturated image that is particularly devoid of any red saturation.

Many people believe that simply making the image blue will deliver the nighttime look.

The other factor that comes in to play in creating day-for-night shots is our learned cultural response to nighttime depictions of scenes in the movies and on TV. Sometimes our color preferences and memory are not accurate, and we believe or prefer colors that are not actually true to the situation. Some of this cultural response comes from watching years of television and film where nighttime is depicted as blue. So despite the truth of the image, adding blue can definitely signal an audience that your shot occurred at night.

Colorist Bob Sliga also provided some suggestions for this correction. His additional suggestion was to pull a matte using the luminance of the sky that could be used to separate the corrections done to the sky from the corrections done to the castle. This key could actually be used to insert a whole different sky into the image. The separation of these elements allows you to create a specific feel for the kind of a night that it is because the tonal differences between the building and the sky give you your best clues as to how dark the night really is.

Sliga also likes to add a little bit of defocus to the highlights to simulate the way the eye has trouble detecting edges in low light situations. You could accomplish this in Color's Color Effect room.

For this correction, let's switch over to Adobe After Effects. Download the file closecastle.tif (Figure 8-20) from the Tutorial folder of the DVD and import it into After Effects.

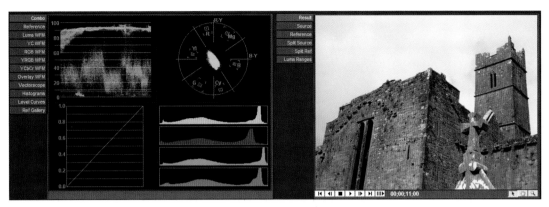

Figure 8-20 Closecastle.tif original image in Color Finesse UI including built in scopes.

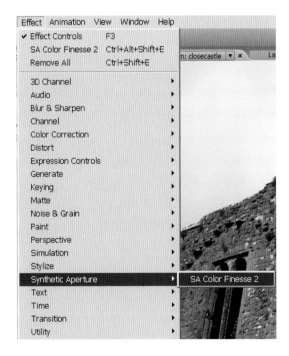

Figure 8-21 Effects pulldown menu showing Synthetic Aperture's Color Finesse 2 selected.

1. Drag the imported file down into the time line and then go to Effect > Synthetic Aperture > SA Color Finesse 2 (Figure 8-21). If you don't see the Effect Controls, hit F3 to call them up. You should see the Color Finesse effect. Click on Full Interface (Figure 8-22) to bring up the Color Finesse plug-in in its own window.

2. I started working on this in the Curves tab (Figure 8-23). I wanted to quickly get it into a place where I could see what I needed to do to sell the image further. I started by pulling the right side of the Master curve down (luma) and also added a point at about halfway and pulled down the gamma

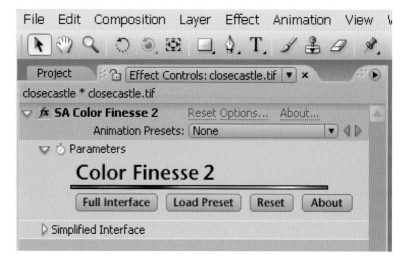

Figure 8-22 Color Finesse 2 effects control in After Effects. Click on "Full Interface" button to enable the UI seen in Figure 8-23.

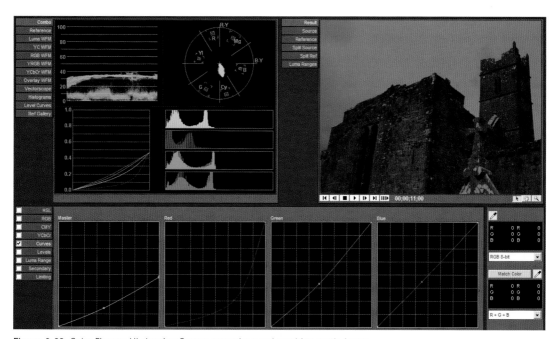

Figure 8-23 Color Finesse UI showing Curves corrections and resulting castle image.

a little as well. Then, keeping in mind that our eyes can't see red very well in low light, I pulled down the gamma of the red curve a lot. I did very minor tweaks to the gamma points of the green and blue curves as well.

3. The biggest telltale sign that this is not nighttime now is that the sky is simply way too bright. So I moved to my RGB tab and went to my Highlights tab. Color Finesse and Avid have a strange little group of controls that break the high-

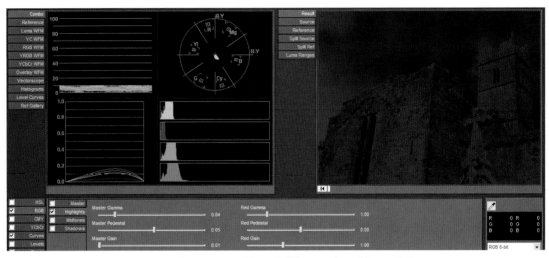

Figure 8-24 RGB Highlights parameter data—note positions of sliders—and resulting castle image.

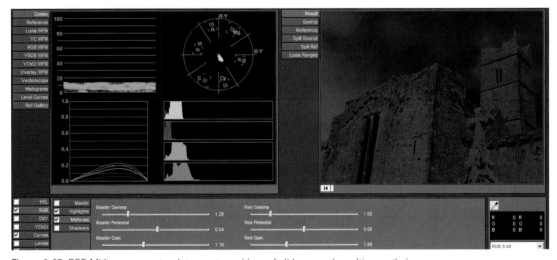

Figure 8-25 RGB Midtone parameter data—note positions of sliders—and resulting castle image.

lights, midtones, and shadows down into three even further tonal ranges that are—confusingly—called Master Gamma, Master Pedestal, and Master Gain. You can actually control the "highlight of a shadow" or the "pedestal of a highlight." So inside of the Highlights, I brought down the Master Gamma a little, brought the Master Pedestal up just a bit, and really brought down the Master Gain. That makes the sky look much more nighttime but also lowers the overall levels too much (Figure 8-24).

4. In the Midtones tab, I raised the Master Gamma, raised the Master Pedestal a touch, and raised the Master Gain a bit as well (Figure 8-25). This makes the green moss and some

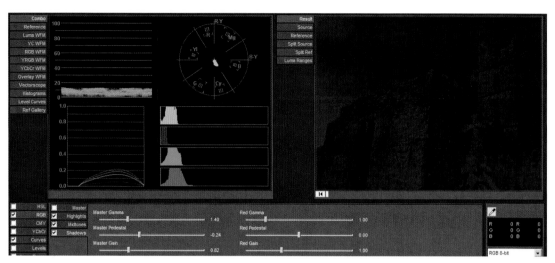

Figure 8-26 RGB Shadow parameter data—note positions of sliders—and resulting castle image.

of the highlights a little weird looking, but sometimes you have to break stuff and fix it later.

5. In the Shadows tab, I raised the Master Gamma quite a bit, lowered the Master Pedestal to keep a nice crisp look, and lowered the Master Gain a bit (Figure 8-26).

6. I'm still not really getting the separation I want in my color corrections of the individual tonal ranges because so much of the original image is midtones, so I went to the Luma Range tab and increased the amount of the image that is considered to be either Highlight or Shadow (Figure 8-27). As you adjust the curves of the Luma Ranges, you'll see that the corrections you applied in the previous step shift slightly. This really starts to make the image pop a bit.

7. I could have gone back and tweaked some settings in step 5, but I decided to go to the HSL tab to make the final corrections because it would allow me to easily undo any bad changes I made. This is similar to the concept of adding Secondary corrections without qualifications that we discussed in the Secondary Color Correction chapter. The changes I made were bringing down the highlights just a bit so that the sky got a bit darker and the highlights on the stone weren't quite so prominent. Then I lowered the saturation of the highlights almost completely so that the sky went a much less blue and a little more neutral. I raised the midtones, and I lowered the saturation in them to make the moss on the walls a little less prominent. Finally, in the Shadows I brought down the brightness and brought up the saturation a bit so that the picture wasn't too desaturated overall (Figure 8-28).

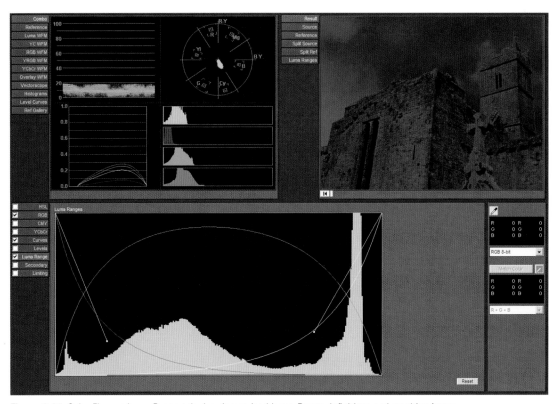

Figure 8-27 Color Finesse Luma Range tab showing revised Luma Range definitions and resulting image.

Figure 8-28 Note the positions of the sliders and the resulting castle image.

Figure 8-29 Final castle day for night color correction.

The final correction is quite convincing (Figure 8-29) with a nice feel that definitely leans toward blue without being awash in blue.

Creating Looks

Creating "looks" is where the big boys and their fancy toys really earn their big-league paychecks. If you want to see great, current examples of this, do a web search for any of the big-name postproduction companies that you see in the credits of your favorite shows. Most of these post houses have reels of demo work by their finest colorists. The post industry has undergone a huge revolution in mergers and name changes, so I won't point out any of the big current names in postproduction. Many of the big players are in Hollywood, but don't forget to check out colorists from across Europe, Asia, and the rest of the world. There's some amazing work being done by colorists everywhere. TV spots and music videos are probably the main places to find cool looks that push the image far beyond what was originally captured on film.

When you're trying to determine what the colorist did to achieve the look, pay special attention to skin tones, grass tones, and sky. These are colors that you inherently can relate to, so it's easier to see how they've been manipulated. Are the skin tones cool? What about contrast? Are the blacks crushed? Are the highlights clipped? Have certain colors been accentuated? Has a vignette been applied? Are there defocus effects?

> *When you're trying to determine what the colorist did to achieve the look, pay special attention to skin tones, grass tones, and sky.*

The Importance of Story

One of the things that color correction can really do well is tell a story. Colorist Bob Sliga told me about his experience grading a TV spot that illustrates the importance of how color can be used to tell a story. The client hadn't arrived yet, so he put the film up on the telecine and balanced it to the TAF. The first shot was a beautiful image of a woman in a flowing dress carrying milk bottles out to a barn under a huge tree. Sliga started to turn it into a picture-postcard "Kodak moment" with lush colors and a clear, blue sky. But when the clients arrived, they made it clear that the direction Sliga had taken was completely wrong because the woman had a terrible illness (that the drug they were advertising would cure). So Sliga pulled all of the color out of the image and pushed it much cooler creating a sense of "despair" and added contrast to increase the tension. As soon as the image comes up on the screen, the audience instantly knows that something is wrong before the first word of voice-over is ever spoken.

One of the things that color correction can really do well is tell a story.

In my book *The Art and Technique of Digital Color Correction*, an entire chapter is devoted to the idea of telling the story with color. Here are a few excerpts from that chapter:

Level 3 colorist Larry Field, the colorist for *24*, explains one of the ways he works with color to promote the story in his work. "With *24* if one of the main characters is doing something bad we'll make it a very gritty and aggressive look to go with the action."

Director of photography David Mullen, ASC, responds, "Everyone wants context. Without context, you can make a billion different choices, but as soon as you know the context of the shot, it narrows the choices. To me to know whether that scene is late in the day, or whether a character turned off half the lights in the office, so this office is not as bright as it normally is. So if they haven't seen the shot where the character turns off the lights, they might try to match the look of the office from the last time they saw the office in the movie, so you need the kind of story context in order to make the final decisions on stuff. Especially since some cinematographers shoot a kind of flat image and then create the look later, the DP definitely needs to be there to give an idea of what the intent of the scene was."

"Without context, you can make a billion different choices."
—David Mullen, ASC

CBS's Neal Kassner, colorist for *48 Hours* agrees, "You've got to know the story because color is part of the storytelling tools." Kassner related several stories about how he had corrections go

TAF (telecine analysis film)

 Kodak developed this technology, and it became the industry standard for colorists in being able to set up a given film stock to a kind of "default" setting. Each TAF has 8 color bars, an 8-step gray scale, and 16 surrounding gray chips. Specific instructions tell the colorist exactly where all of the chips should fall on a waveform and vectorscope. This gives a base setting for properly exposed and filtered footage.

off track because he sometimes started grading before he understood the story.

LA freelance digital intermediate colorist Greg Creaser, who worked as the digital timing supervisor on *Seabiscuit, Terminator 3, Spiderman*, and *Pirates of the Caribbean: Curse of the Black Pearl*, believes the story is so important that he likes to read the script before he works on a film:

> *I think story is really important. I know any time I'm going to grade a film I'd either like to read a script or at least see a cut of the movie before I do it to know what's involved or to know what the genre is because I think that has a lot of say on the color as well. I think that's really a key. I think that's extremely important to do that.*

Roy Wagner, ASC also elaborates on the importance of color and contrast to tell a story:

> *Well, everything in life is a symbol of something. We are interpretive beings, and colors have a very significant interpretive power and emotional response in a human being. Blues have a symbolic meaning and reds have a symbolic meaning and all of the variations in between. Not only colors have a symbolic meaning, but the composition of how the color space fits within the frame, where it sits within the frame, how we respond to that wherever it is. I think that for a cinematographer it's extremely important to not only initially interpret the story in terms of light and contrast and color and composition, but it's important that we pursue that to a final presentation. Where I learned that for myself was with my initial relationship—by chance, I got to work with Ansel Adams as an assistant. And I saw his passion for the final image, and he constructed the final image in the darkroom. He did not construct the final image on the negative. He interpreted what he saw before him and put that on the negative, but the final interpretation was done in the darkroom. So for me, I understood that it wasn't important that you have a perfectly exposed negative, but what was important was that you capture your interpretation on the negative, and then you follow it through in the darkroom.*

"Colors have a very significant interpretive power and emotional response."—Roy Wagner, ASC

I prompted Wagner with the analogy between what a photographer does in the darkroom and what a colorist does in the color correction suite.

> *Yes, very much so. And at the time that he was doing it, cinematographers had very little power because once you captured your image you were pretty much stuck with what you had on the negative because film processing and film printing was a linear process that was not—aside from*

slight adjustments in color and contrast—something you could change.

Creating Story Looks

On the front cover of this book are a series of stills taken from the short film *Susannah* by director Evan Nicholas (www.evannicholas.net). The cinematographer was Brian Hamm (www.brianhammfilms.com). Nicholas's script is provided as a .pdf file on the DVD. An excerpt from the script gives us an idea of the mood for the film:

The inland empire is just a memory as we stare out the window at the desolate land. Starving for its next drop of water the landscape envelops but can't quite hold onto a Green, 1970 Chevelle SS powering along the highway—cutting forcefully into its gut. Across the expanse only dry heat and quiet—on the road the violent whir of pistons chugging ever louder and with more expression as the car shifts into fourth gear.

Meet the driver: Jacob (late 20s): sweat droplets have formed on his creased brow—the open window offers only blasting hot air. His aviators reflect nothing man-made but his car and the road. This frontier only exists because people just wouldn't want to live here. His car, his life and legacy, gulping gas but whispering in his ear all the sweet satisfaction a man could ever want.—Copyright 2007 Evan Nicholas

The script then describes the actual shot that we'll work on:

Jacob … freezes when he hears a loud BANG—he glances over his shoulder to see a MAID (60s) who is picking up the cleaning supplies she just dropped—he exhales, satisfied all is well after his scare and puts the key in the door and turns the lock. The room is dark—he looks behind him one more time—no one's around. Sure he hasn't been followed he opens the door, turns on the light, and shuts himself inside with relief. —Copyright 2007 Evan Nicholas

The opening description is pretty powerful and gives a sense of desperation and foreboding. The heat is almost a character in the film. When I started working on a specific look, I concentrated on portraying the heat through color. I went for a yellow, tobacco-filter feel. Yellow is often used to portray heat, though the reference is different with each culture. Spike Lee used the color yellow and other warm colors to portray the oppressive heat of the summer in his explosive and powerful film, *Do the Right Thing*.

The original image—a 2 K file from a RED camera down-converted to HD—is fairly well balanced though fairly low in contrast (Figure 8-30). Import the jacob_susannah.mov file from the Tutorial folder of the DVD. I'll be doing this correction in Apple

 Watch the video tutorial "Jacob_Susannah_looks" in the Video tutorials folder on the DVD.

Color, but this will be very straightforward, so following along in another application or plug-in should be easy.

Figure 8-30 Original image from Evan Nicholas's short, *Susannah.*

1. Watching an RGB Parade waveform display, set the black level and highlight levels of each color channel using the Advanced Tab of the Primary In room. If you want to, use the technique of isolating specific portions of the picture— like the deep black in the opened door or the white on the side of the air conditioner (the section just to the right of Jacob's shoulder, not the blown-out portion on the far right side) by zooming in to them in the Geometry room. If you are using another application, you can also do this by creating a crop or wipe or by zooming in using an effect. Create a nice rich black at the open door. The side of the air conditioner should definitely clip at 100%. My numbers and intermediate correction can be seen in Figures 8-31 and 8-32.

Figure 8-31 Intermediate correction, balancing the colors and spreading the tonal range; compare to Figure 8-30.

Figure 8-32 Data from the Advanced Tab of the Primary In room for the intermediate correction.

2. With the image balanced and the tonal ranges within normal levels, let's increase the tension of the image by increasing the contrast. I lowered the Master Lift to −0.046400. As a guide, in "focusing" this setting, I looked for a rich black in the open door but pulled back on how much the blacks were crushing when I started to lose detail in Jacob's hair. Also, when the darker, dirtier lower part of the door started to look crunchy I pulled back a bit.

3. After pulling down the blacks with the Master Lift, I noticed that the highlight levels in my RGB Parade waveform were no longer balanced, so I went into the Advanced Tab and raised the red and blue gain so that all three color channels peaked at 100%.

4. Play with the Master Gamma level in the Basic Tab to create a nice, punchy image that doesn't look too dark or too light. I set mine just a bit lower, increasing the contrast between the side of his face that is highlighted and the side that is shadowed.

5. Using the Color Balance wheels in the Primary In room, I left the shadows balanced. This is a common thing for colorists to do because if everything in the image is pushed the same direction, your eyes have a tendency to automatically "rewhite balance" the image. Leaving something that retains a true black or white helps the unbalanced colors really stand out. I pushed just a little yellow into the highlights and did most of the warming of the image with the midtones, which is where the majority of the image sits. When I warmed the midtones, the blacks looked too warm, so I actually ended up pushing the blacks slightly cool, making a nice color contrast with the rest of the image. Traditional artists—painters and illustrators—also often add blue to the shadows.

The final correction (Figure 8-33) feels much stronger than the original raw image. It has a sense of purpose. The data from the Primary In room for the final image is seen in Figure 8-34.

Punchy

 When referring to contrast and tone, punchy means a contrasty image where the image stands out. When used to describe color, it describes higher saturation with good color contrast.

Figure 8-33 The final grade makes the dry heat of the desert a palpable presence; compare to Figures 8-30 and 8-31.

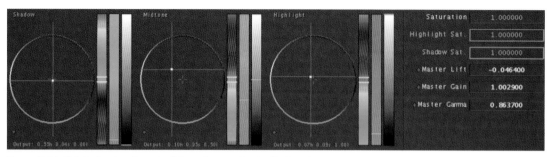

Figure 8-34 This is the data from the Primary In room for the final grade.

There are other stories and looks that could be tried and presented to a client. I thought that matching the distinctive look of *CSI: Miami* would be a good experiment for this image.

I spoke with the original director of photography for the first season of *CSI: Crime Scene Investigation*, Roy Wagner, ASC.

> *Mr. Bruckheimer wanted a more dynamic, more hip style. I chose to pursue the look in the negative to tape transfer. I steepened the gamma, concealing most of the middle values. I also pushed the pedestal until the grain structure was more visible. By making the gamma steeper, the color palette became more limited and more surreal. By over-lighting the highlights and by not using fill light, the film didn't have a chance of ever appearing normal.*
>
> *The color choices were based upon the golden tones of the hot Las Vegas desert and the Technicolor saturation of Las Vegas nightlife. The murder scenes were cold and green, making the event grizzlier, uncomfortable for the viewer.*
>
> *Frankly, the other intention was to create a look that was so striking that it would halt "channel surfers." Surfers don't stop on a channel because they hear a word that lures them. They are halted because something striking catches their eye. This is becoming a more prevalent requirement when creating a visual language for a new television series.*

So let's get started with the same image from the last tutorial, only this time making it look like a scene from *CSI: Miami.*

1. Balance the shot as we did for the first tutorial. You can copy and paste a previous grade or save and load a previous grade as a starting point for a variation of the grade. You could save and load the "tobacco" grade and then reset the Color Balance wheels to eliminate the "tobacco" color as a starting point.

2. As Wagner mentioned, we'll steepen the gamma by pushing the highlights up and really crushing the shadows. We'll also bury the midtones (lower the gamma), crushing the shadows even more. Notice that this increase in contrast

and lowering of the gamma has already resulted in higher saturation. Look at the colors of Jacob's shirt (Figures 8-35 and 8-36).

Figure 8-35 Intermediate correction with increased contrast.

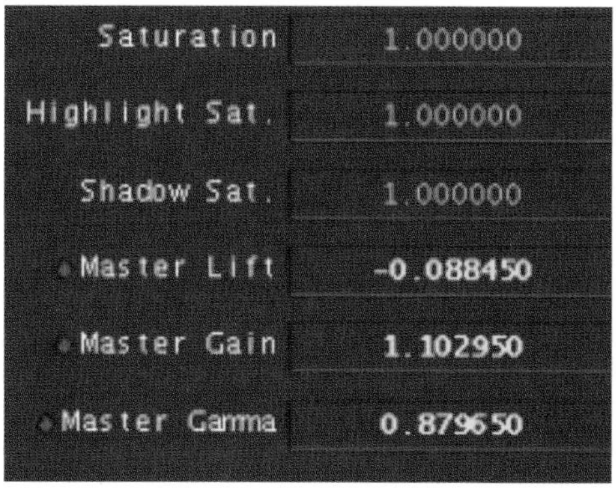

Saturation	1.000000
Highlight Sat.	1.000000
Shadow Sat.	1.000000
Master Lift	−0.088450
Master Gain	1.102950
Master Gamma	0.879650

Figure 8-36 Data from the Primary In room for intermediate correction.

3. Increase the saturation of the image even further. The objects in the scene are all fairly monochromatic, with the skin tones, wall, and door color all matching fairly closely. As we increase the saturation, we'll also be able to create more separation and color contrast between these colors, increasing the visual interest of the scene. I increased the overall saturation while decreasing the saturation of the highlights and shadows.

The final correction doesn't really tell the story of the original script, but it does convey the same look and feel of our target show, *CSI: Miami*, with its saturated colors and surreal, contrasty punch. The saturation on the printed page is definitely over the top, while the image on my video monitor is less saturated, especially in the skin tones (see Figures 8-37 and 8-38).

Saturation	2.670399
Highlight Sat.	0.601250
Shadow Sat.	0.355250
Master Lift	-0.088450
Master Gain	1.102950
Master Gamma	0.879650

Figure 8-37 The final "CSI" grade. The printed version here is much more saturated than the actual video monitor shows.

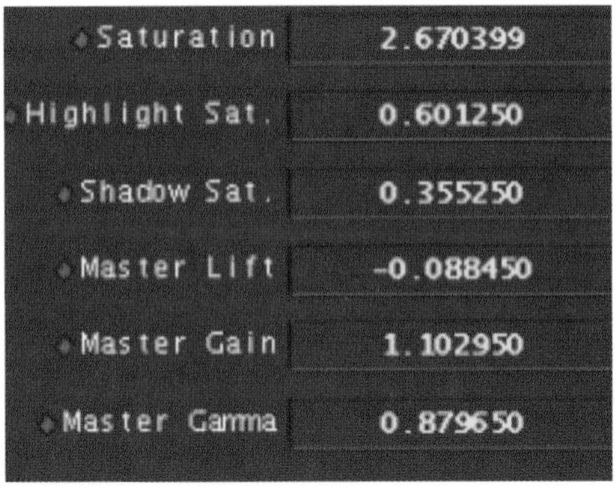

Figure 8-38 This is the data from the Primary In room for the final grade.

Let's do one more grade telling a different story with the same shot. This time we'll do a contrasty, desaturated, postapocalyptic feel.

1. Start by balancing your image and spreading the tonal range, like in the previous two examples. It's always good to start from this position so you're not fighting a color cast or tonal tendency from the original image.

2. With the image balanced, we want to remove most of the saturation from the image, especially in the shadows and the highlights. Then create some pretty extreme contrast by blowing out the highlights and crushing the blacks and pulling down the gammas. We are not looking to keep detail anywhere. Basically we want deep blacks, harsh whites, and very compressed midtones (see Figures 8-39 and 8-40).

Figure 8-39 This is the balanced image with crushed blacks, blown-out highlights, and reduced saturation.

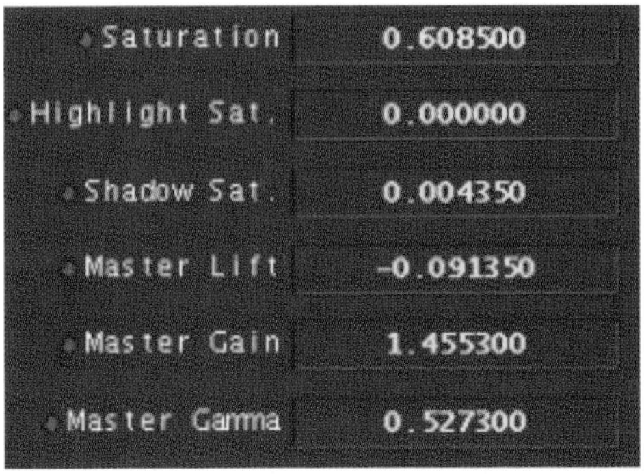

Saturation	0.608500
Highlight Sat.	0.000000
Shadow Sat.	0.004350
Master Lift	-0.091350
Master Gain	1.455300
Master Gamma	0.527300

Figure 8-40 This is the data from the Primary In room.

3. With the Color Balance wheels, take the midtones very blue-cyan. You can try going green-cyan if you want for a more twisted, sick look. I also pulled my highlights slightly in that direction, though when I went too far blue, the highlights seemed to get too harsh and unwatchable. I actually went slightly warm with the shadows to counterbalance the heavy blue of the rest of the image (see Figures 8-41 and 8-42).

Figure 8-41 This is the image with the color balance skewed toward blue.

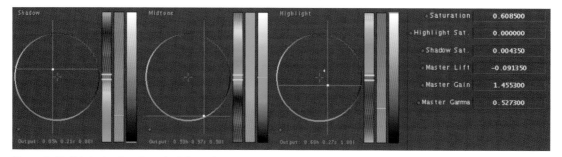

Figure 8-42 This is the data from the Primary In room.

4. Finally, the bright foreground wall and the highlights on the air conditioner are really distracting because of the amount of contrast that's been added, so let's go to the Secondary room and add a vignette that is tall and narrow and centered on Jacob. Then we'll pull down the highlights and the gamma on the outside of the vignette and also kill as much of the chroma as possible. This really centers the attention back on Jacob because he's the center of the bright area and has the most chroma (see Figures 8-43 and 8-44).

Now we've told three very different stories with three different looks applied to the same original image (see Figures 8-45 through 8-49).

Figure 8-43 Final correction with secondary vignette applied to darken and desaturate the sides of the image.

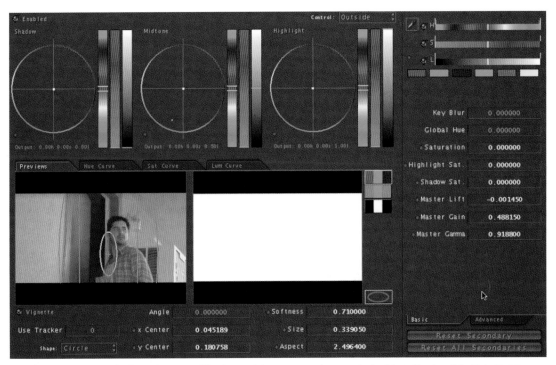

Figure 8-44 Data from the Secondary room. The shape of the matte can be seen in the Matte Preview Tab. Note that the Control pulldown at the top of the figure indicates that the correction is being applied to the outside of the matte.

Figure 8-45 Original raw image from RED 2 K to HD down-convert.

Figure 8-46 Tobacco version to indicate heat.

Figure 8-47 *CSI: Miami* version.

Figure 8-48 Postapocalyptic version. All images courtesy of director Evan Nicholas from his short, *Susannah*.

Other Cool Looks

There are tons of ways to make your footage just look cool. Most of those have to do with lots of experimentation with the tools that you have available to you. You can certainly create cool looks with just your Primary and Secondary tools.

Here's a quick experimentation with some footage of a band shot by veteran filmmaker Charles Vanderpool and telecined by Bono Labs, which has a service that transfers film footage directly to QuickTime movies and ships them out on a hard drive. Very cool for those that don't want to invest in HD videotape decks.

Figure 8-49 Original footage, courtesy of Charles Vanderpool at Vanderpool Films.

Watch the video tutorial "cool_looks" in the Video tutorials folder on the DVD.

Load up the band.mov shot from the Tutorials footage folder on the DVD (Figure 8-49). I'll be doing these corrections in Apple Color.

1. Balance the shot and spread the tonal range (Figure 8-50).
2. Qualify the skin tones using the eyedropper in the Secondary room and add a slight Key Blur to the matte.
3. Using the Control pulldown, choose to correct Outside the matte and crank up the contrast by crushing blacks and gammas and cranking up the Master Gain. Also, pull all of the saturation out with the Saturation, Highlight Sat, and Shadow Sat controls. This makes a very high contrast, stark black and white image. Then switch to control of the Inside of the matte and pull the saturation down on the skin tones so they're not quite so orange (Figures 8-51 and 8-52).

Figure 8-50 Results of Primary color correction before look is created.

Figure 8-51 Secondary correction creates a stark, high contrast black and white image of everything but the skin tones.

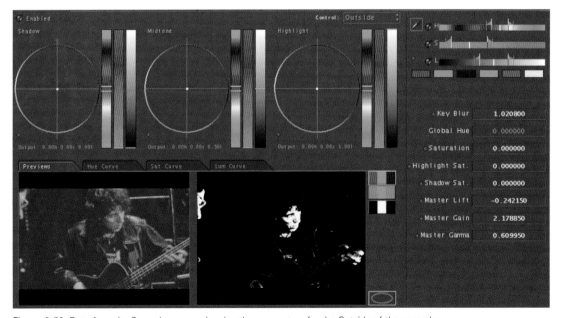

Figure 8-52 Data from the Secondary room showing the parameters for the Outside of the secondary.

Apple Color's Color FX Room

I could devote an entire book to just this one room. The possibilities are endless. For those readers that don't use Apple Color, many other applications have a host of plug-ins and effects filters that do similar things. I encourage you to try out different effects filters and experiment with their parameters. By combining the effects, you can come up with some truly original looks.

Let's quickly walk through some of what's possible in Apple Color. The Color FX room is a node-based or effects-tree or process-tree concept. Each effect can be combined and linked in many ways by means of a treelike graphic interface that doesn't simply stack effects like Final Cut Pro or Avid, but it works more like Shake.

Watch the video tutorials "Color FX room" and "ColorFXRoom_effect" in the Video tutorials folder on the DVD.

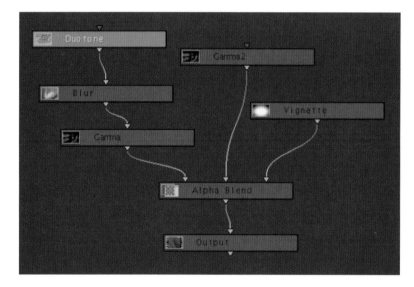

Figure 8-53 Color FX room effects tree showing how effects are linked graphically instead of simply stacked.

Apple Color's Color FX room is populated with quite a list of effects to get you started. Plus more and more vendors are coming out with additional plug-ins that work with Color. The first and best collection for Color is by Graeme Nattress (www.nattress.com). Not only does it include many useful effects, but the plug-ins also include many process trees that show interesting applications for the combination of the effects.

To create an interesting effect for our shot of the band, I'll show you the process tree and resulting image first then break down each "branch" of the tree and what it did. This won't be a tutorial as much as a simple explanation of what I did to create the look.

The process has three main branches that all lead into an Alpha Blend effect and then down into the Output node. The Alpha Blend effect combines or blends the two branches on the left

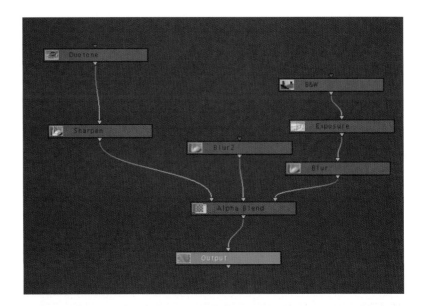

Figure 8-54 This is the effects process tree for the guitarist shot.

Figure 8-55 This is the resulting image from the effects process tree.

Figure 8-56 Duotone effect.

using the alpha channel (really a luminance matte) created by the branch on the right.

So let's go from top to bottom and left to right to explain how this effect works. At the top left is a duotone effect (Figure 8-56). If the effect has a little triangle above it, like duotone does, that means that the effect is actually being fed by the source footage coming from the Primary and Secondary rooms. This Duotone effect creates something similar to a black and white image, but instead of black and white, it uses two other colors that you can choose with parameters. In this effect, I used a bright yellow and a dark yellow, creating a sepia tone look.

Each effect can be linked to any other effect in the tree. In this case, the duotone feeds a Sharpen effect. I cranked up the sharpening until I could see grain and grit (Figure 8-57). The duotone/sharpen image feeds the Source 1 of the Alpha Blend effect. The

Source 1 side is revealed wherever Source 3 (the alpha channel) is black.

The next branch is simply a Blur effect (Figure 8-58). This blurred image feeds the Source 2 of the Alpha Blend effect. This source is revealed wherever Source 3 (the alpha channel) is white. You could make this a more interesting effect if you wanted. This is the part of the effect that makes the nice glow wherever a highlight is.

Figure 8-57 Sharpen effect added to Duotone effect.

Figure 8-58 A simple Blur effect on the original image.

The final branch of the tree starts with a B&W (black and white) effect. The B&W effect feeds in to an Exposure effect that allows me to control exactly how much of the image is black and how much is white. This is the effect that really controls how much of the first branch of the effect is blending into the second branch of the effect. The Exposure effect then feeds into another Blur effect to soften the way that the two branches would key into each other. The resulting alpha channel (Figure 8-59) feeds into the Alpha Blend effect and then to the Output node for compositing of the final image (Figure 8-60).

Figure 8-59 Alpha channel created by a Black and White (B&W) effect, fed into an Exposure effect, fed into a Blur effect.

Figure 8-60 Results of the final effect using the luminance of the original image to create glowing highlights on a sharpened duotone.

More Experiments

There's no reason to stop here. Find some images that you've come across recently that need some work. Take a few minutes to analyze what the image's deficiencies are. Figure out how to fix them. Use several different approaches. Learn which ones yield the best results for you or which ones are the best ones for certain problems.

Color correction is like any other skill. It must be practiced. Challenge yourself. Try to experiment when you don't have a client or when there is no deadline. If there's a tough image in a production that you don't have time to perfect in the course of your deadline, save it and experiment with it after the job is done. You need to have the freedom to experiment and make mistakes.

Color correction is like any other skill. It must be practiced.

Develop your eye by analyzing the images you see on TV and in the movies. How are they using color to affect your perception of a product, character, or moment in a story? Fashion magazines are always visually striking. How can you incorporate those looks into your next project? Save various images that appeal to you so that if you are having trouble communicating a look to your client, you can show them a range of possibilities. Often, the look they want will not be in your folder of clippings, but it can act as a springboard to start a fruitful discussion.

Good luck exploring this brave new world of color correction.

9

THE HISTORY AND ROLE OF THE COLORIST

As you probably understand by now, the intended audience for this book is not really the full-time pure colorist whose sole job every day is to grade images. The real audience is the vast majority of artists and technicians who have access to the great color correction technology that's available today but have much more on their plate than just grading. This book focuses on the editors, auteurs, directors of photography, compositors, and graphic artists who realize that the power to make their *footage* look better is a huge asset to making the entire *project* look better.

With that said though, when you set your main job aside to take on the role of colorist for a few hours, you really want to inhabit that role completely to do your best work. So this chapter gives a little backstory on the history of the job and the technology and presents a glimpse into the day-to-day life of what the colorist does beyond the button pushing and knob turning. In the first edition of this book, this chapter was the first chapter. To allow the reader to dive in to the nitty gritty of learning how to color correct, we moved this chapter to this spot, but in many ways, it's still where our story begins.

Figure 9-1 Modern telecine suite, Finish Editorial, Boston, Massachusetts. Courtesy Terry Lockhart.

To begin the discussion, colorist Mike Most (*NYPD Blue, LA Law*) explains the need for colorists:

> *It's the nature of film and or videotape that you can't just develop it and put it on a telecine in some automated way and make it look okay. I mean, somebody's gotta be at the controls, controlling balance and brightness and color and there's a whole bunch of reasons. But the basic fact of the matter is that it's not locked in. That's the beautiful thing about shooting film is that you have a lot of range and you can change it in post. That's one of the reasons why a lot of cameramen are loathe to go to HD video, because that range is severely cut down. And the nice thing about shooting film is that you can play it straight ahead and straight down the middle, or you can turn it into something special and that's where a colorist comes in. It's not just about balancing both sides of a scene. When things are shot single camera, they're not shot at the same time under exactly the same lights, you shoot one angle, you relight, you turn around you shoot the other angle, and those two things have to match. Even if you have the greatest cameraman in the world shooting tape, they're not gonna match perfectly. Somebody has to sit there and balance them. So that's where the colorist comes in.*

> **"You can play it straight ... down the middle, or you can turn it into something special and that's where a colorist comes in."—Mike Most**

Video-to-Video Color Correction

Twenty-five years ago, the term *colorist* did not exist. We lived in a world where what you shot was pretty much what you got. The only methods of adjusting color were primitive and coarse.

Video had a unique set of issues. Video cameras in the 1970s had indoor and outdoor filters and white balancing. All too often, the person behind the lens would use the wrong filter or forget to white balance. Some color cameras had monochrome viewfinders. Other viewfinders had color, but it wasn't a reference you could trust. As a result, the filter mismatch was a common issue. And fixing the problem was, as they say, like taking glue off of a cat. No matter what you did—fix it or leave it alone—you got a bad result.

The only common means of correcting video in a postproduction suite was with a time base corrector (TBC). The TBC controlled video brightness, black levels, hue, and saturation. There were no settings for midtones, individual color channels, or any other commonly used color correction parameters that we see today.

For those postproduction facilities that served the high-end clientele, video color correction was made available in the mid-

1970s. These controls, by today's standards, were quite primitive, and yet they had the ability to adjust the picture enough to correct for improper camera filtering with individual control over each color channel, but that was the extent of the control. The systems that were available at that time were considered to be revolutionary and at the same time, basic.

Video-to-video color correction wasn't particularly common or practical in the mid-1970s. The video signals were analog, measured by variable voltage. Creating a corrected master meant the loss of one generation of your original master. In most cases, the color correction was done during editing to prevent any further generational loss. The early correctional tools often generated more noise. There were no noise-canceling filters, no video-safe filters to regulate output, and the only analysis tools were a waveform, a vectorscope, and your eyes.

The biggest problem with early color correction was that it was not easy to recreate settings. Most, if not all, of the first-generation color correction systems had no memory or storage capacity. They could not use templates of previous setups. Although they used electronic manipulation, there was no computer control. As a result, one minor bump of a joystick could spell disaster.

Telecine Color Correction

Figure 9-2 State of the art da Vinci 4K Resolve, image courtesy of da Vinci Systems, LLC.

The modern telecine started out as what is now known as a *film chain*. The film chain was a camera pointed at a film projector, usually 16 mm. The film was projected directly into the camera lens. The signal from the camera was sent directly to a transmitter and was broadcast directly, or in some cases, transferred to videotape for later broadcast in one continuous pass. The camera on the film chain had some control over the amount of primary colors—red, green, and blue—as well as luminance and set-up values.

"All of this stuff is much more recent than people think it is."
—Mike Most

Aged film is hard to watch. The color and contrast fade. Much of the color has a magenta tone. As a result, film chain engineers could adjust the camera to compensate for these issues. By adjusting the color on the cameras, these engineers became the first colorists.

Years later, the telecine developed. The telecine actually is different from film chains in two key aspects. First, it has the ability to scan an image with a gas electron beam rather than by shining light through it. Because this beam does not generate the intense heat that old film chain lamps did, it was impossible to melt or burn the film with a telecine. Combined with a capstan-driven transport, the film in a telecine is handled gently enough so that even original negatives can be used in a transfer session. Another important development was that telecines use a method of synchronization to video so that the film passes through at a regular interval. Because film is 24 fps and NTSC video is (approximately) 30 fps, the telecine would hold each frame for a number of fields, based on a 2:3 ratio of film frames to video fields. This 2:3 pulldown, sometimes referred to as "3:2 pulldown," enabled a precise synchronization of the video images to the film. A simple film chain was not that precise; whatever passed through the projector went to the camera. There was no synchronization of the two devices.

Noted cinematographer Roy Wagner, ASC, remembers the early days of experimentation as film moved from the film chain to more sophisticated methods of transfer:

> My initial involvement with this was in the sixties with the EBR—electron beam recorder. I was in the Air Force, and we were doing studies with the electron beam recorder. We were doing it way before Rank was involved, at least commercially involved. When the C5 bomber came out we shot the first flight of the C5 with the electron beam recorder and also with 16 mm. I was, at that time, pretty ignorant about the process, and I was startled at the quality of the image.
>
> Then years later, when I was doing the very first Showtime project, which was called The Family Tree, we transferred on the Rank, which was a baby. It was the first one that I'm aware of in Los Angeles, which was at Compact Video. And I looked at the beam that they were using and said, "This looks awfully, awfully much like an electron beam recorder." And they started laughing and said, "This is (very much) like an electron beam recorder." It was a horrific experience, but what was exciting for me was that what I was seeing was significantly better going from the negative to tape than what I was seeing going with a film chain, which was what had been done before.

"What I was seeing was significantly better ... than what I was seeing going with a film chain."—Roy Wagner, ASC

Jim Barrett, senior colorist at Downstream Digital, has some similar recollections:

> *I entered into video postproduction while attending film school at Long Beach State University during the early 1980s. My first job was in mastering feature films for a company that made laserdiscs, the predecessor to the DVD format. We transferred films to video using the first device made at that time to create high-resolution video, a flying spot scanner by a company from England, Rank Cintel.*
>
> *The Rank, as it was called, would evolve during the next few years to find a permanent place in the process of how film shot for commercials would be transferred to broadcast quality video. I found myself in the unique situation of just starting a career path in video postproduction at the same time as a new technology was emerging. It wasn't long before I was threading film onto the Rank and sitting at the remote controls to set the brightness and color settings for a particular film. The controls at the time were very rudimentary, allowing an operator to merely brighten and darken a scene, add or subtract the overall chroma levels, and set a basic white balance. The goal was to merely make a positive video print from a film internegative. It was nothing more than an elaborate and sophisticated film chain.*

The Rank made film transfers to video possible. But one of its biggest features was its ability to handle film. The Rank was a scanner that was capstan driven, so it didn't have the jerky motion of a projector, which frequently could cause film breaks and melted film from hot projector bulbs. Jim Barrett remembers how it felt to be at the forefront of a revolution:

> *Up to this time, 1985, there was no device that would safely handle camera original negative film. You always had a print made by a film lab. Now that we could create the positive intermediate from the original film, video postproduction companies started the film to tape transfer process.*

Mike Most relates his early experiences with those first telecines:

> *I started on a Dubner system, which basically doesn't exist any longer. I was taught to run things basically on the fly. I had the joysticks in front of me and we'd transfer off of prints, which had basic timing (grading) built in.*
>
> *Most people use trackballs today, which is basically the same thing. Rank Cintels, which were the primary machine for many years, basically came with a control system called Color Grade. It was controlled by three joysticks. Basically it was the joystick for black, gamma, and gain and basically the direction of the joystick where you controlled*

balance, and there was a rotating center pot that controlled level. It was designed to run print on the fly at the BBC. That's who commissioned the design of the joystick panel.

The trackballs that are used today are exactly the same control. Rolling the trackball is the same as moving the joystick, and the outside ring is the same as the inside ring on a joystick. I think the trackballs are probably a little more exacting.

At the time, this was not a process that could be done with individual settings for each scene. Most continues:

I was responsible for running things on the fly for as long as I could and then stopping and taking an edit where I needed to pick it up. And that was how things were done. Computers came into the picture in the early 80s, and at that point we could start scene to scene programming. That's also when we started going off internegatives, and interpositives came in a little bit.

It all changed at that point because you were running original negative, you were doing it as dailies. A lot of things really changed then. And of course, dailies didn't require doing computers except for editing computers, which didn't come into the picture until the mid- to late-80s. All of this stuff is much more recent than people think it is.

From Color Corrector to Colorist

Over time, the controls for color correction, particularly with telecine, became more elaborate (Figure 9-3). As a result, the people associated with the task of correcting color—many of whom were video engineers—began to experiment with the controls, developing different looks or styles with film.

Figure 9-3 At the controls: A colorist manipulates a film with the da Vinci Renaissance 8:8:8 Color Correction System.

At first, it was more experimental, something to do between sessions. But in San Francisco, a director named Leslie Dektor had a novel idea. Jim Barrett recalls one of the first telecine sessions that produced a style rather than just correction:

> *Once the film was threaded up and you sat at the controls, it wasn't long before the more artistic commercial and music video directors figured out that they could have a multitude of "looks" and "treatments" from the same piece of film. I got to see this early on when I watched a colorist work with the commercial director Leslie Dektor. They took film footage from the streets of New York, put it on a Rank, made it dark with a heavy blue wash and created the Levi's 501 Blues campaign. Why would you take beautiful photography and mess it up? It seemed like a mistake. Weren't we supposed to be "color correcting?" That was the beauty of that moment. I finally understood what a colorist is and how pliable a piece of film can be.*

"I finally understood what a colorist is and how pliable a piece of film can be."—Jim Barrett

When it became clear that elements of style could be implemented through the use of modern color correction, the use of style became more widespread. Today, everything—television commercials, programs, and feature films—reflect the use of this modern technology. The role of colorist had clearly changed to color stylist.

A modern colorist has a wide range of sophisticated tools to create dazzling effects and to push the original camera negative further and further in the pursuit of an image that is truly unique and compelling.

Jim Barrett discusses the creative process of the colorist at Lucasfilm on *The Young Indiana Jones Chronicles*:

> *The most demanding job I ever had as a colorist was in taking over the colorist duties for the television series of* Young Indiana Jones *produced by George Lucas. I spent three years on this project, and to this day it was the most rewarding. The typical episode would have many layers that need to blend together. But it is the Lucas approach to the colorist's duties that was unusual. A normal session with a colorist will occur in real time.*
>
> *The colorist will manipulate the look of a film image and through a process of comparison and elimination get an approval from the client who is sitting with him. Not so with George Lucas. I was asked to spend some hours on an episode, unsupervised, for about a month's time with all of the layers and then sit for a screening. The screening would take place in a small living room setting with myself, George Lucas, an editor, and a producer or two seated on couches in front of a large screen television. We would watch the*

edited show that I had done color correction and scene-to-scene matching on. And with a yellow pad of paper and pen I would scribble notes in the darkened room whenever George Lucas would comment. "Too yellow." "Make that scene look like The Godfather.*" "That looks a little red." I remember thinking, "This guy knows a thing or two about technology, and here I am writing notes on a yellow pad." I would leave this screening with my notes and spend an additional 2 weeks on the changes, and we would have another screening. It was an unusual way to work but satisfying in that he didn't need to rush things. It was a very traditional approach in film where a "timed" trial print would be screened from the original negative. A film lab technician would take notes on the desired changes and make a new "answer" print that would incorporate those changes.*

With the growing power to manipulate the image comes the need to deliver a look that is not simply driven by what the technology will allow, but to use an artistic eye in manipulating the image.

Jim Barrett stresses the need for stylized skills for the successful colorist.

I like to look at fashion magazines for inspiration. Sometimes the style that they use is more important than the actual clothing. That's important to remember when you're working as a colorist. You don't wait for someone to suggest something when they come into the suite. You have to come up with a few ideas to get a reaction from the client. That way you can determine the direction they want to go. The image itself suggests what you might want to try to do with it. First I take a look at the image the way it was originally exposed. I store that in memory. You'll hear comments right away. Maybe they want to see more detail. So I'll adjust the detail. I'll try to introduce new looks. It's a great way to keep the session moving by getting a decision from the client. I'll show them something, and they'll say, "Hmmm." Then I'll change it, and they'll say, "Hey, that looks great!" So we'll run it that way. A lot of it is intuitive, based on your experience and exposure to different styles. With each film, it's a different approach. Even the same clients will approach each film differently.

Probably the best known colorist among other colorists is the legendary Bob Festa. It was probably Festa at the controls for the Levi's 501 commercial that Barrett witnessed. Festa agrees that one of the paths to greatness in color correction is finding inspiration outside of the color correction suite:

I think the most important thing is to absorb cultural influences. You kind of have to steal ideas from your cultural upbringings, whether it's art or culture.

Datacine and DI

Figure 9-4 Thomson Grass Valley Spirit 4K High-Performance Film Scanner and DataCine.

Today telecines have expanded their capability to what is known as a datacine. A datacine works much the same as telecine, with one major exception: Instead of transferring the image directly to a videotape that is limited to standard definition or high definition, the datacine has the ability to create large image files that are saved as pure data, similar to a frame from a digital still camera. This resolution is suitable for transfer back to film. The first of these datacines recorded at 2K resolution (2048 × 1080 or 2048 × 1556 for DPX, or Digital Picture Exchange file format).

Some datacines go beyond the 2K standard and produce 4K files (4096 × 2160) or even larger. The datacine scans the film image and transfers it through a high-speed parallel protocol interface (HIPPI), which records the scan in an image file. The images can be stored on drive arrays for transfer to a film recorder, which reads the image file and scans it back onto film.

Datacines are very popular these days, and as a result, colorists are busier than ever. The reason that filmmakers love datacines is simple: Using a datacine creates a highly manipulatable digital intermediate.

Figure 9-4a

Peter Mavromates, postproduction supervisor, *Panic Room*, speaks about DataCine:

> *One of my roles is discussing with the director and the DP what it is we're doing on this movie and how we're going to get there. And can we get it done with the time and money that we have? With* Panic Room, *David [Director David Fincher] wanted to do this digital intermediate process. So "Is that doable?" That's the first question. In building a comfort level that it is doable, one of the things I have to do is—at different parts of the process—say, "Well, let's do a test." Then I have to design that test. And to make it a valid test, we need to take it from point A to point B.*
>
> *In the case of this digital intermediate process it means, "Let's take some shots." In this case, we took some hair and*

*makeup tests, which are going to begin to reflect the condi-
tions of the movie, and did a film-out test. "Let's do a film-
out test at different places and see what we think about it."
But the film-out test is only partially valid. That only tells
us that in theory the process works. But is this process robust
enough to take it to a release print? So then we go to the
next step, and we take this negative and go do a release
print on it. We'll do an IP and then take a release print. And
then let's take it one more step and say is this photochemical IP as good as if we filmed out a digital IP? And then we
did that test, and we said, "It does look like we actually do
improve quality by doing a digital IP instead of doing a
digital negative and going photochemical from that point."
So my point is that part of my contribution is designing
and executing testing. Again, this is where David sort of gets
what he wants by having a post supervisor around.*

*In other movies the DPs have to coordinate those tests on
their own. By my doing it, I take some of the burden off the
camera department so that their energies are not going to
coordinating these things and the follow-through issues. So
they can concentrate on the artistic part of their job and
not get bogged down by having somebody produce those
things for them.*

*[Color correction is] one of those things that is valuable
so that when the person sitting down watching the movie
is watching the movie. They are not distracted by things
that they shouldn't be distracted by.*

Prior to the digital intermediate, an interpositive would be
created photochemically by a person called a color timer. The
color timer would adjust colors and exposure of a film. These
adjustments are referred to as *printer points.* You can still see the
remnants of this technology in many color correction applications
(Apple Color being one of them) that allow the colorist to specify
corrections in printer points. The main reason this terminology
has continued is because for a long time it was the common language with which directors of photography collaborated with the
negative timer or colorist.

For example, a director would tell the color timer, "Increase
brightness in scene 53 by two points," which meant that the
exposure was to go up by a set amount. Or, "Make it two points
redder." When these directions were given, the negative timer
would make a new print of the film from the interpositive,
changing the exposure of the film by the determined amount
during those scenes. The director, cinematographer, and timer
would not actually see the results until the film positive was
printed, developed, and projected. On simple theatrical trailers,
this was a process that took several hours. And because the corrections were done basically "blind" (you couldn't see the affect

of the exposure changes until after the film was printed) it was truly a matter of experience and experimentation that took many passes. When done, the new print was shown, and the director could readjust the film. Film editor Lisa Day recalls the process of color timing:

> *The first time through I would sit with the director, the DP, and the timer in the lab, and we would just run the film straight through, mostly commenting as we went. From that point, the timer knew where we were going, so the DP usually wouldn't have to come back to look at the answer print until we were finished.*
>
> *For the second run, I would look at the answer print and make notes with the timer without the director. We had to go over and over it again to get a good mix. For example, on* White Fang *it took several prints to get the snow the right color. Once the DP was happy with the snow color, the rest of the color sort of fell into place. Usually once the initial notes were made, the director and DP wouldn't screen the print until the timer got it to a point where I thought it was right. But that often took several prints.*

With datacine, the director sees the results on the screen as they are being graded. Also, instead of the gross adjustments of printer points, which basically only allowed rough adjustments of exposure and color balance, the entire toolkit of the modern color correction suite is open to the colorist and director, allowing the use of secondary color correction and highly finessed control of the full tonal range of the image.

When the film is electronically graded, the disk images are scanned back to 35 mm and projected. For the colorist, who works with the director to achieve the proper grading, it can be exciting. Julius Friede, senior colorist for *O Brother, Where Art Thou,* confirms:

> *Working on commercials or music videos, you often get to work with the director, but in traditional film mastering, the grading usually happens farther down the line, and the director (and DP) too often, unfortunately, have moved on to other projects. When they are involved, you get immediate feedback on what is desired by the people that are most intimately involved.*
>
> *Joel and Ethan Coen, along with Roger Deakins (the DP), knew what they wanted to see on screen, and I was the one that had to technically figure how to best achieve that. The closest I can claim to development is in preproduction discussions whereby it was determined that it was best to shoot without filtration or other production techniques so as to give the widest palette possible during grading.*

One of the issues with datacine transfer is the lack of real-time capability. Some datacines transfer at somewhat slower rates than the 24 fps norm. It is crucial for the colorist to see the film as it will appear when projected.

After the film is transferred by a datacine, it is possible to play back the created files from the disk array to a coloring station. This is known as phantom datacine because the scanner is not used. The colorist can play back from the disk array in real time with a phantom telecine and adjust the levels properly. Whether it be a telecine, datacine, phantom telecine, or a plug-in on a nonlinear editing system, the person in charge of such equipment today can be called a colorist. Colorists understand range, contrast, gamut, chromaticity, and luminance. They understand how much latitude they can expect from a given source, be it a particular film stock or a video camera.

Diplomacy and Client Skills

An often forgotten but most important trait of both colorists and editors is the art of diplomacy. Julius Friede comments:

> About the best tip I can give is to listen to your client and don't always assume that you know best (as hard as that is to imagine). Of course, you know your equipment better (I hope), but you can always learn something new. I can't even begin to list the times I scoffed (to myself) when I was asked by a client to try something, only to discover that he/she was right. Even if you prefer one setting or look over the client's preference, that is not necessarily better, just different. The big trick, in my opinion, is not to try and impose your own POV over the client's, but to enhance what the client is looking for, even if you would do it differently.

"The big trick, in my opinion, is not to try and impose your own POV over the client's."—Julius Friede

Bob Festa elaborates in his simple working method for collaborating successfully with his clients:

> I think that it wasn't so much techniques or tools that helped me communicate more with my clients, but I actually started listening. I would actually not say a damn word, but I would tell people, "Before we get started, tell me in 20 words or less what today's theme is going to be." And we might actually look at the work picture while we're doing that. I'd rather let them spill their guts for 20 words or 20 minutes and then turn around and deliver the goods, because then I have a good idea about what their perception is and what their ambitions are for the session. So if anything, I've become a good listener in my old age.

Also, you give them a choice. Work like an eye doctor. Show them A, B, or C and before you know it, you've worked your way into something that's really in focus. And not only have you listened to them, but you've shown them and they've made the decisions as you've worked your way down into it. After a while you get into a very close place. Then the brushstrokes become much more fine and more dynamic.

"Show them A, B, or C and before you know it, you've worked your way into something that's really in focus."
—Bob Festa

For Chris Pepperman, who is a colorist at NFL Films, client skills is a major reason why some colorists are so successful:

I'm one of those guys who verbally expresses or talks out loud what I'm doing. A lot of my clients actually like that because as I'm doing it, I'm talking my way through it and explaining to them what I'm doing, and that's a habit that I picked up very early in the business. I always found it to be a very good tool. I consider myself not to be a technical colorist.

There are two aspects to color correction. One is being able to emulate the aesthetic look or direction that the DP or director is expressing to you, and that's essentially your primary objective, right? That's what you want to do. Somebody comes in and they have a visual idea of what they want and you try to give them that. The other one is being able to have the "room savvy," and what I mean by that is being able to communicate effectively with the client. It's a personality thing. I try to be personable. That's one of my strong points why people like to come here. Not necessarily because I can take this thing apart and put it back together again, because I can't, but I think it's a combination of the two. You definitely have to have talent, technical-wise, to be able to interpret what they want visually. But you also have to have the personality to sit in a room with an "A" type personality or a "B" type personality, understand what they want, give it to them and all along keep them comfortable.

The Future

With the popularity of color correction on nonlinear systems, color correction—like video editing and desktop publishing—has truly become democratized. Consumers and professionals alike can benefit from the tools and skills of the colorist.

Mike Most comments on the changes in the role and capabilities of the colorist:

Figure 9-5 da Vinci Systems Impresario control panels. Image courtesy of da Vinci Systems, LLC.

Well it's gotten more exacting. It's turned into less of a finishing step and more of a collaboration step. I think colorists are brought into the loop a lot more, they're paid a lot more. The need for the job has changed. It's grown quite a bit. With the dawn of digital intermediates and things, clearly it's an extension of those same skills, and a lot of those skills are going to be put to a bigger use.

You may think that many veteran colorists are resistant to the kind of change in the industry that is happening with desktop color correction tools, but Festa is looking forward to the rapid changes taking place in the industry:

**"I think we're really witnessing the Avid-ization of telecine."
—Bob Festa**

I really think it's going to be an application like the Color app, where people are exposed to it on a fundamental, early level. The youngsters who are familiar with Final Cut ... today's runners or assistant editors, they're all familiar with Final Cut—maybe it'll seed the industry at an early age and these people will all be influenced early on that there's no reason to pay big money and spend an inordinate amount of time slinging film.

Frankly I'd rather have the flexibility and the speed to make contributions that are satisfying on a more artistic level (than with the old methods). The way I see it, I've only got so much patience left and I'd rather spend it color correcting something in context than threading film up.

I think we're really witnessing the Avid-ization of telecine, where hopefully color decisions and color correction as we know it can be a lot more interactive and face to face and project based as opposed to service bureau based. I mean, I've been doing this for a long time and we're charg-

ing x-thousands of dollars an hour, just as a traditional laboratory might. Quite frankly, I'd be much happier if I was working on a per project basis, face to face, much more interlocked with my client as opposed to just acting as a service bureau. I'm excited about the future, because I think that's what it's going to be.

10

VISION AND COLOR THEORY

The Science of Color

This chapter is designed to give you an understanding of some of the scientific and technical details of how color is recorded for video and perceived by our eyes. Originally this chapter was at the beginning of the book to give readers a basic understanding of these color concepts, but through in-depth discussions with dozens of skilled and experienced colorists over the years since the book was first released, the importance of the facts here to the day-to-day experience of color correction seems to be more secondary. However, the information provided in this chapter definitely helps inform judgments that the colorist must make and has an impact on some decisions or problems that a colorist may encounter, so we've kept this valuable information in the book but shifted it to the back of the book, allowing the reader to more quickly immerse themselves in the actual task of color correction.

It's All in Your Head

Light is emitted at different wavelengths; each length corresponds to a different color. The visible portion of the electromagnetic spectrum starts at wavelengths of around 380 nm (nanometers), generally perceived as violet, and continues to wavelengths around 700 nm, generally perceived as red. Any waves above and below that spectrum are unseen by the human eye. Still, they exist. In the model shown in Figure 10-1, the visible portion of the spectrum and adjacent waves are shown, but the visible portion is actually a very small part of the entire electromagnetic spectrum. It's easy to remember the color order of the visible spectrum by using a simple code: *Roy G. Biv* (red, orange, yellow, green, blue, indigo, violet). The code begins with the longer wavelengths and proceeds to the shortest wavelength, that is, violet. Another simple way of remembering the spectrum is: *Richard Of York Gave Battle In Vain.*

Figure 10-1 The electromagnetic spectrum.

Color is a sensation created by a combination of three factors: a source, a modifier, and a detector. Each one of these components must be properly working in concert to create the perception of color.

Source Light

The source of light can come from any light-emitting object. That is, any object that emits electromagnetic energy at 400–700 nm. The sun, a lightbulb, a flashlight, or a firefly—these are all sources of light. Sometimes the color of light is altered by the medium through which it travels. For example, the light of the sun is refracted somewhat as it travels through our atmosphere, or a the light from a lighting instrument on a set is altered when it passes through a colored filter.

Color Temperature

Any source that emits light has a color temperature. Color temperatures are measured in degrees kelvin. The kelvin scale is derived from astronomy. The observation of light emitted from a black body when heated determines its color temperature. As the black body is heated to varying temperatures, the color of light emitted changes.

At the lower end of the kelvin spectrum is red. The higher degrees of kelvin temperatures emit blue. Lava emits a very red light at 1200 K. Incandescent light, usually emitted by tungsten light bulbs, is a warm yellow at 2850–3200 K. The sun emits about 6500 kelvin. The light of the sun is bluish.

At the lower end of the kelvin spectrum is red. The higher degrees of kelvin temperatures emit blue.

There is no perfect, uniform, untainted, white source of light in the universe. The sun, which is used as a reference when adjusting images, is known to radiate at a certain color temperature. The average color temperature of the sun is 6500 K. But even this constant fluctuates, depending on variants including the earth's atmosphere, which can affect the color temperature of the sun before it reaches our eyes.

When we express the color temperature of light in degrees kelvin, the most accurate representation of a "pure" light source, aside from the sun, is any light source that radiates 6500 K, or D_{65}. When adjusting computer monitors, it's important to be sure their white points are set to correspond to this color temperature, or else all other factors of color correction will be inaccurate. Broadcast video systems are defined as having a D_{65} white point.

The color temperature of light can alter our perception of modifiers.

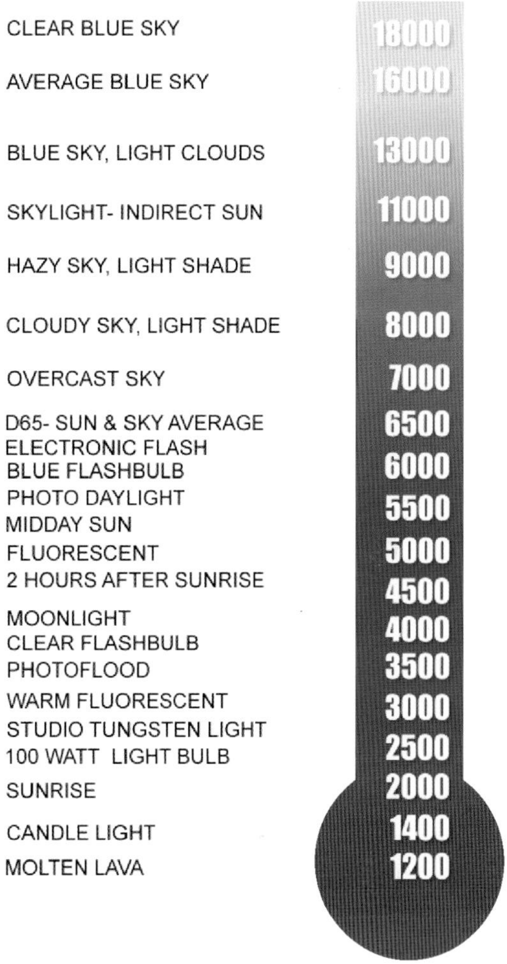

Modifiers

When light is emitted, it illuminates objects that can reflect (or transmit) and absorb different wavelengths of that light to varying degrees. These objects are called modifiers. When a modifier strongly reflects certain wavelengths of light, we perceive those reflected wavelengths to be the "color" of that object. For example, an orange tends to strongly reflect longer visible wavelengths and is generally seen as orange. A concord grape strongly reflects shorter visible wavelengths and is generally seen as purple.

Modifiers can also reflect and even emit some electromagnetic waves that are not visible to the naked eye. For example, infrared sensors and night vision scopes can pick up emitted infrared heat or waves from people, animals, and plants. And bugs with ultraviolet vision see plants in a completely different way than we do. Some plants even have specific color patterns that are only visible under ultraviolet light.

Modifiers can also absorb different wavelengths of light. The orange mentioned previously reflects relatively more of the longer visible wavelengths of light, but when illuminated by wide spec-

CLEAR BLUE SKY	18000
AVERAGE BLUE SKY	16000
BLUE SKY, LIGHT CLOUDS	13000
SKYLIGHT- INDIRECT SUN	11000
HAZY SKY, LIGHT SHADE	9000
CLOUDY SKY, LIGHT SHADE	8000
OVERCAST SKY	7000
D65- SUN & SKY AVERAGE	6500
ELECTRONIC FLASH BLUE FLASHBULB	6000
PHOTO DAYLIGHT	5500
MIDDAY SUN	
FLUORESCENT	5000
2 HOURS AFTER SUNRISE	4500
MOONLIGHT CLEAR FLASHBULB	4000
PHOTOFLOOD	3500
WARM FLUORESCENT	3000
STUDIO TUNGSTEN LIGHT	
100 WATT LIGHT BULB	2500
SUNRISE	2000
CANDLE LIGHT	1400
MOLTEN LAVA	1200

Figure 10-2 The different color temperatures of light. The scale is in degrees kelvin.

trum light, it also absorbs much of the light of shorter wavelengths, generally seen as purple or indigo, which you normally wouldn't perceive when looking at an orange.

The spectral reflectance of modifiers is especially important to the colorist.

The spectral reflectance of modifiers is especially important to the colorist because the spectral reflection can cause a phenomenon known as a *color cast*. Color casts affect the immediate area surrounding the modifier. When an orange is illuminated, other objects near it that are capable of absorbing or reflecting orange-colored light, in addition to their normal spectral reflectance of a shared light source, can change the perception of that color.

Detectors

The final component of color is the detector. In human beings, the detector is an interaction between our eyes and our brains. While the eye might be in perfect condition, our brain must correctly decipher the information received from the eye. It is known that babies cannot process all of the information that their eyes give their brains; thus they can become overloaded visually with too much information. The color sensation is encoded in the eye and decoded in the brain. Without the proper elements to encode this sensation and the ability to decode it, we would be (and many are) color blind, or partially so.

How Eyes Work

Your eyes are the only true detectors of the sensation of color. Other means of color and light detection are artificial, derived from measuring electromagnetic waves. Eyes are a sophisticated and accurate tool. They consist of two sensors that receive and encode the light reflected from or transmitted by the objects that you see. These sensors, located in the retina, are long in shape and are oriented so that they can determine pinpoint direction of a light source and adjust to different viewing conditions. Incoming electromagnetic waves are detected by these sensors and sent to your optic nerve, which takes them to the brain for deciphering.

Rods

The first of these detectors are the rods. Human beings have approximately 130 million rods in each retina. Because they do not discriminate color, we could say that they detect brightness information only.

The rods in your eye are located on the outside edge of an area of the retina, the center of which is populated by cones, which detect color. Because of this, you might notice that your perception of color detail in your peripheral vision is poorer than it is in your central field of view.

Cones

Cones come in three different varieties that are either red, green, or blue sensitive. But it isn't quite that simple, as you can see in Figure 10-3. Red cones can be achromatic, like rods, and also red-green and yellow sensitive. Blue cones can be achromatic and blue-yellow sensitive. Green cones can be achromatic, red-green, and yellow sensitive. You'll also notice that the yellow-only channel is a subchannel of the blue-yellow channel. So light that enters your eyes as a continuous spectrum are converted to two channels of chrominance (blue-yellow and red-green) and one channel of luminance (achromatic). This method of visual perception is emulated in color video systems as we will see later on. Cones are located in the fovea, the center of your retina, adjacent to the optic nerve. The fovea is the region where highest resolution is perceived. Consequently, color detection is difficult within our peripheral vision. In darkness, when detecting color is nearly impossible, the rods and cones work together to try to compensate, improving our peripheral vision somewhat.

We have far more sensitivity to variations in luminance than we do variations in hue and saturation.

Your eyes have many more rods than cones—there are only 7 million cones in each retina compared to 130 million rods. Thus we have far more sensitivity to variations in luminance than we do variations in hue and saturation. This comes into play when we determine the best methods of sampling color in video systems. Eyes are far more sensitive to variations in luminance than they are to hue or saturation differences.

Cone Resolution

Eyes have a different response to the varying wavelengths of color that we see. While our eyes are sensitive to all colors, some colors are not as resolved as others. The eye has little ability to detect high resolution in the color blue.

The reason for this is simple and related to the ratio of green and red cones to blue cones. Along the periphery of the fovea, the ratio of red and green cones to blue cones is 14:1. As we enter the center of the fovea, the ratio can increase by as much as 20:1.

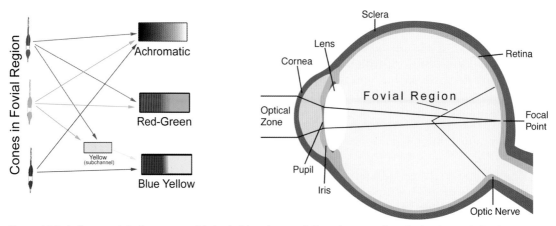

Figure 10-3 A diagram of the human eye with the fovial region noted. Note that cones have both achromatic (luminance detection) abilities as well as color information. The two color channels are red-green and blue-yellow, with an additional subchannel of yellows. Cones are in the fovial region of the eye, while rods are on the periphery, making color detection difficult within our peripheral vision. In darkness, when chromatic detection is near impossible, the rods and cones work together to try to compensate, making our peripheral vision somewhat better in darkness.

Thus, our eyes do not perceive enough blue physically to obtain as much resolution from it, compared to red and green.

As a result, we have a tendency to see blues as less resolved or even fuzzy. To prevent this phenomenon from hindering our ability to perceive higher resolutions of red and green, the eye has a blue filter on top of the fovea called the macula lutea. The macula lutea blocks any blue light from green receptors in particular, which perceive some blue light. By blocking blue light in the center of the fovea, the macula lutea enables us to perceive high definition in reds and greens without blue interference.

Try focusing on the two blocks in Figure 10-4 for about 20 seconds. Note that after a while they both appear to be fuzzy. Our visual system cannot perceive higher resolution blue. As a result, your vision adapts, and you perceive both blocks as being fuzzy.

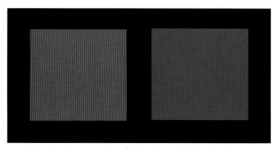

Figure 10-4 Blue and red blocks.

The Two Kinds of Vision

Our eyes, like most organs in our bodies, have the ability to adapt. Significant changes take place in our visual system when adapting from light to dark situations. These two conditions result in physiological responses from our visual system, providing us with two different types of sight:
- Photopic (where light is plentiful)
- Scotopic (where light is scarce)

Photopic Vision

Under well-lit conditions, our eyes use cones as primary receptors. As mentioned previously, cones have the ability to detect brightness as well as color information. With photopic vision, the cones receive plentiful color information. We have excellent visual acuity because these cones, located in the fovea, are at the center of our retinas.

Scotopic Vision

Scotopic vision, or night vision, uses rods as our primary receptors. During these dark or near-dark conditions, our ability to see color is absent. Cones are not used in scotopic vision, which prevents the perception of color. Another interesting fact is that scotopic vision is less *defined* because the foveal region of the retina is unused, thus the center receptors are not active, preventing visual acuity. Bob Sliga's tip in the "Day for Night" tutorial concerning defocusing highlights is based on this biological response.

Perception

It is impossible to discuss color without perception. Perceptual phenomena can alter the way in which we think and even feel about color images. For purposes of definition, we have divided perception into three categories:
- Color dynamics
- Cultural adaptation
- Viewing environment

Color Dynamics

Colors can stimulate, excite, calm, depress, increase your appetite or thirst, and create an external feeling of warmness or coolness. The science of how color affects us is called color dynamics.

The Luscher Test

In 1947 Max Luscher, a Swiss psychologist, developed a color test using colored chips. The patient would lay the chips in order, depending on their preference. Luscher developed methods of interpreting the patient's state of mind (and thus, required therapies) by interpreting the chips.

Many of Luscher's observations were already commonly used (red and yellow are warm colors; blue and green are cool colors). This also opened the door to interpretation by corporate marketing and advertising executives, as well as the development of light and color therapies.

Color for Advertising and Marketing

For a marketer or advertiser, the Luscher test gives some insight into how our minds react to color. For example, red is widely known to excite or agitate us, to keep us moving. Yellow, to which the human visual system is particularly sensitive, excites us. And what are the two most popular colors for fast food restaurants? Red and yellow, of course.

Hot and Cold Colors

There are some studies that relate to our reactions to color. Red can convey danger and risk taking. It was proven that people take bigger risks when exposed to red light for a period of time. As a result, casinos are full of red light. It has also been proven that, when exposed to red light for long periods of time, our blood pressure rises.

Alfred Hitchcock knew this when he inserted frames of red into the motion picture *Marnie*. By adding the red frames, Hitchcock tried to excite the audience during key scenes. Other directors, such as David Lynch and Federico Fellini, use reds frequently to foreshadow tension. The viewer can be made to feel uncomfortable during a scene but not know why.

Alfred Hitchcock inserted frames of red into Marnie *to excite the audience.*

Hues of blue and green, on the other hand, tend to calm and relax us. A person's blood pressure drops when cooler colors bombard the visual system. Hospitals use greens and blues to calm us. Greens and blues have a tendency to relax us, make us stick around for a while. Blue can be a good color for bookstores and other places where we're encouraged to browse. Cool colors are also popular with corporate interiors to keep the excitement to a minimum. These colors also have a tendency of making us feel colder physically.

One company had received complaints from employees that the temperature in the cafeteria was too cold. Employees were wearing sweaters and coats when going to lunch. The plant manager made temperature readings in various parts of the building and found no detectable difference in temperature between the cafeteria and any other office on the premises. A color expert was brought in to consult, and the walls of the cafeteria were repainted from the original mint green to peach. The employee complaints ceased.

Color and Depth Perception

One of the important discoveries about perception and color has a definite application in color correction: Warm colors appear closer than cool colors. For example, using warm colors in the foreground of a picture and cool colors in the background enhances depth, a trick that many cinematographers and art directors use. Figure 10-5 shows two pictures, one with a warm foreground and a cool background, the other with the same foreground but a warm background. Why does the picture with the cool background appear to have slightly more depth?

Figure 10-5 (a and b) Sense of depth is determined by color.

Color and Culture

Color also has different meanings for different cultures. In fact, some cultures do not have words for all of the colors in the color wheel. Traditionally, the Japanese used a single word for the colors blue and green. Imagine sitting at a stoplight and being told that the light is blue! However, in recent years, more descriptive terms of color have been added to the language.

While some cultures don't use all the spectrum colors by name, many reserve certain colors for purposes of reverence, joy, sadness, and other emotions. In many cases, they differ from western tradition.

Also, the cultural references to even such basic things as warm and cold colors can be different. When I wrote *The Art and Technique of Digital Color Correction*, I spoke with director of photography David Mullen, ASC, who is sometimes asked to accent certain emotions with specific colors. For him it's not about dwelling on preconceived notions of how we perceive colors but in imposing a structure on the film using a "code" of colors that is specific to that film only:

> *Generally there are certain cultural associations like warmth for passion or coldness for badness or isolation or something like that. It's not always true. I've read interviews with directors from northern Europe who feel that cold colors are pleasant and relaxing and warm colors are aggressive and disturbing. I remember once reading in an interview with I think Ingmar Bergman and John Borman that they find hard sunlight to be very disturbing. So the opening screen in* The Wild Strawberries *is set in this bright, dead sunlight, and it was actually shot in the middle of the night in northern Sweden where they have those endless days, so the light is very strange because it's bright and sunny, and yet the streets are empty.*

"Directors from northern Europe feel that cold colors are pleasant and relaxing and warm colors are aggressive and disturbing."—David Mullen, ASC

> *So not everyone associates sunlight with happiness and overcast with sadness. Similarly, you can pick a symbolic style for the film in terms of color and contrast and as long as you clue the audience as to what your symbolism means … I mean it's sort of like a code, when someone comes up with a code in the spy business, they also have to come up with a key to break that code so the person at the other end can decipher that code. So you can decide that red symbolizes something or blue symbolizes something, and as long as the audience is told in the beginning what that structure is, they sort of accept it for the rest of the film.*

> *When you look at* Little Buddha *[cinematographer Vittorio] Storaro has all of the scenes in Seattle in very cold, blue/gray colors, and wherever possible he tries to have the scenes set at twilight with deep blue light out the windows. So there's always a blue accent in the frame somewhere. And all of the scenes in Tibet are very golden.*

Viewing Environment

Much of how we perceive color is based upon the environment in which we see it. The relationship between colorimetry and the appearance of color in a viewing environment is affected by image luminance levels, surround types, and adaptive white points.

> ***Much of how we perceive color is based upon the environment in which we see it.***

The colorist must determine the environment in which the audience will be viewing his or her work. If the finished program is going to be viewed on a computer or video monitor, there are many considerations to take into account. The colorist can be sure of two things:

- The finished program will not always be viewed in ideal conditions.
- No two viewing environments will be exactly the same.

Image Luminance Levels

Image luminance levels are also affected by *flare*—extraneous light that reflects off of the monitor faceplate or from some other source into the viewer's eye. If you've ever tried to work on a PC outside on a sunny day, you have experienced an intolerable amount of flare firsthand. While there are glare reflectors that can reduce flare, they also reduce the luminance of the viewed image. As a result, the picture will not be seen in the best possible manner.

But flare can exist in most any environment. Where light and reflection are present, flare is present. So how can you adjust for flare when setting up your working environment?

Figure 10-6 shows an example of indirect light in a color correction suite. The indirect light came from a specialized dimmer of colored fluorescents that maintained a constant color temperature of 6500 K. The background used to reflect the indirect light was of textured neutral colored fabric to disperse the light evenly but indirectly over the working area.

Adaptive White Point
Color stimulus that an observer— adapted to a set of viewing conditions— would judge to be perfectly achromatic and white.

Figure **10-6** Color correction suite with indirect lighting.

Adaptive White Points and Chromatic Adaptation

Look around you and determine what colors you see. If you're in a white room, take a look at the walls. Are they really white? Chances are, you've adapted from what *truly is* white to what *should be* white. If the room is illuminated by tungsten light, notice that the walls probably appear yellowish. If the light in the room is fluorescent, the walls may be tinted slightly green or green-yellow. Our ability to adapt to different light sources is guided by what is known as *chromatic adaptation*. In a sense, the human visual system white balances itself to allow us to perceive the correct colors in most environments.

> **The human visual system white balances itself to allow us to perceive the correct colors in most environments.**

Whenever we are placed in a situation where the lighting doesn't provide correct white color, no matter how extreme, our visual system will adapt toward that color of light and try to determine which elements that surround us are achromatic. As a result, we mentally adapt and use that adaptive white point as a reference subconsciously, seeing it as an achromatic source.

If a viewer is surrounded by a light blue cubicle, the amount of reflected blue light would be significant, so much so that any references of white would probably have some color cast of blue. This would ultimately lead to the viewer's eyes being somewhat desensitized to lower wavelength blues. As a result, a subtle blue color in the environment could appear to the viewer as neutral.

Thomas Madden, Eastman Kodak's color scientist, explains:

> *A given color stimulus presented under different viewing conditions will likely result in different color appearances. In an imaging system, input devices are "looking" at these stimuli, not human observers. Devices are not subject to the adaptive effects our visual systems are. An instrument or device sensing a given color stimulus presented under different conditions would confirm the stimuli to be equivalent (which they are!). A human observer, on the other hand, would view those stimuli in each condition and perceive them to be different (which is their correct perception!).*

The colorist's suite often has an item known as a reference spot. It can be framed on the wall or on a table. A source of light at 6500 K is cast on the spot area. The reference spot is not only good for adapting to the right white point, it also serves as a tool to use for placing colored objects or swatches for reference. If the director shows you a color or a picture that he or she wants as an overall tone to a scene, you can place it on the reference spot and look at it while matching the colors on the screen.

Surround Types

As we discussed in Chapter 2, another perception issue deals with the environment around the monitor. Perhaps the biggest advantage of going to the theater is that the image is so large that it is difficult to be distracted. In addition to the image size, a dark movie theater offers little if any visual references, so our visual adaptation is focused on the projected image, not surrounding stimuli.

But in the case of computers and televisions, we are bombarded with color and luminance information that surrounds the medium. The brightness and color of the image surround can affect our perception of the viewed image. For example, a darker surround gives us the perception that the image has lower luminance contrast than would be perceived if the image were viewed under lighter surround conditions. Thomas Madden clarifies the point:

> *The adaptive white point for dark-surround images will depend on a number of factors, including the degree to which the image fills the observer's field of view, the luminance of the image, and the fact that an observer adapts somewhat to the image itself in this viewing condition.*

In Figure 10-7 we see how surrounds interact with a neutral gray. In this figure, the gray dot is identical in every square, but the surrounds create an illusion that causes the viewer to believe that each dot is of a different luminance. As the surrounds grow darker, the dot appears to be brighter.

As the surrounds grow darker, the dot appears to be brighter.

Figure 10-7 Different shades of gray surround five circles that are all the same shade of gray. Yet our perception is that the circles have different luminances because of the surrounding shade.

Additive and Subtractive Color

Putting the biology and psychology of our vision aside, it helps to understand additional principles when doing color correction. Among them are the science and art of color reproduction.

There are two methods of reproducing colors: additive and subtractive. Color produced by video monitors and projectors are generated using three additive primary colors of red, green, and blue (or RGB) light. In some cases, these devices use optic splitting devices—prisms—that create separate images corresponding to each channel of red, green, and blue light in the picture. As a result, a separate monochromatic image of each of these primary colors is generated. The light of the combined image is detected by your eye, and the colors are recreated in your brain. When we use additive methods, we start with black, combining light of the primary colors red, green, and blue. When added in the right combination, these three colors can create white.

Inks, dyes, or pigments subtract light by using three subtractive primary colors. These colors are cyan, magenta, and yellow. Subtractive color works on the principle that a support material (a white piece of paper, for example) has colorants added to it, absorbing light of different wavelengths. So subtractive color starts with white, which is selectively filtered by the colorants.

When combined in the right formulation, the subtractive primaries can create black. A problem with subtractive inks, dyes, and pigments is that they are inherently impure, that is, they do not absorb light of only one primary color. Instead of a black, they can sometimes create a murky dark brown when combined. To remedy this, an additional black colorant is usually added to the subtractive process, so the colors are referred to as CMYK, where K represents black.

Although it may seem strange, the medium of film is actually a subtractive process. By combining different dyes, the print is created. One of Kodak's color scientists, Thomas Madden, explains the advantages and disadvantages of video and film gamuts:

> Since a video display works additively, it can do a good job of making certain saturated colors of high lightness because as more primary-colored light is added, the lightness of the color increases. Film, on the other hand, is good at producing dark, saturated colors because as more colored dye is added, the lightness of the color decreases. Depending on the particular video and film systems, there, of course, will be a volume of colors where the video display and film gamuts intersect, and there are other regions of color where one gamut may exceed the other.

This distinction in the strengths and weaknesses of film versus video is actually one of the important reasons why colorists are needed in the transfer process from one medium to the other.

Color Spaces

How do we define a specific color or family of colors? Scientists have been working on this problem for years. In 1633, Sir Isaac Newton was quarantined at home and could not return to Cambridge for the entire year because the plague was sweeping across Europe. To cure his boredom, he cut holes in his curtains and conducted experiments with light using a prism. Newton discovered that white light was comprised of a spectrum of colors at pure wavelengths. His experiments resulted in the invention of the color wheel, which is much like the color picker used on some computers. The color wheel defined the spectrum of light as a continuous 360° circle with complementary colors opposed at 180° from each other. While this may seem to be common knowledge today, remember that in Newton's day, scientists were working more through observation and had fewer proven facts. Note that rainbows have no magenta color in them. They are composed only of those colors found in the spectrum. The combination of red and violet, which are at opposite ends of the rainbow, are not displayed. Thus, Newton had to find the missing link to complete the color wheel (see Figure 10-8). He completed the wheel with the addition of magenta.

Space versus Gamut— What's the Difference?

A color space is a universally agreed upon description of color. There are two different kinds of color spaces: device dependent and stimulus dependent. But these color spaces only define the descriptions of the space, not the color variations within them.

> *A lot of people incorrectly use the term* color space *when referring to a color gamut.*

A lot of people incorrectly use the term *color space* when referring to a color gamut and *color gamut* when referring to a color space. The two are ideologically different but can be easily confused. When we say that a color space is a universally agreed upon description of color, we mean that it is just that—a description, usually mathematical. Color gamuts, however, are the actual colors or variations of color contained in that space.

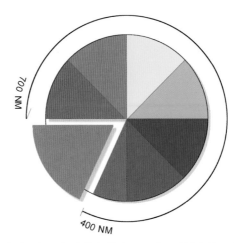

Figure 10-8 Newton's color wheel. Note that magenta, which bridges the spectrum boundaries of red and violet, is inserted.

A color space can be defined as a three-dimensional representation of a theoretical space defining the color coordinates of that space. It can be defined in density, units of measurement, headroom and footroom parameters, and so on. It broadly represents all of the colors within a given space. What it does not show are the color differences within the space. That is the definition of the gamut. When referring to color, 9 times out of 10, we are referring to the range of color variation within the space, or gamut.

Stimulus-Specific Color Space

In 1931, the Commission Internationale de l'Eclairage (CIE)— or International Commission on Illumination, an organization responsible for international recommendations for photometry and colorimetry—recommended a mathematically defined Standard Colorimetric Observer for characterizing the trichromatic characteristics of color stimuli. It should be noted that the CIE color spaces do not emulate adaptive states of our visual system or take into account any psychological processes.

The CIE Standard Colorimetric Observer resulted from a survey of human observers who were given sample colors and asked to match them with red, green, and blue light sources. As a result, the XYZ color space was derived where colors are described in terms of the amounts of the three primaries—denoted X, Y, and Z—that would combine additively to produce a visual match.

Device-Dependent Color Space

A device-dependent color space is determined by any device that reproduces color within a predefined color gamut. The color space determined by a device in theory would be the same as any other similar device. Although we could say that in today's world, many devices reproduce color accurately, many factors relating to each individual device determine how accurate the reproduction will be.

Perhaps you have attempted to create an image on your computer screen that, when printed, looked entirely different than when it was previewed on your monitor. This is a common problem with device-dependent color. The color variations and specific gamut that can be reproduced by the device are entirely dependent on the device itself.

> **The color variations . . . that can be reproduced by the device are entirely dependent on the device itself.**

To solve this problem, device vendors have created color management modules or color profiles. Many of these modules are in use on computers without the user being aware of it. The modules provide translations between peripheral devices to ensure some accuracies in color reproduction between those devices. These can include video cameras, printers, scanners, and monitors.

Video Color Spaces

Video cameras are all device specific. A film camera is not device specific, but the medium, a certain film stock, is specific in terms of its spectral sensitivity and other imaging characteristics. So, for example, when we color correct YCbCr-component digital video in an RGB nonlinear editing system, some complicated processes are taking place. The camera, not the monitor, dictates the gamut of the image.

The monitor must reproduce it as faithfully as possible. But when switching between color spaces, the gamut is remapped from one to the other, based upon their predefined equivalents. In some cases, one color space may have the exact same color in its gamut, but it will not necessarily be remapped to that color. So when you switch from one color space to another (in this case, YCbCr to RGB), what happens?

Thomas Madden explains:

> *Well, strange things can happen if you're not careful. Artifacts such as changes in hue or objectionable lightness or chroma can occur. If the color gamut of your starting colors is much greater than that of your output device or medium, you must decide what to do with the starting colors your*

output device is not capable of reproducing. That technique is called gamut mapping. *There's quite a bit of research going on, trying to find preferred ways of doing this. It boils down to what trade-offs are you willing to make in choosing an achievable output color to substitute for the original out-of-gamut color. If it is desirable, for example, to maintain the original color's hue, then compromises in chroma and lightness must be determined, which result in a least-objectionable substitute color displayable by the smaller gamut. The exact trade-offs in hue, lightness, and chroma will likely depend on the disparity between the two gamuts. There may well be different trade-off mappings in different areas of the gamuts depending on the disparity in each area. The topic of gamut mapping is as at least as much art as it is science.*

Some color information generally is irretrievably lost when mapping colors from a larger gamut into a smaller gamut. When colors are brought into the smaller gamut space, there is no way of knowing, without some form of tagging, whether a color value was originally in the intersection of the two gamuts (brought in without alteration) or if the color value is a substitute for an original color that was beyond the smaller gamut.

"Some color information generally is irretrievably lost when mapping colors from a larger gamut into a smaller gamut."— Thomas Madden, Kodak color scientist

The Y Factor

More relevant to the discussions of general color spaces is the specific knowledge of how video deconstructs and then recombines color components to reproduce color. This is stuff to kind of keep in the back of your head, but for the most part it is information that is "way under the hood" and not really necessary for understanding color correction.

Video signals generally come in two flavors:
- Composite, which consists of a single signal
- Component, which consists of two or more individual components of the picture

When discussing the differences between device-dependent color spaces, it's important to note that some terms used are general, and others are more specific. The letter Y is used to denote the presence of luma, or a quantity of luminance in the picture. Because we're using additive colors, the Y signal is computed from a weighted sum of the red, green, and blue color primaries as follows:

$$Y = 0.3R + 0.59G + 0.11B$$

So the "recipe" for luma would be approximately one part blue to three parts red to six parts green. Now that we've defined luma or Y, let's take a look at some of the various color spaces used for video and discuss their differences.

Y, R-Y, B-Y

Y, R-Y, B-Y is an encoding and decoding signal used for PAL and NTSC component analog and digital video. The subcategories for this signal would be YPbPr and YCbCr, which are mentioned later in this section on page 256. The Y, R-Y, B-Y components are encoded by these formulae:

$$Y = 0.3R + 0.59G + 0.11B$$

$$R\text{-}Y = 0.7R - 0.59G - 0.11B$$

$$B\text{-}Y = 0.89B - 0.59G - 0.3R$$

Note that R-Y and B-Y are color-difference channels, where the difference of Y in the encoded signal is subtracted from each channel, and the rest of the R and B channels is added in each, respectively. The remaining 0.41 of the green signal is combined through a combination of the color-difference channels.

YUV (Y,U,V)

YUV consists of the luminance and color-difference channels used in PAL and NTSC systems. The components are actually Y, R-Y, and B-Y, the same as previously mentioned. But in composite NTSC, PAL, and S-video signals, the R-Y and B-Y are scaled down so that the combination of these signals is within the range of $-\frac{1}{3}$ to $+\frac{4}{3}$. These limits are due to limitations of composite signal recording and transmission. Note that YUV, while containing separate components, is actually an intermediary for composite signals, not a component signal. This is frequently misunderstood.

YCbCr

The International Telecommunication Union (ITU) makes recommendations for universally accepted standards for the video community. ITU's recommendation for encoding digital component video signals is ITU-R 601 BT. This document recommends use of YCbCr. YCbCr is essentially the same as the general term Y, R-Y, B-Y.

However, there are some differences. The specified range for YCbCr is based on values between 0 and 255, where 16 is the normal unit measure for video black and 235 is the normal unit measure for video white. So the range of the color and luminance channels is limited by headroom and footroom based on these values. Therefore, the excursion of this color space, defined in terms of steps or units from black to white, could be said to be 224 (255 – 16 – 15). But in the case of YCbCr, the excursion of the luminance channel, Y, is specified to be 219 rather than 224 units. As a result, the YCbCr specification differs somewhat from the more general Y, R-Y, B-Y color space.

YPbPr

YPbPr is very similar to the values expressed in YCbCr, with two major exceptions. The YPbPr color space is used for analog, not digital, video. The other exception is that each channel of YPbPr has the same excursion. Because it is an analog signal, YPbPr is measured in millivolts (mV), where video black is 0 mV and white is 700 mV. Each color-difference channel has a signal between –350 and +350 mV, half the bandwidth as the Y signal. YPbPr is also used in the ITU-R 601 BT standard for high-definition video, although different luma coefficients are used.

YIQ

The YIQ color space is very similar to YUV. It is an intermediary of components used to form a composite analog or digital signal. The YIQ space differs from YUV in that its color-difference channels lie in a different area than YUV. Scientists discovered that the human visual system has less visual acuity in magenta-to-green transitions than it does for red-to-cyan transitions. As a result, when the U and V color channels from a YUV signal were shifted 123° on a vectorscope, the Q color channel could be more heavily filtered than the I channel, and the results would be almost imperceptible to a normal television viewer. YIQ was developed in 1953 for use in component analog video (CAV) using NTSC systems.

Bit Depth

Now that we've analyzed color spaces used in encoding video signals, let's look at the concept of bit depth and how it can vastly improve the overall image. The quality of a video signal is determined by a number of factors. These can include the format, signal type (analog or digital), and whether the signal is divided into components. Contouring is affected by one significant factor called *bit depth*. Bit depth describes the number of bits used to encode each channel—luma and color differences—of the video signal. The higher the bit depth, the finer the definitions of color are encoded in the signal. Higher bit depth is always desirable for improving signal quality, though it also increases the processing speeds and storage requirements needed for recording and playback.

The ITU-R 601 BT recommends a bit depth of at least eight bits per channel, with the option of using 10. There is quite a difference between these two sampling rates. For example, let's consider an NTSC component video signal digitized with 8-bit samples for each component channel of the video at 13.5 MHz. This is a fairly common video signal. In this case, a YCbCr image (digital component video) has each channel (luma, R-Y, and B-Y) digitized at eight bits (256 levels per channel), and the reading of the luma or Y component is taken 13.5 million times per second.

Beyond the 8-Bit Standard

Some video production and postproduction equipment goes well beyond the 8-bit rate, allowing for a better overall picture. This is particularly good in cases where the signal is processed through several different sequential pieces of equipment and is switched from digital to analog frequently.

By maintaining, for example, a 10-bit sampling, there are 1024 individual levels per channel—four times the number of levels using 8-bit sampling. Ten-bit sampling is also excellent for use as an intermediary in signal processing, where processing can reduce the number of signal levels. Starting with 10 bits of information makes it possible to push the image further in color correction without compromising the quality of the signal.

Another advantage of 10-bit sampling is that the picture will always be better when it can be presented in a 10-bit mode. In some cases, such as multimedia presentations, 10-bit signals can be maintained from production through display. That's when the color differences are really spectacular.

The performance capabilities of 10-bit color are staggering when compared to 8-bit sampling. For example, the use of 10 bits can increase signal-to-noise ratios fourfold compared to that of an 8-bit signal because it has four times the number of discrete values. The number of discrete values is especially important in the darker regions of the picture, where most of the noise is generated. As a result, there is a potential increase in signal to noise of as much as 8–12 db.

The performance capabilities of 10-bit color are staggering when compared to 8-bit sampling.

By virtue of the greater number of discrete values, 10-bit sampling reduces signal artifacts, particularly in areas that vary slightly in brightness. For example, a picture of a bright sky with a slight variation from left to right might cause *contouring*. Contouring occurs when quantized data is converted to an image that looks much like a contoured geographical map. The artifacts of contouring are frequently referred to as *quantizing errors*. In such cases, an 8-bit image displays rounding errors where the image data passes from one value to the next. But each value in a 10-bit signal is one-fourth as large as that of an 8-bit signal. Thus, the discrete steps are finer, resulting in a smoother-appearing image.

Figure 10-9 reveals some of these differences. The 8-bit picture on the left is exactly the same as the 10-bit picture to the right, with the exception of the sampling. There are more contours or *banding* visible in the 8-bit picture. Why is this so? Because there are more potential color values, that is, more levels in a 10-bit picture. Thus, the changes in color from pixel to pixel are finer in the 10-bit picture, making the image changes appear more gradual. Without 10-bit encoding, the picture might not be acceptable for use. This can also be said for situations where pixels in an image are so closely related in value that the image appears posterized. This can happen frequently in 8-bit images, depending on their subsampling ratios described later in this chapter. It is important for the colorist to remember that each tweak in the color of images with lower bit depth produces a greater change overall in the pixel values.

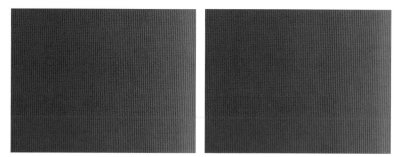

Figure 10-9 (a and b) An 8-bit image versus a 10-bit image. The 10-bit image appears to be smoother because it has four times the number of discrete values as the 8-bit image.

Perhaps the biggest advantage of 10-bit imaging (and beyond, when possible) is that the finer increments between discrete values allows for greater flexibility in contrast and gamma control for the colorist. As a result, there is more control of the picture, with the possibility for greater contrast, brightness, and blacks in the picture and a greater ability to "push" the picture beyond its current look.

Subsampling

One of the biggest challenges in the development of video formats is the issue of bandwidth. The videotape revolution began with 2-inch reels of videotape, which were loaded onto huge VTRs. Then came the portable camera and deck combinations of the 1970s. Now much of our footage can be captured with a DV or HDV camera onto a very small mini-DV cassette or even memory chips. With each evolutionary reduction in media size, issues of bandwidth continue to grow. How can you send a normal video signal to such a small medium without reducing some of the information originally captured by the camera head?

The answer is that you cannot. As a result, subsampling was introduced into video signals. Subsampling defines the ratio of samples taken for each component in the video signal, that is, Y, R-Y, and B-Y.

The reduction of samples in color-difference channels of component video was a result of the observation by scientists that the human visual system has much more luminance acuity than chrominance acuity. (As mentioned previously, there are many more luma-detecting rods in our retinas than color-detecting cones.) By reducing the sampling rate in the chrominance components of the image, significant bandwidth can be saved. The result? To the human eye, there is very little difference.

Subsampling is not the same thing as compression.

Each format uses a single subsampling method. It's important to note that subsampling is not the same thing as compression. Compression works by averaging or consolidating pertinent information, throwing away unnecessary data that takes up space.

Compression can be:

- Lossy, where some original image information is lost, or
- Lossless, where information is consolidated and the unnecessary data is thrown out, but the original image can be exactly reconstructed

So when someone refers to an image as "compressed," it isn't always a bad thing. Subsampling works by sampling the luma channel and the two color-difference channels at a predefined ratio. For example, in expressing a subsampling ratio, we could say that for every four samples of luma, there will be two samples of chroma for each color channel. The sampling ratio is in direct relationship to a sampling frequency. Earlier in the chapter, we defined an 8-bit image as having a sampling frequency of 13.5 MHz, which is the ITU-R 601 BT recommendation. So in the case of a 4:2:2 sampling ratio, we could say that the color-difference channels are sampled at 6.75 MHz, half that of the Y sampling ratio of 13.5 MHz.

The notation used in the subsampling ratio is not only indicative of color difference to luma channel ratios but also that of horizontal and vertical subsampling. Thus, a 4:2:0 subsample would have four samples of luma, two horizontal samples of R-Y and R-B, and 0 samples of R-Y and B-Y vertically. In other words, the color-difference channels would sample every other line, effectively.

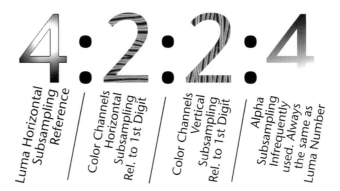

Figure 10-10 Diagram of a subsampling ratio.

Figure 10-10 shows a diagram of subsampling ratio. A subsampling ratio can consist of four numbers, with the fourth number indicating an alpha or key channel. The fourth number is always the same as the luma sample and is used infrequently. The ratio of the second and third coefficient is for both color channels, divided into horizontal then vertical sampling of the image.

The most common professional subsample is 4:2:2, where for every four pixels of luma (with green signal encoded) we sample two pixels of red minus luma and two pixels of blue minus luma. The diagram in Figure 10-10 shows how this is done. Examples of formats that use 4:2:2 subsampling are: Digital-S, BetaSP, D-1, DVCPRO50, Digital Betacam, and D5.

Other formats use 4:1:1 subsampling, where for every four samples of luma, there is one pixel of R-Y and one pixel of B-Y both horizontally and vertically. Even at this rate of subsampling, the picture may be acceptable for broadcast in some regions. The only major limitation is that it is nearly impossible to chroma key with 4:1:1 color because the subsampling limits the ability to consistently key out even the most evenly lit color background. Examples of formats that use 4:1:1 subsampling are: NTSC DV, DVCAM, and DVCPRO. PAL DV uses 4:2:0 subsampling, where for every four samples of luma, two samples of each color-difference channel are sampled horizontally on every other line. Again, the subsampling notation indicates horizontal and vertical sampling and not a ratio for each individual color-difference channel.

11

BUILT-IN SOFTWARE AND PLUG-IN CAPABILITIES

As the popularity and importance of color correction grows, more and more vendors are getting color correction products into the market or beefing up the capabilities of the products that are already there. Despite the rapidly changing and expanding marketplace, this chapter will provide an explanation of color correction capabilities for some of the most popular desktop products and platforms. We'll leave the "big iron" products out of the discussion for now and focus just on products under $10,000.

We'll start with the built-in capabilities of some of the most popular editing applications and then cover some of the plug-ins that also have specialized color correction tools. We'll primarily focus on the specific tools that help you utilize the information in the first couple of chapters. We'll stay away from filters that provide preset looks because that pushes the boundary between color correction and effects work.

Adobe Premiere and After Effects

Adobe Premiere offers a nice array of color correction tools built in to the basic software. Premiere and After Effects both ship with versions of Synthetic Aperture's Color Finesse, which is a very powerful, dedicated color correction plug-in and probably the Adobe user's best choice for serious color correction. (See the Color Finesse heading later in this chapter for more on Color Finesse's capabilities.)

In addition to using Color Finesse, Premiere and After Effects both have other color correction effects. In Premiere these are in Effects > Video Effects. There are three folders with subcategories of effects that are applicable to color correction: Adjust, Color Correction, and Image Control (Figure 11-1).

Most of the effects in the **Adjust** folder are automatic effects. Though there are times when using these may be appropriate or

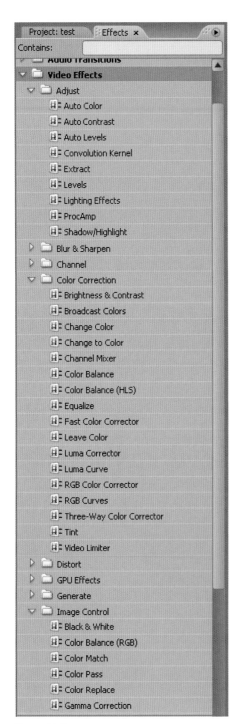

Figure 11-1

helpful under tight deadlines, I won't discuss them in more depth here because they're basically "drag and drop" solutions.

- **Extract** is basically for creating black and white images, with nice control over contrast and exposure.
- **Levels** is similar to the histogram solutions described in the Primary section of the book.
- **ProcAmp** is basically just the kind of control you'd get from a time base corrector (TBC), so I wouldn't advise using it.
- **Shadow/Highlight** allows you to even out an image that has a strong backlight, pulling up the shadows and reducing the highlights.

  The **Color Correction** folder has most of the effects you'll want to access.

- **Brightness and Contrast** don't give you enough control, which this book is all about, so stay away from that.
- **Broadcast Colors** is basically a broadcast limiter that helps keep your video legal.
- **Change Color, Change to Color**, and **Leave Color** are all variations of one another. Essentially they all do secondary color correction. They allow you to choose a color or color range in your image and either change it to another color or change everything else to black and white.
- **Channel Mixer** is a powerful tool but is not very intuitive or easy to use for beginners. It allows you to change the percentages of various channels or to swap them with other channels that are within—or even outside of—their own color spaces (for example, swapping the red channel for the Pb channel or the green channel for the luminance channel). This is useful when you have a severely damaged color channel because you can swap it for another less damaged channel. This obviously will change the color of the image quite radically, but you can fix the color differences with another effect.
- **Color Balance** is similar to the RGB Color Corrector effect, but I think that the RGB Color Corrector effect is superior to this in terms of functionality, so I'd use that instead of Color Balance.
- **Color Balance (HLS)** is basically like the ProcAmp effect and only provides very rudimentary control.
- **Equalize** is a gimmicky automatic effect to even out your pictures.

- **Color Corrector** is good for a quickie correction. It's similar to FCP's Color Corrector effect. It's a single color wheel with sliders for blacks, mids, highlights, and saturation.
- **Luma Corrector** is a powerful tool. It includes the ability to do secondary color correction qualification and to set your tonal ranges.
- **Luma Curve** is limited in its functionality compared to what you can do with RGB Curves, so I'd use that instead.
- **RGB Color Corrector** is basically like the Advanced Tab in the Primary room of Apple Color. It allows you to address specific tonal ranges of each color channel. This is an important effect. Like a few other Premiere color correction effects, it includes the ability to do secondary color correction qualification and to set your tonal ranges.
- **RGB Curves** is similar to the Curves controls available in Color's Primary In room and in Avid. Some people love to do their corrections with this tool. This is good to use while watching RGB Parade waveforms.
- **Three-Way Color Corrector** is similar to the Color Balance wheels in Final Cut Pro and Color and to Avid's Hue Offset wheels. This is an important set of controls for color correction (Figure 11-2).
- **Video Limiter** is another broadcast-safe limiter to ensure legal levels on output.

The **Image Control** folder has a few additional effects, but these are mainly poor versions of effects that are in the Adjust and Color Correction folders. I have the feeling that this folder is a "legacy" folder that was left in place so that long-time Premiere users will know where certain effects are. In any case, the effects in this folder are:

- **Black and White:** This effect has no controls. Use Extract instead.
- **Color Balance (RGB):** This is limited to overall levels for each color channel instead of allowing control over each tonal range. Use RGB Color Corrector instead.
- **Color Match:** This allows you to match colors. You can use this to try

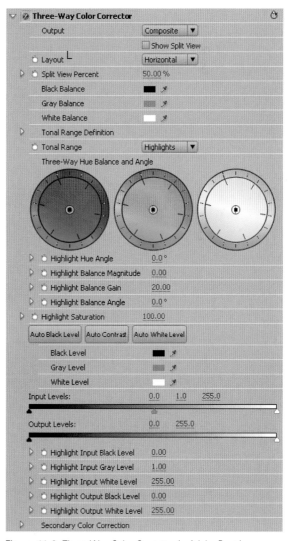

Figure 11-2 Three-Way Color Corrector in Adobe Premiere.

to match shots or colors, but hopefully you've learned enough at this point that you can do a better job than this effect by a little hands-on effort.

- **Color Pass** and **Color Replace:** These are variations of **Change Color, Change to Color**, and **Leave Color**. Essentially they all do secondary color correction. They allow you to choose a color or color range in your image and either change it to another color or change everything else to black and white.
- **Gamma Correction:** This provides a single slider to adjust gamma. Try another tool instead, like the Luma Corrector.

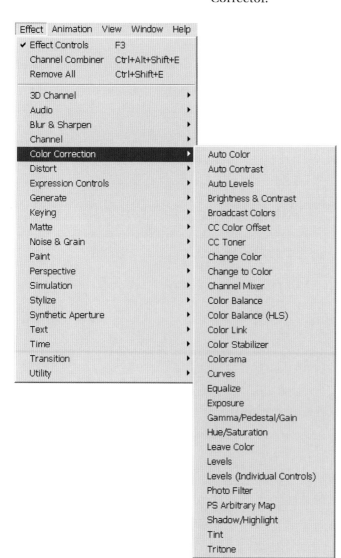

Figure 11-3 Adobe After Effects Color Correction menu.

The effects for color correction in Adobe After Effects are a little more centrally located (see Figure 11-3). These are all the same as the effects just described for Premiere. Adobe tries—whenever possible—to have similar user interfaces and effects between all of its products to make it easier to transition between them. Some of the differences in effects are due to the nature of After Effects as an animation and motion design tool, so even though the effects are in the color correction menu, they're really more design tools, like Color Link, which allows you to colorize a layer based on the average color of the pixels from another layer. That's not really applicable in color correction. There are a few effects that are different between the two applications though:

- **Color Stabilizer** helps to reduce flicker and luminance changes between frames.
- **Exposure** is not really designed for video images, though it does give excellent controls over tonal range and color.
- **Gamma/Pedestal/Gain** is similar to Premiere's RGB Color Corrector effect.
- **Levels (Individual Controls)** has histogram controls for each color channel and the master level.

- **Photo Filter** allows you to add a filter—similar to a glass filter placed over a lens when taking a picture—to add an overall color to the image.
- **Tint** is similar to Photo Filter without all of the preset colors.
- **Tritone** provides controls to break the image down into three distinct color palettes. This is a cool, graphic-looking effect.

Additionally, as of CS3, Adobe Photoshop has the ability to deal with video, and all of its powerful image processing tools can be used to do color correction. Video can be imported, turned into Smart Objects, and manipulated just like a still image.

Avid

Since the introduction of Avid Xpress Pro 3.5, Avid has ported a good deal of the power of their excellent color correction mode from Avid Symphony down into the rest of the Avid line, including Adrenaline and Media Composer. These are accessed from the Toolset menu. By clicking on **Color Correction**, the entire UI reconfigures to a new set of tools specifically designed to put all of the color correction tools you need in one place. The two main tabs are HSL and Curves. In the HSL tab are two more tabs. One is called Controls, and one is called Hue Offsets.

Controls offers the basic TBC controls, Hue, Saturation, Brightness, Contrast, and Clipping controls. There are also color matching controls that allow you to sample colors from reference frames to match colors from scene to scene. I never use the controls in this tab except for Saturation. Instead, use the controls in the Hue Offset tab.

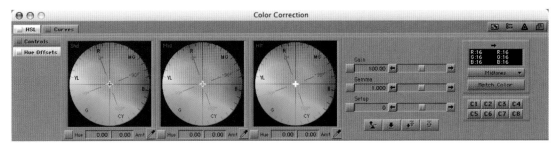

Figure 11-4 Avid Color Correction mode HSL Hue Offset Wheels tab.

The Hue Offsets tab (Figure 11-4) includes three Hue Offset wheels, one for each luminance range, but none for overall Hue Offset. Additionally, it includes controls for gain, gamma, and setup. Also on this tab is another set of color matching controls.

For quick fixes, this is the tab where you can get the most done with the least work.

In the Curves tab, there are four different curves, one for each primary color plus a master curve. There is also another set of color matching controls. The color matching controls on each tab offer a slightly different capability, especially the one in the Curves tab, which provides a function called Natural Match. All of these tabs have buttons called Color Buckets that allow the user to save various setups for quick recall and reuse from shot to shot.

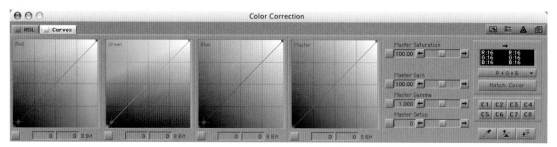

Figure 11-5 Avid Color Correction mode Curves tab.

In addition to the easily accessible Buckets, an unlimited number of corrections can be saved in a bin. These corrections can then be named and used from the bin, like any Avid effect, by dragging and dropping. The naming convention for color corrections is usually to name it after the clip that it corrected, but it can also be a simple description of what the correction does, such as "crushed blacks, cool gamma" or "Kurtis blue fix."

Color

Apple Color has been discussed in pretty thorough depth throughout this book. This application—for Mac only—is a very deep application that has a very thorough toolset organized into rooms, which would be referred to as Tabs in just about any other application. The rooms include:

- **Setup Room:** This room is for general settings and project management including the ability to save entire grades including all of the settings in all of the rooms.
- **Primary In Room:** This room is where the main Primary color correction is done using numerous sliders, color wheels, numerical entries, and Curves.

- **Secondary Room:** This room allows for qualification of eight different secondaries plus the ability to correct inside and outside of each of those qualifications. Vignettes and custom-user shape masks can be applied.
- **Color FX Room:** This room lets colorists apply numerous effects and plug-ins to the image and connect them in unique and complex ways in a user interface known as a process or effects tree. If you want to do selective defocus effects—a common color correction task—this is the room for the chore.
- **Primary Out Room:** This room is identical to the Primary In room except that it allows you to add additional corrections to a shot without altering the initial correction. And, because the rooms feed into one another, the Primary Out room is "downstream" of the Secondary and Color FX rooms, so it allows you to add corrections after the image has gone through those rooms. It also has additional limiting or "ceiling" functions for keeping your video legal.
- **Geometry Room:** This room allows you to rescale, recompose, and change the tilt of shots. As has been pointed out in a few tutorials, this can be useful to zoom all the way in on a certain portion of the picture so that it is the only thing fed to the scopes.
- **Still Store Room:** This room allows you to save and compare corrections on the same shot or to match colors between shots. Parameters allow for various wipes or to cut back and forth between shots.
- **Render Queue Room:** The final stop in Color is the Render Queue. This is the room that controls the output of Color and the return of the corrected material to Final Cut Pro or some other output.

Color Finesse

Synthetic Aperture is everywhere. It is a powerful standalone application for color correction, similar to Apple Color, but it is also a plug-in for Final Cut, After Effects, and Premiere, among others (Figure 11-6). It has many useful features that make it an excellent tool, even when used as a plug-in to applications that already have substantial color correction horsepower. One reason for using Color Finesse within these apps is that you can execute all your corrections with a single filter.

Color Finesse has a very complete range of tools with which to inspect and analyze the footage. There are software waveform and vectorscopes built into Color Finesse. Sampling colors with an eyedropper is an excellent way to analyze your footage. Color Finesse

Figure 11-6 Color Finesse's basic UI. More tools are accessible through numerous tabs.

provides this common feature and adds the ability to choose a single pixel or an averaged sample from a 3×3 pixel area, a 5×5 pixel area, or a 9×9 pixel area. Another nice feature is the Reference Gallery, which allows you to have access to a list of images that can be used as references for matching colors from one shot to the next. They are available across all projects, which is very convenient. You can use this feature for clients who have approved a certain color for their products or a certain skin tone for talent. (This stuff happens, believe me!) When it has been approved for one project, you can then match that color for any other projects. Matching skin tones from one scene to the next is as easy as clicking with an eyedropper using Color Finesse's Color Matching feature. This is a great thing for people looking for more automated corrections. You can also use the eyedropper in the Curves tab to set white balance, black balance, and gray balance. This is a quick and intuitive way to get rid of color casts and to set basic levels.

For more hands-on specific, manual control of your image, there are a wide range of choices that closely match the capability of Avid Symphony. There are Hue Offset wheels, Levels, and Curves, in addition to the standard HSL controls. All of these controls can be applied to specific luminance ranges of the picture, providing excellent control.

Final Cut Pro

Internally, Final Cut Pro provides most of its color correction effects through the Effects Menu > Video Filters > Color Correction path. The main tools that you'll access from here are the Color Corrector and 3-Way Color Corrector (Figure 11-7). FCP also offers a set of scopes, including a histogram and parade waveform, which are accessed through the Windows > VidScopes. These scopes can be arranged in various configurations and, best of all, can be expanded to full-screen size. There are also color correction options in the Effects Menu > Video Filters > Image Control path, which was the main path for color correction before FCP version 3.

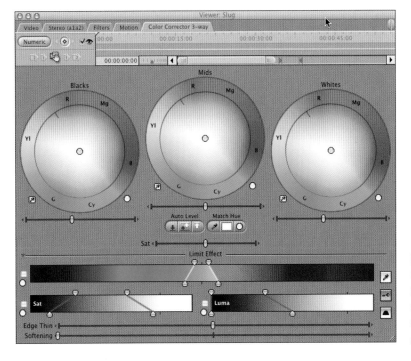

Figure 11-7 Final Cut Pro 3-Way Color Correction effect. The Limit Effect controls at the bottom are revealed by spinning down the small triangle at the bottom left side of the effect window.

Under Image Control, Brightness and Contrast there are simple sliders for general control across the entire image. Color Balance provides sliders for R, G, and B levels for highlights, midtones, and shadows. Gamma/Pedestal/Gain provides sliders for gamma, pedestal, and gain in each of the color channels. Also, Levels provides sliders for master RGB and individual R, G, and B color channels with control similar to that of an editable histogram. Finally, the Proc Amp controls give the basic TBC-like controls that many editors are used to: Setup, Video, Chroma, and Phase.

Plug-Ins

In the first edition of this book, plug-ins were much more important because editing software was just beginning to provide the capabilities that the plug-ins allowed. Plug-ins still allow some functionality not provided by the color correction tools built in to the software. Plug-ins can also help make a more effortless transition between editing or compositing applications by using a color correction application that works as a plug-in in both applications.

Boris

Boris offers a number of color correction options in addition to the 3D effects for which Boris is best known. It allows brightness and contrast control and master RGB color controls. It also offers basic TBC control through the Color Correction filter and Gamma Control filters. Boris also has a set of plug-ins called Boris Continuum Complete, which includes a color correction plug-in that provides brightness, contrast, hue, saturation, output black, and output white controls. Also, the Pixelchooser gives many options for applying secondary-like qualifications to very specific portions of the picture based on a list of matte-generating features, as well as the ability to selectively mix the correction back with the original image.

Digital Film Tools

Digital Film Tools' Composite Suite offers basic HSL (hue/saturation/luminance) control plus sliders for gamma and overall RGB sliders. Additionally, there are RGB sliders for shadows, midtones, and highlights as well as a feature called Flash Amount. This is terminology borrowed from cinematography and describes the optical process of brightening and lowering the contrast of an image by flashing it with light. Basically, Flash Amount just adds a simple tint to the image and is done by choosing a color with an eyedropper or RGB sliders. Digital Film Tools' full Composite Suite package provides these color correction capabilities. They also have a color correction only package called Composite Suite Color Correct.

GenArts

GenArts' Sapphire package also has some color correction capabilities. Sapphire does not put all of its color-related controls together in one effect, so you must stack several individual effects to have full control. For creating interesting looks, Sapphire does have a lot of options for blending effects in unique ways.

Noise Industries Color Correction Effects

Noise Industries has several color correction effects as part of an extensive collection of effects (Figure 11-8). These include Vignettes, Bleach Bypass, Color Temperature, Day for Night, Filmic, and others.

The Advanced Vignette allows similar functionality to the Vignette tool in Apple Color without having to leave Final Cut Pro. Bleach Bypass lets you create the classic film process look in post-production with parameters that control the contrast and gamma and provide a couple of preset looks.

Red Giant Magic Bullet Colorista

The basic Colorista effect is so similar to the color correction controls in Final Cut, Avid, and Premiere that there's not much I can say to recommend it because it seems to work slower than the built-in effects of those applications, but if you want to experiment with some of the techniques in this book that use the individual sliders for each tonal range of each color channel and your application (FCP or Avid) doesn't have them, then the Colorista (sliders) effect is just what you need. It's similar to the Advanced Tab of the Primary In room of Apple Color.

3Prong

3Prong's color correction offering for Avid AVX, ColorFiX provides lots of control for isolating colors and luminance ranges. It also allows the image to be re-white balanced and re-black balanced using eyedroppers. ColorFiX has two sets of controls that it calls *paths*. The Main path provides overall color correction and the Select path is more closely related to secondary color correction, allowing for the replacement of specific colors with different colors without affecting the rest of the image. The controls in this plug-in are very advanced and provide very detailed control,

Bleach Bypass
Sometimes called Skip Bleach, Bleach Bypass is a film developing process where the bleaching process is skipped. Without the bleaching process, film acquires a contrasty, low saturation look because the silver (black) is left on the film along with the film dyes. The look is similar to laying a black and white image on top of a full-color image.

allowing corrections to one part of a picture, such as shadow, to be done without affecting other areas. Also, the Color Difference controls allow for unusual color vector movement that is not available in any other plug-in.

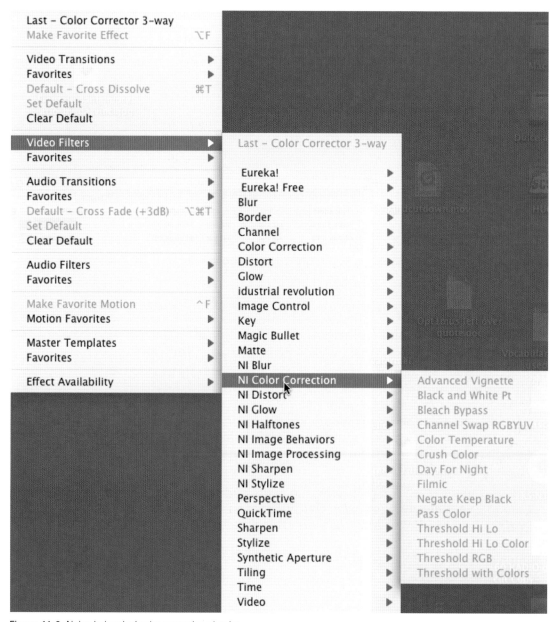

Figure 11-8 Noise Industries' color correction plug-ins.

BIBLIOGRAPHY

Baker, Robert, and Ansel E. Adams. 1995 (reprint). *The Negative, Ansel Adams Photography, Book 2.* Little Brown & Co.: Boston, MA. ISBN 0821221868.

Berns, Roy S., Fred W. Billmeyer, and Max Saltzman. 2000. *Billmeyer and Saltzman's Principles of Color Technology, 3rd Edition.* Wiley-Interscience: Hoboken, NJ. ISBN 047119459X.

Blazner, David, and Bruce Fraser. 2001. *Real World Photoshop 6.* Peachpit Press: Berkeley, CA. ISBN 0201721996.

Eiseman, Leatrice. 2000. *Pantone Guide to Communicating with Color.* How: Indianapolis, IN. ISBN 0966638328.

Eismann, Katrin. 2001. *Photoshop Restoration & Retouching.* Que Books: Indianapolis, IN. ISBN 0789723182.

Georgianni, Edward J., and Thomas E. Madden. 1997. *Digital Color Management Encoding Solutions.* Addison-Wesley: Reading, MA. ISBN 0201634260.

von Goethe, Johann Wolfgang. 1970. *Theory of Colours.* MIT Press: Cambridge, MA. ISBN 0262570211.

Hullfish, Steve. 2008. *The Art and Technique of Digital Color Correction.* Focal Press: Burlington, MA. ISBN 978-0-240-80990-8.

Itten, Johannes. 1977. *The Art of Color: The Subjective Experience and Objective Rationale of Color.* John Wiley & Sons: Hoboken, NJ. ISBN 0471289280.

Itten, Johannes, and Faber Birren. 1970. *The Elements of Color.* John Wiley & Sons: New York, NY. ISBN 0471289299.

Jack, Keith. 2001. *Video Demystified: A Handbook for the Digital Engineer* (3rd edition). LLH Technology Publishing: Eagle Rock, VA. ISBN 1878707566.

Luscher, Max. 1979. *Four Color Person.* Simon & Schuster: New York, NY. ISBN 0671242326.

Scott, Ian A. 1969. *The Luscher Color Test.* Random House: New York, NY. ISBN 0671731459.

Wyszecki, Gunter. 2000. *Color Science: Concepts and Methods, Quantitative Data and Formulae* (Wiley Series in Pure and Applied Optics). 1John Wiley & Sons: Hoboken, NJ. ISBN 0471399183.

Zwimpfer, Moritz. 1988. *Color Light Sight Sense.* Schiffer Publishing: West Chester, PA. ISBN 0887401392.

INDEX